BERCOW

ROWDY LIVING IN THE TORY PARTY

Bobby Friedman

GIBSON SQUARE

First published in 2011 by

Gibson Square

Tel: +44 (0)20 7096 1100

info@gibsonsquare.com
www.gibsonsquare.com

ISBN 9781906142636 HB

Contents

Preface

*"The worst sin towards our fellow creatures is not to hate them,
but to be indifferent to them".*

George Bernard Shaw, *The Devil's Disciple.*

There's something about John Bercow. He is the "marmite" politician
– a man who evokes extreme views, positive or negative, from those
who know him. People may love him or hate him, but they are rarely
somewhere in between. Bercow might exasperate and anger, or inspire
and enthuse, but he is never boring.

In Parliament, true political characters are an increasing rarity.
Boris Johnson has achieved high political office, but he only did so by
running for the London mayoralty, a position which has always been
decided with an unusually strong focus on personality. Throughout his
career Bercow has stood out: for his strong views, his diminutive size
and his odd manner of speaking; and yet, he has still achieved senior
office. In doing so, Bercow has bucked the trend.

At the time of his election as Speaker, there was a significant degree
of hand-wringing amongst the Conservative Party at his victory. I was
intrigued by the headlines and wanted to find out the true story that lay
behind them. I had watched Bercow during his career, as he crossed the
political spectrum, making enemies and friends along the way, and
wanted to discover how all this could be possible.

The result, nearly two years on, is this book, which relies on in-
depth research, alongside interviews with well over 100 of Bercow's
friends and acquaintances, to tell the story of his life and political
journey. My account has no agenda, and does not set out to promote
either side of the marmite divide. Instead, it aims to be an honest

reflection of what I have discovered, putting across the balance of opinion and both praising and criticising Bercow where appropriate.

Bercow himself is wary of the project and always has been. When we met to discuss the idea back in September 2009, he told me that he would not encourage his friends to speak to me, although he did promise not to discourage them either – and many of them did talk to me in the end. He has, however, always been extremely courteous to me personally on the many occasions when we have met.

As for his wife Sally, she was very much in the background when I started researching the biography. She was well-known around Westminster and not much liked by a lot of the Tory Party, who blamed her for turning Bercow – as they perceived it – against his own side. But to the wider public she was largely anonymous.

Her rather colourful past was the subject of much discussion in political circles but I made the initial decision that her private life was off-limits; after all, she wasn't a public figure, she wasn't being a hypocrite and it didn't affect Bercow's ability to do his job. However, following Sally's press interviews, it is now wholly unrealistic that any book about John could ignore Sally and the skeletons that were revealed when she opened up her closet. It is Sally Bercow herself who has courted the public interest, who has made herself a public figure and who has revealed all sorts of lurid details about her past. She has allowed herself to be defined – at least in part – by that public persona and in doing so she has forged her own career as a commentator and aspiring politician. This book is a biography of John Bercow, but Sally is now an integral part of his story.

I have a deep debt of gratitude to the large number of people who have helped me in this process, although space and confidentiality stop me from mentioning them all. In particular I would like to thank Michael Crick for his expert guidance; Joe Gosden for his constant support; and Richard Eschwege for helping me to develop the idea.

I would also like to thank Russell Walters, Peter Golds, John Pinniger, Sarah Westcott, John Stringer, Alex Mason, Ken Cheng, Sara Beech and Charlotte Jenner for their help during the research stage, as well as Patrick Maxwell for his photographic skills. My thanks also go to my superb agent, Andrew Lownie, and to Gibson Square Books.

Preface

Above all, I would like to thank my parents, Caroline and Jonathan Friedman, my sister Katie, and Rebecca Dudill for their unfailing support.

Bobby Friedman
London
2 February 2011

1

Reluctance

"John Bercow doesn't count"

Cameron made his way to the loos near the Commons chamber. There, he stood at the urinals next to a Labour MP, who turned to him and said, "I'm about to vote Conservative for the first time in my life." Cameron replied: "John Bercow doesn't count."

It was June 22nd, 2009 and the House of Commons was about to choose its new Speaker. For John Bercow, the small man with the big ambition, it would be a day of triumph. But for David Cameron, the leader of the Conservative Party, disaster loomed. As MPs waited to vote in the final run-off between Bercow and the old Etonian Sir George Young, they knew that Bercow was about to take the prize.

Later, as Cameron was making his was towards the Commons, he saw one of his MPs approaching him from the stairs at the back of the chamber. He looked at his colleague, who stared back, the two of them appearing momentarily like lorries on the M1 with their headlights up. Cameron gave a look that simply said, 'What has happened?' Then the future Prime Minister saw a Tory MP who had recently announced he would stand down from Parliament at the next election. Such was his strength of feeling, that Cameron turned to him and said, "You're right to leave" – meaning, that thanks to Bercow, he could see why someone would not want to be an MP any more. Cameron checked himself, saying, "You're not actually," but it was clear what he thought of Bercow's election.

It was not just David Cameron: a large number of other Conservative MPs were very, very angry. "I have never seen anything like the tribal wish to thwart someone," says one. "It was much stronger than I was expecting". One of Bercow's supporters, the

Labour MP Peter Kilfoyle, told me, "I realised we'd won as soon as we knew how angry the Tories were – the prize going to someone they didn't like[1]."

The two biggest political facts of John Bercow's career are that, firstly, despite spending his early years in the House of Commons as the archetypical Tory attack dog sticking his teeth into Labour at every opportunity, Bercow had wholly alienated huge chunks of his own side. And, second, that, despite having served on the immigration and repatriation committee of one of the most right-wing Conservative pressure groups, and having infamously called Cherie Blair "Lady Macbeth", Bercow was being swept forward by the unstoppable force of Labour votes, from Blair Babes to old-school socialists alike – with his Labour-supporting wife Sally watching on.

Soon John Bercow was victorious and he was ceremonially pulled to the Speaker's Chair. The traditional reluctance that a new Speaker has to fake as he is "dragged" up to his place above the Commons benches is, of course, a complete fiction. But even so, on June 22nd 2009, that reluctance was perhaps more inappropriate than it had ever been before. Bercow had run the most professional and concerted campaign to be Speaker that the House of Commons had ever seen. It was the culmination of years of work behind the scenes and, as Bercow was taken from the backbenches to the Speaker's chair, his longstanding ambition was finally realised.

However, as the reaction from the Conservative benches showed, there was very real reluctance in the House of Commons that day. It was not just that many Tories wanted George Young to win; it was that they wanted "anyone but Bercow[2]".

But for Bercow, all that counted was the result. For many years he had been wandering in the political wilderness, marooned from his own party but unwilling to cross the floor and join Labour. Now, he was sitting pretty as the First Commoner of the land, in one of the most important and best-paid roles in politics. "Has there ever been a political recovery like it?" asks one Conservative MP.

John Bercow's election as Speaker provides but one snapshot of his life. It is, in a sense, a stopping off point rather than a final destination. The road to the Speaker's Chair was fraught and seemingly full of controversy at almost every step, but Bercow has led no less complicated an existence since he finally won the role. Mr Speaker Bercow has had to stave off concerted challenges to his position both in his constituency, Buckingham, and in the House of Commons itself; and with a significant rump of anti-Bercow MPs and constant rumblings over his wife Sally's behaviour, Bercow remains one of the most controversial and colourful characters in British politics.

However liberal Bercow is now, he has been and will continue to be defined by the right-wing Tory persona that was his calling card for so many years. His moves across the ideological spectrum from right to left are symptomatic of the battles that have been fought in the Conservative Party over the last 20 years as it has struggled with the need for reform; but with Bercow there is something more. His political journey is perhaps more ferocious and more controversial than that of any other Tory.

Bercow is no ordinary politician. He undeniably provides a true hate figure for some, but just as some attack him with a real venom, there are many who argue with equal ferocity that he is a marvel – or "my hero[3]" as one put it to me. The story of John Bercow is one – not of two halves – but of two sides. He is an exemplar of the world of Thatcherite Conservatism, where anything is possible whatever one's background or disadvantages; and yet he is also a uniquely incorrigible character around Parliament. It is remarkable that this little ball of energy and self-belief has managed to propel himself into a senior position in British politics. For someone who had been written off so many times as a joke figure, his victory was a fantastic triumph against the odds.

2

Bercowitch to Bercow

"Throw them into the Danube"

11th October 1923

"The report on him is not exactly satisfactory[4]", wrote the Home Office official. He was examining the naturalisation papers of a Romanian man, Jack Bercowitch, a furrier living in the East End of London. Bercowitch had spent hours meticulously filling in a long series of forms and searching out suitable references in the hope of becoming a British citizen. Like thousands of Jews from across Europe, he had come to England in the early twentieth century in search of a better and safer life and now he wanted to make his allegiance official. Jack wanted to be a citizen, not an alien.

Jack Bercowitch didn't want to go back to Galatz, the Romanian city on the Danube that had been home for his first sixteen years and which later found fame as Count Dracula's port of disembarkation. Jews made up a large proportion of the population there, more than twenty percent, and, as was typical of Romania at that time, anti-Semitism was rife. In 1859 there was a blood libel in the city, sparking three days of riots. A number of Jews were beaten or murdered and their homes were looted.

For many Romanians in Galatz, the answer to the supposed problem with the Jews lay in the river that ran through the city. As the popular nineteenth-century Romanian novelist Ioan Slavici wrote, "The solution that remains for us is, at a signal, to close the borders, to annihilate them, to throw them into the Danube right up to the very last of them, so that nothing remains of their seed[5]".

Slavici was far from unusual. As the Jewish population in Romania rose in the years after 1850, so the fear of them increased. Romanians

12

wanted independence and they didn't want Jews to get in the way. Some even saw Zionism as a plot for Jewish people to take over Romania and make it a Jewish homeland. However fanciful these claims were, many people treated them with respect, and discrimination against Jews was an everyday fact of life. Romanian Jews like the Bercowitches were for a long time denied Romanian citizenship, despite significant international pressure. When the Romanian authorities finally caved in in 1879, the procedure was made so difficult that only 85 Jews successfully applied for full citizenship before the turn of the century[6].

If anyone understood why there was good reason to leave behind your country of birth, it was Jack Bercowitch. But by coming to England, Jack needed the understanding of a national population. He needed their acceptance of a stranger and an outsider. He needed them to be more open-minded than those who had discriminated against him, those whom he had left behind in Romania.

Jack wasn't the first member of the Bercowitch family to cross Europe and make his home in the UK. His father, Sam, a traveller[7], and his mother Annie had come to England in the late nineteenth century and Jack followed soon afterwards in 1900, although two of his sisters remained in Romania. They settled in the East End, Jack working as a gas fitter for three years before going into the fur trade[8]. Jack met and married another Romanian woman called Annie – Annie Rothman, in 1911. He was 27 and she was 23. Annie had also grown up in East London and had spent her childhood living with her parents and three siblings in Spitalfields, squashed up with just two bedrooms between the six of them[9]. Perhaps unusually for more socially conservative times, Jack and Annie were living together – at 106 Shacklewell Road near the Hackney Downs – at the time of the marriage[10]. The ceremony took place at the Wellington Road synagogue in Stoke Newington, one of the growing number of synagogues that were sprouting up as the influx of Jewish immigrants to the East End continued at a pace.

Life in the UK was good to the early members of the Bercowitch family. After his marriage Jack opened up his own shop, on Aldgate Avenue near Liverpool Street, and he later moved to Spitalfields. He had good written and spoken English, and as time went on Jack's horizons began to expand from the small area in East London where he and his family had all lived and worked for their whole time in the UK. His next move was to West Kensington, where he opened a shop at 6a Bank Parade. This time, the name above the door was J.Bercow, the Romanian "itch" falling by the wayside. The immigrant family was fast becoming the establishment.

There was just one final thing to do. Jack Bercowitch wanted the prize that was denied to so many Romanian Jews for so long: citizenship, and with it, acceptance. Why, then, was this hard-working man's report "not exactly satisfactory"? In his short time in the UK Jack had already managed to pick up a criminal record in addition to being investigated for putting in for some very questionable expenses. In 1917 Jack reported that his house in Colverston Crescent had been broken into, but when the police came to take statements they were left unconvinced by the "manner" of Jack and his brother-in-law Morris. They claimed for £185 of lost property, but there was, apparently, "serious doubt" whether the burglary had taken place at all. The police were not convinced and a firm of solicitors appointed by Jack's insurers were also extremely sceptical. Eventually a compromise was reached and Jack received just £75 of the £185 he originally claimed.

However, more seriously, a year later Jack found himself up in court, charged with failing to furnish a statement giving the names of the persons employed by him at his workshop in Spitalfields. He was fined £2. To make matters worse, Jack didn't include the offence on his naturalisation form, although when the mistake was noticed he claimed that he saw the offence as "technical[11]" rather than criminal.

Those indiscretions were relatively minor in the grand scheme of things and Jack was, in the end, considered suitable for citizenship. He was helped by a number of solid referees, who described him variously as a "straight forward businessman" to whom they would give credit of "hundreds of pounds.[12]" So it was that his application was rubber stamped. The man who arrived as a Romanian gas fitter had become a small businessman in the best English tradition.

Jack and Annie had four children: a girl, Bella and three boys, Reuben, Samson and Charles. The Bercowitches' Jewish roots continued to play an important role in their lives and their sons each had a barmitzvah on turning thirteen, just down the road at the Wellington Park synagogue. Then, to celebrate their silver wedding anniversary in 1936, Jack and Annie placed a celebratory notice in the *Jewish Chronicle*.

But by then, the hatred that had made them leave Romania had flared up once again, this time in London. With the backdrop of Hitler's rise to power in Nazi Germany, Oswald Mosley and his blackshirts were creating trouble in the East End, where the majority of English Jews lived. In October 1936 came the battle of Cable Street, in which British Jews, communists, Irish dockers and trade unionists came together to stop Mosley's blackshirts marching through the East End. It was a time of undoubted anti-Semitism, and it wasn't uncommon for people to shout at Jews to "go back to Palestine". The anti-immigrant language of the post-war period would have a different target, but the sentiments were the same.

This prejudice was certainly having an impact on the Bercow family and Jack's son Samson seemed to have the family flair for a good argument. In 1937, the year after Cable Street, he wrote a letter to the *Jewish Chronicle*, saying:

"As a Jew, I am deeply grieved that the splendid work that is being done by the various anti-Fascist organisations should be marred by vituperative extremism on the part of a few well-meaning but misguided persons. Let us combat the Fascist not with his own despicable tactics but with honesty and determination that will rally to our support those who at present hold a neutral point of view."

Samson was the first – but certainly not the last – member of the Bercowitch family to become active in British politics. After the war he addressed the Anglo-Jewish Association's London Branch, talking about "The Jew in politics", with visitors paying more than five shillings to get in[13].

In 1955, Jack Bercow died and two years later his wife Annie passed away. All of their children had been born in the UK and their original surname Bercowitch, which was shortened by Jack for his trading name, was gradually fading out in favour of the anglicised "Bercow". The family from Galatz was assimilating well into English society.

It was Jack Bercowitch's immigration to the UK, and the UK's willingness to have him, despite his "not exactly satisfactory" nature, that paved the way for his grandson John. Jack Bercowitch didn't live to see the birth of his grandson, some forty years after he took the oath of allegiance, but the controversy surrounding immigration and immigrants like Jack lived on. Soon it was John Bercow himself who was a torch-bearer for the voluntary repatriation of immigrants. Back in the late 1800s, Jack might have found it hard to believe that just two generations later, a member of his family, with his anglicised name, would be the First Commoner of the United Kingdom. Not bad, considering Jack would have been very unlikely to become a citizen in the country of his birth. But, then, perhaps there are other things that Jack might not have believed. Having grown up seeing the anti-Semitism in Romania and then the East End, and having been given a new life by the UK, one can only speculate as to what he'd have thought when, decades later, his grandson decided to campaign for the repatriation of immigrants. But, as with most things related to John Bercow, therein lies the contradiction.

3

Little John

"The Jewboy son of a taxi driver"

Precocious, articulate, opinionated? John Bercow as an MP: maybe. John Bercow as a little boy: without question.

As a small child, Bercow used to sit on the wall outside his family home, whiling away the hours by reading the newspaper. *The Times* was his favourite and as he clutched the broadsheet in front of him, devouring all the latest news, the little boy would seemingly disappear behind the mass of news print, as the paper was bigger than he was.

One local acquaintance recalls that Bercow would peer over the top and loftily tell him what was in that day's paper. For him, that made Bercow a "pugnacious little shit". Perhaps it might be more accurate to say that, even then, news and politics were John Bercow's lifeblood. It came naturally to him, a hunger that he couldn't sate. For those less interested, it might make him seem bookish or overbearing. But it's hard to see how he was a "pugnacious little shit". If anything, it tells us that being interested in the news isn't the easiest way for a kid to make friends. All his life, Bercow has seemed willing to take the unpopular path. Not out of spite or a desire to provoke, but merely because he has stuck with what he wanted.

What does come as a surprise is that Bercow was like this at all. This child with an endless appetite for current affairs hardly seems to be the likely spawn of his parents. And it's here that the leap from the migrant Jack Bercowitch to the present day is made. Charles – or Charlie, as his friends called him – was the son of the Yiddish-speaking Jack and the father of John, who knows English so well that he makes a habit of pulling up people when they speak it incorrectly.

During Charlie's early years, he enjoyed local amateur dramatics as part of 'The Lodge', a Jewish theatre group. He was cast in two plays – a comedy called 'High Spirits' and, later, in 'Murder at the Vicarage'. What's striking, though, is that Jack's son wasn't appearing in a dingy theatre speaking Yiddish in the East End. The acting was probably scarcely any better, but amateur theatre in Edgware, north London is happily a very long way indeed from blood libels on the banks of the Danube. So when Bercow now says that, "I am myself the Jewboy son of a taxi driver", this description seems something of an over-simplification. Bercow's predecessor as Speaker, Michael Martin earned the nickname "Gorbals Mick" after the working-class district of Glasgow where he grew up. Martin's world was truly working class, one of unions and sheet metal workers. Although Bercow's childhood was, in some ways, not easy, his family were typically petit bourgeois and admirably aspirational. In some respects, Bercow's description fails to do them justice.

For a long time, it had seemed that Charlie might not get married at all. In the post-war period, the average age of a groom was 26; but in 1956, Charlie was 36 and still a bachelor. The Second World War had of course got in the way – Charlie was 25 when fighting broke out and he had gone on to serve in the RAF. But the happy news came when Charlie announced that he was engaged to the 27-year-old Brenda Bailey, whom he married at Edgware and District Reform Syngagoue on December 13th 1956.

If Charlie and Brenda were older than your average couple, they also did things differently in another, significant way: Brenda was not Jewish. Back in 1956, "marrying out" was frowned upon by many in the Jewish community. Brenda did convert to Judaism, but through a reform synagogue, meaning that, for the most orthodox of Jews, she was not really Jewish at all. So, it follows, her son John is not Jewish either – as the religion is passed down through matrilineal descent.

Does any of this matter? After all, to most of the outside world and to much of the Jewish community, Bercow was – as he put it – a "Jewboy". That term itself is evocative of the anti-Semitism that followed Bercow around throughout his life, not just as a child but also later as an MP. In that respect, Bercow was and is clearly Jewish. But even so, Bercow's in-between status did mean that there was something of the interloper about him. In some people's eyes he was simply not Jewish and the United Synagogue – the UK's biggest synagogual organisation – would not allow someone like to Bercow to marry in one of its synagogues for that very reason. As David Faktor, a cousin of Bercow's, told me, the perception he had during his childhood was that, "They *were* different, they were less Jewish... Brenda was not Jewish...she was a bit of an outsider, I remember somebody laughing at the fact that they had non-kosher chicken." To the non-Jews he was a Jew, but to many Jewish families he wasn't. Neither group would have him.

A recurring theme for Bercow is that he's never quite fitted in. Once again, Bercow was just a little bit different, in the same way that sitting on the wall in front of his house in north London reading the paper, marked him apart. The theme is replicated in his adult life, too – and I've lost count of the number of MPs who've told me that the problem with Bercow is that he's not very "clubbable". To them, he's not the sort of person with whom you'd share a glass of whisky and a cigar at the Carlton Club. Bercow has seemingly always had to fight for acceptance; or merely admit to the fact that he would never be on the inside.

So if the term "Jewboy" fails to tell the full story, then what about the claim that his father was a "taxi driver"? Yes, it's true that Charlie did end up driving minicabs for a living, but as the forays into amateur dramatics show, his was very much a middle class life. After the war, he and his brother Ralph, who'd also served in the RAF as an officer in Bomber Command, set up Bercow Motors, a car business in Warren Street in central London. David Faktor recalls that his impression was that, "Charlie was very much the junior partner, the poor relation" in the enterprise. But even if Ralph took the lead, Charlie was very much a successful businessman. It's unsurprising that when he married, he described himself as a "Company Director" on his wedding certificate. Moreover, he had been living in a boringly middle class house in Wolomer Gardens in Edgware, part of the influx of residents to leafy north London after the Bakerloo line opened and tube trains ran to Stanmore for the first time. Meanwhile, Brenda, who worked as a secretary for a legal firm, had been living at 44 South Hill Park in

Hampstead in London, another middle class address.

Bercow Motors continued to flourish and Charlie and Brenda moved to Abercorn Road in Mill Hill, which was yet another comfortable London suburb. It was here that Brenda became pregnant with their first child, Alison, who was born in 1960. And on 19th January 1963, she gave birth to their only son, John Simon Bercow, at the Edgware General Hospital. Soon afterwards the family moved further up the property ladder, buying a detached house at 108 Southover, in Woodside Park, north London. It was a very middle class road, described by one resident as an "upmarket Coronation Street, everyone talks to everyone." Nicky Crowther, a classmate of Bercow's at primary school, says, "We were middle class, definitely not working class. Woodside Park is basically well-heeled and lots of Jews who made good in the previous generation moved there as it was a bit more leafy[14]." So the early years of John Bercow's life were ones of middle class comfort, a world away from Speaker Martin's deprived working-class Glasgow.

Bercow Motors continued to do well, but then in the late 1960s the council announced that it was putting yellow lines along the road in front of the showroom. Unable to park their cars outside, Ralph and Charlie upped sticks and moved the business to Burnt Oak, closer to the family in North London and free from the dreaded parking restrictions. More misfortune was to hit the business and the family, as Ralph died in 1969 and then, as the national economy struggled in the early 1970s, Bercow Motors felt the squeeze and within a few years it had been forced to close. Out of work and with two small kids, Charlie started driving cabs. John's description of his father as a taxi driver is, of course, accurate, but perhaps it doesn't do Charlie justice. He was a businessman who provided well for his children and who did his best when his business collapsed.

But, even so, Bercow always seemed to be somewhat sheepish about his background. One friend at primary school says that, "John seemed embarrassed about saying that his father was a tradesman and he didn't go about advertising it." David Faktor recalls that within the family, "We were brought up to think that we were better than them and maybe they felt that too.[15]" John and Alison didn't go to private school like their cousins and Faktor says that Charlie and Brenda simply had a different attitude. "Charlie had more money than my father, who was a scientist. [My father] worked seven days a week to send us to private school and we were taught education was very important, whereas there was a feeling with Alison and John that the sport was important".

However, if anything it seems that the Bercows wanted their children to be the best, both academically and on the sports pitches. Bercow says that Charlie was "scrupulously honest" and helped shape his view on the world. "I once asked my father about a business colleague," Bercow recalls. "My father said, 'Son, you ask my opinion, well I will buy him at my valuation and sell him at his and make a healthy profit'.[16]" The influence was political too: "I think my original political views were slightly to do with discussions with Dad," Bercow says. "He had strong, traditionally Conservative views about most matters. For much of his life, he was self-employed and a lot of self-employed people tend to be Conservative. He believed in the creation of wealth, the idea we should stand on our own two feet.[17]"

Brenda has had an even greater impact on her son than her husband Charlie. Bercow describes her as "hard-working[18]" and she was a determined woman, working part-time as a legal secretary throughout his childhood. Her own mother had worked in a laundry. Aside from her work and looking after her children, Brenda was always entering competitions, with a good success rate. She's still at it, winning a Peroni aperitif-making kit in 2010[19]. Even now, in her 80s, she works as a supporting actress and in recent years she appeared in the ensemble in a production at the Royal Court Theatre in London[20].

Bercow certainly didn't seem to need private education to become quite the intellectual and his state school didn't stop him developing into that boy reading *The Times* on the wall outside his house. Charlie and Brenda sent John to Frith Manor, where, in the words of his classmate Nicky Crowther, "He was a small lad but he made a lot of noise. He and I were rivals in Maths and English all the way through junior school; we probably pulled each other on a bit without realising it[21]". Bercow was well-known as a big David Bowie fan, although he wasn't such a talented singer himself: he remembers being expelled "with some insistence[22]" from the school choir.

Bercow's brain was far stronger than his voice and it was immediately clear that he was very bright, although not all of the teachers were able to put up with his precociousness. "You don't go into primary school teaching because you want to be contradicted," says his teacher John Stringer. "You seldom get someone who suggests there's some other way of doing something and John would not be slow in pointing things out.[23]" However, many of the staff were very fond indeed of Bercow and, for Stringer, both his personality and his intelligence were impressive. "I found him fun. I've always felt he was sincere and direct. I always thought he'd go onto great things – or hang, one or the other. I knew one way or the other he would make some impact." It was Stringer's belief in his pupil that helped spur Bercow along. "He was a wonderful, encouraging man," Bercow recalls. "He made you feel if you worked hard, if you were persistent you could achieve anything you wanted to achieve.[24]" Such was Stringer's impact, that the two stayed in touch and Bercow invited him as a guest at the first state opening of Parliament after becoming Speaker.

However, even at that young age Bercow was already ruffling feathers amongst the pupils with his political views. A friend recalls that, "Things started going oddly for him by the fact that he was quite outspoken," and Crowther remembers a young Bercow arguing in defence of Enoch Powell, who had given his infamous 'Rivers of Blood' speech just a few years earlier in 1968. There were other signs of the politician that lay within and by the age of 9 or 10 Bercow was displaying an incredible vocabulary. It was still, though, something of a mystery as to how and why he spoke in such an extraordinary way. His sister Alison talked much more normally and Bercow seemed to have been partly self-taught.

Nonetheless, his ability to perform in public was finally recognised when Stringer cast him as the lead in a school production of 'David and Goliath'. Bercow, who had shoulder-length hair at the time, played David: the short, Jewish boy taking on the taller, stronger enemy. If ever there was a metaphor for the life of John Bercow, this was surely it.

Next up was the chance to test himself out as a potential politician. First came the School Council elections, where Bercow was a keen participant: "At the age of nine I stood as a modernising and reforming candidate with a particular commitment to doing something about the quality of the school dinners, a rather questionable manifesto as the quality of the school dinners was not that bad, I quite liked them and there was no prospect of me being able to do anything about them[25]."

Then, in February 1974, by which stage Bercow was the grand old age of 11, the school held a mock General Election as Harold Wilson attempted to unseat the incumbent Prime Minister, Edward Heath. Bercow stood as a Conservative candidate and had to make a speech in assembly, complete with a giant blue rosette. Even then, he was as confrontational as ever, telling a Welsh nationalist candidate that she was "talking a load of fish" and describing school dinners as "the ghastliest garbage I have ever had," at which point the headmaster suggested the kitchen staff might boil Bercow down to size if he was elected[26].

Crowther beat Bercow into second place, but friends remember that he was still very pleased. "John was ecstatic. He was surprised to have got as far as he did. I suspect he thought to himself, 'I can do this'"; and one of his classmates remembers Bercow talking about Heath as an example of where politics could get someone from an ordinary background.

But perhaps the biggest influence on Bercow's life came from the actions of his headmaster. As comprehensive schools went on the march in the 1970s, the grammar schools around Frith Manor were gradually being phased out, to be replaced by non-selective schools. As Bercow came to the end of his primary school days, the 11+ exam had already been abolished, but there were still some very good grammars in the area. In this interregnum, the power was given to primary school head teachers to recommend children for places at the grammar – or to send them to the local comp instead.

Much relied on Bercow's headmaster, Sam Unsworth. It was he who would choose 4 pupils to be considered, with 2 of them finally winning a place; but, surprisingly, the clever young Bercow did not even make the shortlist. This decision was very upsetting on a number of levels, not least because Bercow was almost certainly good enough to have been in the first four: "On an objective basis, had there been internal testing within the primary school, I am fairly certain John would have made the grade," says a friend. What's more, it seemed hard to understand why so few people from Frith Manor were allowed to be put forward to the grammar. As Adrian Magnus – one of the boys who was selected by Unsworth – told me, "In my year there were 2 of us who went to Christ's College [grammar school], 1 boy from each class, whereas when I got there, there were other schools where quite a lot of boys had gone through – perhaps 6, 10 or 12 a year, maybe more. I didn't think the standard of some of them was any better than any of the boys who didn't get to the grammar, so there were inconsistencies. John was precisely the sort of person who – had the headmaster taken a slightly different approach to these things – would easily have gone to grammar school and benefitted from it."

If the system had allowed for an exam, the outcome might have been different. But in the 70s, kids like Bercow were stuck with it. In his case, it was not clear whether Unsworth merely felt that he was not good enough – a view with which many others disagreed – or if there were other factors that undermined his standing among some of the teachers. One friend recalls that Brenda had not always got on well with the headmaster as she often liked to go in to battle for her children. He says, "She was pushy academically and highly aspirational, more than you'd expect of any parent. She'd not be bothered about alienating the school at any stage...I can still recall the class teacher saying to John, who told me and others, that he wouldn't be recommended for grammar school because of all this. If he'd gone [to grammar school] he'd have been very different. He lost out...John's reaction was to pull the blinds down. He didn't say anything about it, but some kids found out and kids can be vicious. Some taunted or mocked him".

Of course, many millions of children have gone to a comprehensive or a secondary modern and flourished, but then John Bercow was no ordinary child. It's hard enough being a ten year old, but when you're a ten year old who likes reading the broadsheets and talking about politics, you're more likely to flourish around those who are more interested in academic work. Bercow ended up like a fish out of water and once again, he would be on the outside, looking in.

The other big event in young Bercow's life was that his parents decided to divorce, although Brenda and Charlie did their best to make things easy for John and Alison. Charlie moved to a flat in Totteridge, while Brenda and the children moved to the Uxbridge Road in Stanmore, so both parents were close by. Even so, a friend remembers that, "The divorce was devastating. He had all the traits of being a loner, arrogant and inflammatory. These were all magnified by a factor of three or four and he became even more difficult. There was a before and after. There was no going back". Another says, "The divorce affected him a lot and made him more of a survivalist. When you met him as a child, he was very much a boy that was going to stand on his own two feet. He was from a single parent family, [it was as if] he had to look after himself, look after his mother." Clearly it was a tough time and perhaps Bercow felt a little bit more alone in the world. But others are clear that he had a warm and loving relationship with both parents before and after the divorce, even if he was perhaps instinctively closer to his mother. He still saw his father regularly and Charlie seems to have had no less impact on the young Bercow just because they didn't live together full-time.

Moreover, by the age of 11, Bercow's precocious personality was already fully formed. The desire was there for all to see; and the young David was ready to slay any Goliath that stood in his way.

4

To the Manorhill Borne

"Small boy, big mouth"

It was the late 1970s, and a small teenager was being terrorised by a bunch of kids in his class. They were larger than him and there were lots of them, so he didn't stand a chance. They picked him up, kicking and shouting, and marched him to the biology pond, where they unceremoniously threw him in, laughing, "Bercow can be in there with the other amphibians[27]". As an MP, John Bercow is used to surviving with few allies on his side. It seems it was a skill he had to master at an early age. As a pupil at secondary school, he found it difficult to make lasting friendships and as a bright and precocious teenager he was both a joy for his teachers and a target for abuse.

His school, Finchley Manorhill, was what would now be termed a 'bog-standard' comprehensive. Bercow started there in 1974 and spent his first two years in the lower school, a great big square, old-fashioned brick building, with concrete corridors and painted iron railings on the stairs. Later he would transfer to the upper school, a more modern site.

Manorhill was a real north London melting pot, with significant numbers of Asian and Greek pupils. It's interesting that Bercow – who later came to have such uncompromising views on immigration – was so used to mixing with people who had only recently come to the UK. Certainly there was no chance that he was merely ignorant of other cultures – in his formative years he sat in lessons with pupils from ethnic minorities. His next-door neighbours in Southover were also Asian and Bercow was friends with their son.

The school had more than a thousand pupils but Bercow soon began to make his mark. As Manorhill was in the same catchment area as the grammar schools the competition wasn't as strong as it might have been, but Bercow was a clear star performer. He was widely recognised as one of the most talented students in his year and his eventual rise in politics did not come as a surprise to his contemporaries, although, as one says, "It was an inadequate comprehensive so you might say it's a wonder he did anything at all". Bercow certainly wasn't a quiet boy, either. He was incredibly witty, with one classmate recalling that he was, "One of the funniest kids in the school. He was years ahead of his time with his cutting remarks".

However, despite his biting humour, Bercow found it difficult to settle down. Beneath the high-achieving exterior there was a teenager who was deeply unpopular and a regular target for the bullies. Undoubtedly his intelligence marked him out as different and Bercow was never one to play down his intellect. Nicky Crowther moved to Manorhill with Bercow and says that, "John was a small man with a big mouth. He annoyed people because he was very clever, pompous and headstrong[28]." Certainly Bercow wouldn't take it lying down when he was teased. Julian Baker, who was also in his class, says that, "Bercow didn't really ever try to avoid the abuse by keeping quiet. He was gobby and opinionated and pretty unpopular[29]."

Bercow's appearance didn't help. He was extremely spotty and some of the scars from his dreadful acne are still visible today. Like any number of teenagers who are unfortunate enough to have deep-set, persistent acne, Bercow was mocked for it. His hair was greasy and worn over his ears and he was about 5'2 in his mid-teens, so he became a natural target. Often when he would outsmart another pupil verbally they would come back at him with a comment about his appearance. Fights were commonplace at the school but Bercow wasn't the fighting kind. As a small boy he would have found it difficult at a school where physical might rather than intelligent argument was king.

Bercow enjoyed getting his revenge on the students who disliked him and unsurprisingly it only served to push him further down the popularity stakes. Baker says, "He was a clever lad and there was no question that he'd go far. We didn't bother with a nickname for him but people would usually just turn to him and say, 'shut up and fuck off Bercow'. He was just constantly unpleasant[30]." The crueller kids would go to extreme lengths to harass him. Bercow was terrified of bees and wasps and would go into a screaming panic if one came into the room, pushing tables over to try to get out of the way. His tormentors would herd bees and wasps through the window so they could watch him freak out. It's a fear that has lasted through to adulthood and when Bercow was dining outside at the London restaurant La Poule Au Pot in 2010, he ended up hiding with his head in his jacket after a wasp gate-crashed his lunch[31].

Although Bercow was cruelly ostracised for his intelligence and his appearance – two things he could do nothing about – it was his manner that really cemented him in the bad books of his classmates. He often flaunted his superior ability, seemingly goading the other kids. Crowther says he, "Had the most extraordinary vocabulary, but he always used it in a manner that said 'I really do know this awfully well[32]'." Others describe the young John as a parody of himself, acting up to the stereotype to wind up the other students. There's a similarity between him and Disraeli: for both of them oratory became an affection, an exercise in superior intelligence even though it made them less popular. Perhaps trying to compensate for his size, Bercow would often try to humiliate bigger kids in his class. One in particular used to make mistakes with his reading and Bercow would write them down and recite them back to him. Incidents like these would certainly have contributed to the view that Bercow was an "odious little toad[33]" who was probably the most unpopular person in the year.

After school, John would hang around just like any other teenager, although he would often still be found with a copy of *The Times* in his hand. He and other local kids would wander down to Sweet News, a newsagent at the bottom of Southover, and buy candy from the shop's owner, Mr Nadim. But the same themes emerge and, as one other resident of Woodside Park told me, "He was very precocious. He had a fabulous brain, but tended to discuss with you what your faults might be and in the end you just gave him a wide berth. He looked down on everyone and was determined to be running the country. He told me one day he would be an MP and in the Cabinet."

Manorhill hardly seems like a happy environment for Bercow and he had to accept that his parents were unable to send him to private school, despite knowing that he might have fared much better in a more academically-driven environment. He was not to receive the privileged schooling enjoyed by his future wife Sally, who attended Marlborough College, where fees are now verging on £30,000 per year, as a sixth-former in the 1980s – a time in which Sally experimented with smoking cannabis[34]. The future Queen, Kate Middleton, went to the school and David Cameron's wife Samantha was a student there at the same time as Sally. The rough and tumble of north London could scarcely be further away from the beautiful buildings and extensive grounds of Marlborough. Perhaps driven by this idyllic setting, Sally was so determined to become a student there that she used part of her inheritance to pay the fees. Although Sally says she, "Didn't really fit in with those girls in Alice bands and everyone coming from a house with a long drive[35]," Bercow must have at times longed to be anywhere apart from Manorhill. Posh would beat the biology pond any day.

One source of respite, though, came from the teachers, with whom Bercow got on a lot better. A key figure in his time at the school was his English master Alan Jobson, who found Bercow to be an excellent student and a "pleasure to teach[36]". Bercow did have an easy wit and was often extremely charming – attributes that might not have endeared him to teenagers but which adults would have more readily appreciated; and which stood him in good stead as he went for selection for a seat in the House of Commons.

Many of Bercow's contemporaries left the school at the age of sixteen but he was easily clever enough to stay on, making his way into the sixth-form in the autumn of 1979. At around this time his mother Brenda also moved back to Dollis Hill, to 105 Dollis Road, just round the corner from the house where John was born.

Bercow also began to develop an interest in girls as he matured, although he didn't have any proper girlfriends at school. He did have a number of potential targets and was particularly keen on one student there who was widely thought to be the prettiest girl in their year. Like him, she was sharp-witted and Bercow enjoyed verbally jostling with her, but she didn't reciprocate his romantic interest. Crowther says that she is, "Continually astonished he got married and had three children. He was not an attractive young man. He was very loud mouthed and had no gentleness or mellow good humour. If there were thirty boys in the year, you wouldn't have had him in your top thirty[37]."

Politics was also becoming more important to Bercow and it wasn't a subject he was afraid to talk about. He moved into the sixth form in the year that the local MP, Margaret Thatcher, became Prime Minister and it was a time of political volatility. He says, "I had started to develop a keen interest in politics and a horror at how Britain seemed to have become ungovernable. In the Winter of Discontent, the streets went un-swept, the sick went untended and the dead went unburied[38]." The 1979 election brought Bercow into active politics for the first time when he went to hear Thatcher speak at the nearby Woodhouse School. He recalls that he met her afterwards: "[I] expressed my support and was promptly advised by her to join the Young Conservatives, which I later did[39]."

With Manorhill in the Conservative leader's Finchley constituency, politics was a hot topic of conversation at the school. A fellow pupil, recalls, "I remember well, him asking me who my parents were going to vote for in the '79 general election. When I said Labour, he was flabbergasted and wanted to know if there was something wrong with them[40]". Julian Baker says that Bercow was, "pretty right of centre and even then was saying some of the stuff about immigration that he was coming out with later [as a politician][41]." For Nicky Crowther, "He got worse through secondary school. By sixth form it was generally known that he had opinions which were very, very strong and out of keeping with everybody else. He must have been an angry young man.[42]"

However, his former classmates say that, although Bercow continued to openly support Enoch Powell as he did at primary school, they never heard him saying anything which was remotely racist. What's more, he was actively friendly towards some of the Asian kids in his class. However, Crowther says that, "Underneath all of this was this strain of him going in a different direction. He was at a liberal, multi-racial school but it had no effect on him[43]". A fellow pupil who was from an ethnic minority told me, "I once said, 'John, are you thinking about what you're saying?' He was in denial and he wouldn't accept that he [too] was of immigrant descent." Here, then, were the first signs that while Bercow ostensibly signed up to policies that were extremely right-wing, he balked at their implications in practice. It was a theme that would develop over the coming years.

Bercow was fiercely loyal to the Conservative Party and soon after that meeting with Thatcher, he acted on her advice. One weekend, he arranged for a local friend to take him to the Hendon North Young Conservatives, renowned as one of the most right-wing branches in the Greater London area. The Hendon YCs met on Sundays in the bar of the Edgwarebury, a tudor-fronted hotel on the Barnet Road in Elstree. One member says that, "Like all Young Conservatives, we were only interested in i) how to get ahead in life; ii) politics; and iii) getting laid". Bercow got a lift from Charlie's flat in Totteridge and started making friends and having fun as soon as he arrived. He was right-wing enough to fit in well and his visits to the Edgwarebury became a regular occurrence. It was his first real step in Conservative politics.

But Manorhill itself also provided him with a chance to take his Conservatism to a wider audience – when Jobson organised a trip to watch the BBC's *Question Time* programme being recorded in January 1981, just a few months before Bercow completed his A-Levels. It was to be his first appearance on television. Bercow was the keenest member of the party that went to the recording. "It was typical of John", Jobson says, "he was the only one that day to ask a question[44]."

The panel that night consisted of Barbara Castle, the former Labour Minister who had left the House of Commons and moved to the European Parliament; the Conservative Home Secretary Willie Whitelaw; the Chairman of the British Railways Board Sir Peter Parker; and Cyril Smith, the popular Liberal MP best known for being hugely overweight – at one time he was thought to tip the scales at twenty-nine stone. Big Cyril, as he was known, was joked to be the Liberals' "heavy artillery". It was said that before he was elected only one taxi was needed to transport the whole Parliamentary Liberal Party; after he won his seat, they could fill two taxis.

Bercow has never spoken publicly about his appearance on the show. But watching the tape back, it's easy to see that at the age of just eighteen he was already very charismatic, pugilistic and blessed with great oratorical skill. When Castle said that Whitelaw had been talking "economic nonsense", Bercow stuck up his hand and the presenter Robin Day picked him out of the audience to ask a question. The camera turned to him, dressed in a shirt, tie and jumper and with his greasy hair and spots visible under the lights. This "question" turned out to be the comment of the night, as he jumped to Whitelaw's defence:

"For Mrs Castle to describe what Mr. Whitelaw said about financial assistance as economic nonsense really is utterly absurd," he began, with an older lady sitting at his side beaming at him, clearly charmed. He began to wave his arms and jab his finger at Castle, who was sat on the stage, as he got into his stride. "Mrs. Castle recalls in her recent book, Mr Callaghan once said that if he were a young man he would emigrate because he didn't have any of the answers to Britain's economic or any other problems. I would suggest to Mrs Castle that the reason she sought to join the European Parliament is precisely the same". The audience burst into laughter and applause, while Castle struggled for an answer. Cyril Smith shouted presciently back at him, "Wonder which Young Conservatives he's chairman of?", but Bercow had stolen the show.

5

The Tennis Champ

"John Bercow bites yer legs"

As a 10-year-old boy, John Bercow was far more interested in the umpire's chair than the Speaker's chair. Tennis is the only activity that has ever come close to usurping the pre-eminent position of politics in his heart and for a long time it seemed that his tennis career, not politics, was going to propel Bercow to national prominence. Back in the early 1970s, Bercow looked every bit the tennis player. He had long, flowing hair down past his shoulders, a forerunner perhaps of Andre Agassi's early hairstyle. And he had confidence, because he was very, very good.

It is hard to do justice to quite how impressive Bercow was as a young tennis player. He was probably the best in the country for his age group; the player that all the others wanted to beat and the number one seed at the national championships in the under 12s category. Ashley Fuller who is now the head professional at the Roehampton Tennis Club, remembers that Bercow used to regularly outplay him. He told me that Bercow was, "Unbelievably talented, practically unbeatable and invincible. The first three times I played him, I didn't win a game. I lost 6-0, 6-0; everyone did. If you played Bercow it was the end of the tournament." Stuart Bale was introduced to Bercow when they were both 12 years old: "You felt that if you beat him, you'd make it as a tennis player. He was the benchmark for all the Middlesex guys[45]."

Bercow was so good that he regularly played and beat eighteen year olds and his fame spread throughout the Middlesex tennis circuit. Bale's father was such a fan that he had some T-shirts printed. Their message: "John Bercow bites yer legs". In return, Bercow affectionately called him the 'hamburger' due to his luxuriant waistline.

Tennis was a serious business, even for twelve-year-olds. On Saturday mornings, Bercow and Bale used to go to a gym on Paddington Street in Marylebone, perhaps somewhat ironically for them called "Tough Guys". As Bale puts it, "I was trying to get stronger and John was trying to get taller![46]" Tough Guys had one room, rented out from the Church of the Good Lord Shepherd – presumably the people in adjoining rooms had very different ideas of a higher power. A quite bizarre mix of stars would use it to get into shape, ranging from the Star Trek actor Patrick Stewart, who was then with the Royal Shakespeare Company, to professional wrestlers; Ronnie Corbett; and the celebrated ballroom dancer Victor Silvester. Other visitors to the gym included the notorious gangsters Reggie and Ronnie Kray. The owner, Wally Schulberg, would work out individual programmes for his clients and arranged routines for Bercow and Bale.

Bercow was coached at Finchley Manor Lawn Tennis Club by the former Wimbledon quarter-finalist Bobby Wilson, and Bercow was the club's junior champion in 1974, when he was 11. Wilson remembers Bercow as a talented young player and called his serve the "Bercow bullet" because of its strength. "He was a very good junior for his age. He was very, very difficult to beat," Wilson says. "He was extremely good because he worked on the principle that if he got the ball back one more time than his opponent then he would win the point[47]." Bale remembers, "When I tried to get lessons from Bobby Wilson, the first question he asked was 'how many games did you get off Bercow?' I lied and said 2 or 3 as actually I lost 6-0, 6-0. But he was perhaps the best player in England then[48]".

Bercow had a lot of natural talent but it was his determination that really set him apart from his contemporaries. He hated being beaten and tennis helped to channel his aggressive streak and develop a killer instinct. As Wilson says, "He much preferred winning to losing. He wasn't always the best of losers. Sometimes if he didn't play as well as he should have he got angry. But he had a strong desire to succeed, which is what you need to be successful[49]." He was, for Fuller, "Ruthless. He would run for every ball, high and deep and just get it back[50]." Even though Bercow was a head smaller than any other boy playing on the Middlesex circuit, he wouldn't let that stand in his way.

He stood behind the baseline, playing balls forty feet into the air that would land 6 inches inside the court. This unusual style lead to him being labelled "Bercow the plonker," but for a long time it was effective. For Bale, Bercow, "Loved the pressure and wouldn't have folded to it. He was a fighter, you had to be twice as good to beat him, if you were the same standard you'd lose, he was a tougher competitor than most.[51]"

Bercow was a dominant presence in the tournaments going on round Middlesex. As he was reaching his peak in the under 12s, he played competitions for five consecutive weeks during the summer holidays. First up was North Middlesex; then Pinner, Coolhurst, Temple Fortune and finally, the biggest prize of all, the Middlesex Championships. Bercow won the lot. His mother, Brenda, was always there to cheer him on. As well as taking him to practice, she also ferried him to whichever tournament he was going to win next. Her reward came in seeing her son stuff the opposition.

Bercow also enjoyed doubles matches and he was a surprisingly understanding and cooperative partner. Fuller played with him on a number of occasions and always enjoyed it. He says, "When we played doubles he was fine if I messed up. He was very supportive and very encouraging on court, he'd always shout "great shot" at me and he was good fun to play with[52]". The pair won a number of tournaments together, with Bercow hogging the baseline and Fuller playing at the net.

Bercow might well have dreamt of national stardom and a place at Junior Wimbledon. Going into the national championships in the under-12 group, he was the number one seed and it seemed as if he was completely unbeatable. In Middlesex, winning was easy and he was so good that he was expected to breeze to the title when the rest of the country joined in. Shockingly, he lost in the first round. Perhaps it was because the match was played on grass and he was used to shale and hard courts at Finchley Manor. However, it seems that the defeat might have been a sign of deeper-lying weaknesses. Bercow's opponent in the nationals had a fast serve and the small boy on the baseline was powerless to do anything about it. As other players became ever-stronger, the problems would only increase for Bercow.

Tennis was a useful outlet for Bercow outside of his school life and it's intriguing that his tennis friends put a very different, more positive slant on the young Bercow's pomposity. For example, Fuller says that he was "a bit conceited, very intelligent and very strong minded and very well spoken. He spoke like a politician at the age of 10. He'd come in and see my father and say, 'Mr Fuller have you heard what's in *The Times* on page 3? It's outrageous, I have to show you'. He was very strongly spoken, but we got on well.[53]" Stuart Bale also remembers Bercow as pompous but a good friend[54]. For whatever reason, Bercow seemed relaxed around his tennis mates and he found making friends easy.

That compares with his school life, where everything seemed to be a battle. It seems rather sad that the same person could be understood by one group of people and yet wholly eschewed by another. When Bercow was put on the defensive, tennis became a sword to help the fight back against the attacks. As Julian Baker recalls: "At school, he was able to use it as a way of getting one over on those who liked to put him down...Bercow was really ambitious with his tennis and he couldn't help but talk grandly about it. He created this 'I could thrash all of you, you're all a bunch of oiks and peasants' caricature of himself. My mother [who worked at the school] played him at tennis when he was 14 and she beat him. He was absolutely furious.[55]"

Perhaps his defeat at the hands of one of his schoolmate's mothers was a warning of the decline to come. The reason Bercow didn't become a top tennis player is not because politics took over. Rather, it seems that politics filled the void left by his tennis as he was gradually outflanked by other players. Bercow himself admits, "I wasn't good enough[56]" to become a professional player, although many media profiles suggest that he *could* have made it if he hadn't contracted bronchial asthma. The truth, though, is that Bercow's tennis skills gradually weakened as his teenage years wore on. Wilson says that around the age of fifteen Bercow began to find tennis more testing. "As players get older, they hit it harder and volley it more, so John found it more difficult. His was not an aggressive attacking game[57]".

His downfall must have been a difficult pill to swallow. As Fuller says, "From being the best, he suddenly was one of the worst. He was still OK at under-14 level but by 14 everyone just started beating him. He fell out of the top 10 in Middlesex and never even got to the nationals. It was quite sad. The first time I beat him when I was 13, at the North Middlesex tournament, he didn't take it well.[58]"

The real problem for Bercow was that he was simply too short. No 12-year-old is tall enough to play a really attacking game, but as boys turn into men they develop bigger serves and become more aggressive. Bercow just couldn't compete. When he came into the net it was easy to lob him or hit a passing shot, so, in the words of Wilson, "He would never have been more than a good club player[59]". Ultimately, Bercow wasn't built to be a tennis star. According to Wilson, even when Bercow was eighteen he "wouldn't even get a point[60]" off his much older coach in a match – but when you're playing a former Junior Wimbledon Champion that is probably not too great an insult. It does, however, demonstrate that Bercow would never have been good enough to play at the top level.

Bercow seemed to emerge well from the test of character. It would have been easy enough to throw away his racket for good, but he seemed to accept his fall from grace well and used the talent that he still had to benefit others. He was still an excellent player – just not a superstar – and he used to spend his free time at the club helping to coach younger players. Wilson says that without Bercow's help he wouldn't have been able to cope with giving Saturday morning lessons and there was a definite altruistic streak behind Bercow's decision to help out.

Most of all, though, tennis provided an important means of self-justification. For someone who has often been written off by his peers, whether it was his classmates calling him spotty and a swot, or an MP calling him a "dwarf", his undoubted talent allowed Bercow to say that in the physical, as well as the mental, he was just as good as anyone else. In contrast to his school life, his tennis life was a happy one and made Bercow realise that if he put his mind to it, he could emerge a winner.

6

Monday Clubbing

"More right-wing than Marie Antoinette"

It was "utter madness[61]", he says now and so it probably was. John Bercow's decision to join the far-right Monday Club, where he was a member for three years, is one that has dogged him throughout his career.

It's not hard to see why it's been a constant black mark against him. Even at the time the Club faced vigorous opposition within the Conservative Party – and the dislike went further than a mere disagreement over policy. As a One Nation Conservative told me, the Monday Club during Bercow's membership was "Racist. It was absolutely simply that. It was racist. This was an intolerant, racist organisation under the cloak of being sceptical about Europe and the impact of immigration. But it was racist."

Despite the views of others in the Conservative Party, many Monday Clubbers saw the Club as an effective pressure group – and they vigorously denied that it had a racist outlook. It was undoubtedly influential, with many hundreds of members, including a large number of MPs – at its peak in the 1970s, six Monday Clubbers were Ministers in Edward Heath's government. Gregory Lauder-Frost, a prominent member for a number of years, says that the Monday Club has received a bad press. "Over 100 MPs have passed through the Monday Club and they can't all have been raving right-wing lunatics", he told me. "It has gone from 'right of the Tory party' to 'far-right' in last 18 years. As the media has moved further to the left, the description of the club has moved further to the right. The Monday Club position is really quite static and so if we were lunatics in the year 2000, we must have been lunatics when [the Club member] Julian Amery was a Minister."

Samuel Swerling, who was the Club Chairman from 1980-1982, says, "It was a mainstream organization with a varied membership. There were some extremely clever people in it and others as thick as a brick. It was an unusual organization and it had its good points as it had its failings[62]." The Club has never replicated the influence it had in the 1970s and during Margaret Thatcher's time in power its membership began to drop away. Today it is a marginalised and largely ineffective set, with a PO Box address in Bishop's Stortford in Hertfordshire instead of its old central London building, but when Bercow joined the Monday Club it still had the ear of a number of senior politicians.

Bercow certainly threw himself into Monday Club activities with gusto, and made great efforts to become an integral part of its work. At first, though, he came across as a bit of a loner and struggled to make friends. "He always stood at the back," says Eleanor Dodd, the head of the Club's youth section. "It was very male-dominated and quite a lot of [the members] were lawyers who would talk shop a lot of the time. John was doing tennis lessons and hadn't even started at university when he first joined us, so he was different. After meetings a lot of us would go off to have supper, but John never joined us as he didn't seem to be part of our coterie.[63]" Others remember Bercow as a dishevelled boy with grubby cuffs and wearing his infamous raincoat. It was a long mac that went down to his ankles and it only added to his slightly odd appearance as he stood at the back of the room, huddling himself up in it. But even from his position in the shadows, Bercow did still make his presence felt. Whenever a speaker took questions, Bercow would always take the opportunity to make a point, although as his fellow young Monday Clubber John Pinniger recalls, "It was nauseating because you knew he was making a speech rather than asking a question. He liked the sound of his own voice.[64]"

However, the frosty welcome did thaw over time and Bercow struck up a number of friendships. One of those was with Swerling, who found Bercow to be, "Ambitious. He wanted to make his own way and he had very strong opinions on immigration and free market views on the economy[65]". Pinniger says that Bercow seemed to look up to him, although the interest was not wholly reciprocated. "He latched on to me," Pinniger says, "and phoned me every morning at 9am.[66]"

Becoming a Monday Club member was definitely controversial, but perhaps his interests lay in some of the Club's other activities away from immigration. It had strong views on a number of other issues, opposing further European integration; promoting the traditional family unit and "Conservative values"; and calling for a tough stance on law and order. Those ideas fitted in nicely with what was then a popular combination for many Conservatives of economic liberalism and social conservatism. The two articles that Bercow wrote for the Club's magazine, *Monday World*, both argued in favour of free market economics. The titles – "Throwing off the shackles of the state" and "The Choice: Laissez-Faire or Creeping Socialism" – spoke for themselves[67].

Despite Bercow's membership of The Monday Club, he was not racist and he never at any stage advocated racist policies. However, the one area that Bercow concentrated on above all others was the one for which the Club attracted most criticism: immigration. He decided to join the Club's Immigration and Repatriation Committee, even though there were committees dealing with a host of other areas, such as economics or Northern Ireland. Indeed, even amongst some members of this right-wing organisation, he was considered particularly virulent in his views. As Eleanor Dodd says, "He was more right-wing than Marie Antoinette. He was very strong on immigration...and I can't think of any subject on which he wasn't to the right of the party. He was certainly not a middle-roader...he was very, very much in the Monday Club mould.[68]"

Bercow became the Secretary of the Immigration and Repatriation Committee in September 1981, under the chairmanship of Harvey Proctor, who was then the MP for Billericay. At the time, the Monday Club was broadly split between the moderates – led by George Gardiner, the MP for Reigate – and the "extremists", headed by Proctor and a number of others on the Immigration Committee. Like Bercow, Proctor also came from relatively humble origins – his father was a baker in York – and Proctor was a key member of the Club, sitting on the executive alongside his duties on the immigration committee. As an avowed right-winger, Proctor campaigned on the issue of immigration to win his seat in Basildon in the 1979 election by a narrow margin. He was later forced to resign in disgrace in 1987 after the *People* newspaper alleged that he had held "spanking" sessions with a number of teenage boys in his London flat. With the financial backing of Jeffrey Archer and Michael Heseltine, he then opened two luxury shirt shops, where he hung a sign saying "Shirtlifters will not be prosecuted[69]". Bercow soon became friends with Proctor and they started playing tennis with each other – yet another occasion when Bercow's prowess on the tennis court proved a useful way of making friends with powerful figures.

The committee was unequivocal in its stance towards immigration and it resolved to work for "an end to new Commonwealth and Pakistan immigration, a properly financed system of voluntary repatriation, the repeal of the Race Relations Act 1976 and the abolition of the Commission for Racial Equality. Particular emphasis on repatriation[70]". It was Bercow who minuted these recommendations. Such policies speak for themselves and Bercow was a fully signed-up participant in the affairs of the committee. Moreover, it's hardly likely that Bercow was surprised by the strength of feeling amongst the other members. Throughout the 1970s the Club had been actively calling for a scheme of voluntary repatriation and for the scrapping of the Race Relations Act 1976, which had prohibited discrimination on the grounds of "Colour, race, nationality or ethnic or national origins".

It was voluntary repatriation that really caught the imagination of the Immigration and Repatriation Committee. For their inspiration, they looked to s.29 of the Immigration Act 1971, which allowed the Secretary of State to make payments for the expenses of immigrants to allow them to leave to go to live permanently in another country, although it had to be shown that the person's interest was to leave the United Kingdom and that he wished to do so. Pinniger explains the stance, saying, "Repatriation was awkward and people then started trying to make it compulsory. But there was a case [for repatriation]. People from Ethiopia came to see us and wanted the help[71]". However, the policy faced staunch opposition and, as the then Secretary of the Confederation of Indian Organizations argued, people had "made this country their home. They want to be part of it. The question of resettlement does not appeal at all[72]."

It wasn't just the Committee as a whole which was big on immigration – it was also Bercow himself. In 1981/82 he sat on the Executive Council – the Club's highest body – as a representative of the Young Members' section, but he also wanted to join the Executive in his own right. So, in April 1982, he stood unsuccessfully in the elections for that body – and, in doing so, he produced his own personal mini-manifesto. In it, he argued that, "The strengthening of our national identity demands a programme of assisted repatriation[73]"; while "immigration" was listed first amongst his political interests, Bercow also described himself as "professional tennis coach" and an "active member of Finchley Young Conservatives".

For many of Bercow's contemporaries – even within the Tory Party – there was something unforgivable about his decision to sign up to the Club. On simple policy matters it was perfectly acceptable to hold an opposing view and then change one's mind – but, even back in the 1980s, the Monday Club was a very different story. As such, although Bercow was very young – when he went to his first Monday Club meeting he was barely old enough to order a drink in the bar afterwards – people question how he could ever have subscribed to their views. Bercow explains his decision by saying that "[Enoch] Powell convinced me that it was right to fear large-scale immigration. This was 1981, the year of the inner-city riots, and my fear was that we were in a politically explosive situation.[74]" It is true that race was high on the agenda, with Powell warning of a "racial civil war[75]" and widespread racial unrest breaking out across the UK. None of this, however, explains why Bercow ended up coming down on the side of voluntary repatriation.

In one sense, the answer is very simple. Bercow grew up in a time of right-wing politics, in an area of north London affected by immigration and he was therefore particularly open to these sorts of ideas. At the Hendon Young Conservatives, for example, there were plenty of right-wingers who might have equally felt at home in the Monday Club. There perhaps need be no further explanation, other than Bercow believed the ideas at the time and he later changed his mind. As Pinniger says, "He chose the Monday Club as he was an absolute devotee of Enoch Powell... He was very intense and obsessed with politics[76]".

Another explanation, then, might lie in the events going on in Bercow's life around the time he joined the Club. The great orator, the intellectual who read *The Times* on the wall outside his house, had failed in his schoolwork; and rather than heading to university, he became a tennis coach instead.

The Monday Club offered Bercow acceptance – it was, after all, the most high Tory of pressure groups. For the son of a Jewish cabbie, who must have often felt himself to be considered as "the other", to be accepted by the Monday Club would have given him a sense of truly belonging. For someone who was not a traditional Tory, making his way in an organisation like the Monday Club would have been a sign of coming into the fold. In joining up, Bercow was firmly casting himself in the role of assimilated British citizen.

As with many pressure groups which have a relatively small number of active members, it offered a good forum for Bercow to meet influential Conservatives. For someone who was obsessed by politics and who wanted to be an MP, it gave him an outlet to discuss political issues and to meet people who could help propel him towards a seat in Parliament.

However, as quickly as Bercow immersed himself in the Club, he suddenly decided to make an exit. Bercow stood down as secretary of the Immigration Committee in February 1983 after 18 months in post and then left the Club altogether, a year later in February 1984[77]. His explanation is that, "It became clear that there were a lot of people at the meetings who were really unpleasant racists and so I left[78]," although it is not completely clear why there was such a long gap between Bercow stopping active involvement and giving up his membership. The Monday Club was well known for its political positions well before Bercow joined and it was hardly a great leap to work out that some of the members would be racist. Perhaps it was Bercow's naivety – he was, after all, just 18 when he joined – that led him to underestimate the extent to which there really would be racists in the Monday Club.

It is obvious that the Monday Club was not a complete flash in the pan for Bercow. As late as 2000, Bercow said of Enoch Powell that, "Perhaps he should have used different language, in retrospect. Powell gave an impression of hostility to immigrants. But Enoch was not a racist. He was a patriot, and he served all his constituents, whatever their skin colour or origin... The professional critics of Powell, such as the Campaign for Racial Equality, blamed him for promoting violence. But to what extent he really was guilty of that... we'd have to think carefully[79]."

Bercow has since completely revoked his earlier views on voluntary repatriation, saying, "I'm guilty of errors in the past, subscribing to wrong and damaging views, but there is such a thing as the rehabilitation of offenders. I've more than made up for it.[80]" However, this does not completely explain the move away from his Monday Club views back in the mid-1980s, so soon after he held them. The key factor might well be that, a year after joining the Monday Club, Bercow went to university. He was away from north London and amongst a wider set of people, who were constantly challenging his political ideas.

Also important was that the tide of opinion within the Conservative Party was moving away from the Monday Club. As Samuel Swerling says, "He was a very young person with quite unformulated opinions of politics, but with certain political sentiments. He passed through it, came to a view that there were a few people who were pretty nutty, which was not true of most of the members, and he decided it was not the political vehicle for his advancement. It's perfectly reasonable that if don't want to make enemies, you head for the centre.[81]" Indeed as he began to make his way in student politics, out and out libertarianism was the popular cause. The authoritarian side to his politics would not have made him many friends amongst his peers in the Federation of Conservative Students. If the Monday Club was a convenient and influential vehicle in 1981, by 1984 it, like so many other movements, was being pushed aside by Thatcherism. If Bercow was tying his colours to the popular mast, that mast had changed by 1984 – or at least, the organisation most relevant to propelling Bercow's political career forward in 1984 was a libertarian, rather than an authoritarian one. Bercow had always been a free-market fan, but by turning his back on his earlier Monday Club views on immigration he performed perhaps as big a political conversion as when he turned from right-wing attack dog to liberal Conservative. His later political journey might therefore be seen as part of a continuing movement from right to left and one of a series of significant changes in his views.

But amidst all this, there was another driver behind Bercow's decision to leave the Monday Club. Fittingly, perhaps, it seems to have been his Jewish background that finally convinced him the time was right to go, no doubt influenced in part by his student politics. Anti-Semitism was a significant problem in the Conservative Party at the time and amongst Bercow's contemporaries, one was quoted in the press as calling a rival a "horrible little yid[82]". The Monday Club did accept all sorts of members and Derek Laud, the black Conservative who later rose to some sort of prominence by appearing on Big Brother, became one. Bercow was not alone in being a Jewish Monday Clubber, but there was a difficult confluence of the two. Dodd recalls that Bercow never brought up his religion and was reticent about his background: "Most people, over a period of time you get to know little snippets about them and a jigsaw emerges, but with John he was very much a closed book[83]". On one occasion when it came up in conversation, Dodd asked him if he was Jewish. "He said, 'Well I'm not Jewish really, my mother isn't Jewish but my father is, so I'm sort of only half-Jewish', she recalls. "He was very defensive about it and didn't want to talk about it any further, although I didn't care one way or the other if he was Jewish or not[84]". Dodd then asked Bercow what his father thought about his being a member of the Monday Club, but he "just said 'well I don't see much of my father' and made it out to be a distant thing." Dodd's account seems to provide quite a contrast to Bercow's views on his religion in his more mature years. For example, speaking to the Board of Deputies of British Jews in 2010, Bercow told them that his father taught him to be proud of his Jewish heritage, "to stand up for what I am...and not to seek to hide it[85]".

Whatever the other members of the Monday Club say, Bercow's Jewishness did not sit easily with the aims of the club. He was, after all, the grandson of Romanian immigrants and his father had been born into the Yiddish-speaking East End. In researching this book, this author spoke to a large number of people who'd been involved in the

Club at the same time as Bercow. On mentioning Bercow's religion to one senior figure, he said to me, "Oh those Jews, yes they're all the same." That statement was made to this author, with a Jewish surname, thirty years after Bercow was a member – and those are thirty years in which it's become totally unacceptable to be racist. If one of the members was prepared to talk like that to a virtual stranger, then one can only imagine what the atmosphere must have been like towards "those Jews" in the Monday Club back in the early 1980s.

So what was it that helped to change Bercow's mind? John Pinniger, who was by that time on the Club's Executive Council, recounted the story to me: "Why did he leave? Not because of immigration. It was about Israel and Palestine." Pinniger put a motion before the Council arguing for a two-state solution in the Middle East, which was not a popular position at the time. It came just a few years after Israel had almost been annihilated by a combined attack from the Arab countries around it in the Yom Kippur War and this was a very touchy subject for Bercow. He was extremely loyal to Israel and had been taken there by his father as a Barmitzvah present in 1974, just months after the war ended. He would have seen at first hand the destruction caused by the Arab invasion and the fear that pervaded in Israel at the time that the Jews, would, as promised, be thrown into the sea – a similar solution to throwing Jack Bercowitch and his fellow Romanian Jews into the Danube.

Pinniger is vehement that he himself is and was not anti-Semitic – and he had even worked with the Israeli embassy for a number of years, trying, he says, to promote awareness of Israel. However, on hearing of the motion, Bercow was furious. "Bercow knew I was going to do this," Pinniger told me. "He phoned me up and we had a blazing row. In the end I put the phone down on him and we didn't speak again till 1986 [when the pair were on Lambeth Council together]. We never saw him at the Monday Club again." Most tellingly, though, Pinniger remembers that Bercow called him "anti-Semitic" for putting forward the motion. Undoubtedly the issue went far deeper than just Pinniger himself and as the Club's Executive was voting on it, a number of Bercow's closest friends at the Monday Club would have had their say on the Israel question. But it's not so hard to think that in a place where a leading member would talk about "those Jews", inevitably discussion of Israel would have brought up deeper prejudices. As Bercow himself recounts, during his time at the Club he, "Encountered a degree of anti-Semitism.[86]" This, then, was the denouement of John Bercow's strained anti-immigration beliefs. His Asian schoolfriend who felt that Bercow's own background, of Jack Bercowitch on his way over from Romania, made him wholly incompatible with a rabidly anti-immigration policy was probably right. Mixed up with the politics of anti-immigration is, inevitably, antipathy to the Jews who came to the East End and later to the streets of north London. For Bercow, who was from the very background that so disturbed so many Monday Clubbers, his position was hard to reconcile. Perhaps Bercow only truly realised that they were racist when the target was not Ethiopians or Ugandans, but people like Jack Bercowitch, like his father Charlie, or like Bercow himself.

7

The Essex Boy

"We'd quote Monty Python, he'd quote Disraeli"

Wivenhoe Park on the outskirts of Colchester doesn't look like the sort of place where Great Men are made. But it was this small part of Essex that helped propel a pimply John Bercow towards a successful political career.

As Bercow had soon found at the Monday Club, being a tennis professional didn't exactly impress the higher echelons of the Tory Party. There may be enough former barristers in the House of Commons to set up a different sort of chambers, and as many journalists on the green benches as in the press gallery above, but tennis pros? You'd be lucky. Buster Mottram, the former world number 15, came closest in trying to be selected as a Tory candidate, but was never successful. So when Bercow, who was merely a club pro not a national star, was considering his options in the early 1980s, he knew that it would not be easy to step up from the tennis club to the Commons.

With his intellect, he realised there was more out there in the world for him than tennis, however much he enjoyed the game. Harvey Proctor, his mentor from the Monday Club, was an important influence and recommended that Bercow should consider studying for a degree. Despite having initially decided against it, Bercow realised that he was smart enough to go to university and that it would be useful politically, too. He was right, because student politics put the wheels in motion for his career in Parliament. If he'd decided to carry on working in tennis, it's debatable whether he would have made it in politics at all.

Bercow didn't have a wealth of options as he'd underperformed in his A-levels. Even though he was probably clever enough, he didn't have the grades to get into Oxford or Cambridge. Instead he got in touch with Shamit Saggar, who had been in Bercow's year at school and had just started his degree at Essex University. Saggar told Bercow that if he wanted a university education then he should go for it. Bercow took his advice to heart and went up to an open day at Essex, liked it, and put it down as one of his choices. As for the subject, it was only ever going to be Government and Politics.

Essex wasn't his only option and Bercow also applied to Brunel University in London, where the renowned public policy academic Prof. Maurice Kogan was on the interview panel. He later told a friend that he didn't want to teach Bercow as he thought he was too much of a blagger. The omens seemed little better when Bercow turned up at Essex and discovered that his interview was to be with Ernesto Laclau, a Marxist professor who had a substantial portrait of Marx behind the desk in his office. Bercow took one look at Marx and thought he was done for. But he need not have worried: he made such an impression that Laclau bent the rules to tell Bercow straight after the interview that he would be offered a place[87].

So it was that Bercow re-started his academic career at Essex, settling into his dormitory accommodation outside Colchester in the autumn of 1982. Essex was a relatively new university, having only been set up in 1962, but it was already carving out a niche in the humanities and social sciences. The campus itself was a set of uninspiring 1960s buildings that housed the small population of around 1,200 students. Essex had already managed to establish quite a reputation as a hotbed of left-wing activity in its short life and there was plenty for Bercow's leftie contemporaries to get their teeth into. Britain had just emerged triumphant in the Falklands War but unemployment stood at over three million. As the Labour Party moved to the left under Michael Foot, British politics was at its most polarised.

Bercow was there to work hard and as soon as he arrived in Colchester he made sure he was introduced to the key figures in the Government Department. When he put his mind to it he could be extremely charming and, as a fellow student told me, "John was quite the most sycophantic when he thought no one was watching...my jaw dropped watching John across the corridor". It seemed to many at the time that he was already gearing up for a political career. One of his professors, Anthony Barker, remembers that Bercow visited his house, along with the other students, for drinks. "I thought, 'Here's a young Cecil Parkinson!' He held court, sat on the floor in the middle of our drawing room. The others listened and it was all very amiable. He'd have been 19 or 20 and saying 'thank you' and 'good evening' to my wife in a totally different manner to the rest of the students, as if he was already in training for buttering up the ladies of a certain age in the Conservative associations where he'd want to be adopted. I wondered at the time, is he veneer all through? But I don't think [with hindsight] that's right.[88]"

But if it was a fascinating time to be studying politics, Bercow was even more interested in putting it into practice, and he sought out the University's Conservative Association at the Freshers' Fair in his first week. At that time the Tories had a marginal presence on campus and, in one of the country's most left-wing universities, there were few people willing to stick their heads above the parapet to speak up for Thatcherism. The Association's membership was in double figures but there were perhaps only five or six active members, so, in that context, when Bercow and two other students signed up at the Fair it was something of a coup. Andrew Crosbie, who was Chairman of the Association when Bercow arrived at Essex, says that his first impression was that Bercow was, "Very well-spoken and a bit out of place at the University of Essex. He was very keen, very eager, very passionate about politics.[89]"

Bercow soon began to play an integral role in the Association, becoming Crosbie's Vice-Chairman within months and then focussing on gaining the Association a much more vocal presence on campus. Whereas the Essex Tories had previously been wary of engaging with their left-wing opponents for fear of validating them, with Bercow's debating powers at their disposal they were soon able to get their message across. As Crosbie told me, "John became one of the key speakers for us. He was articulate and very witty, so John delivered the message in such a way that we got an audience. We were the enforcers and John was the consummate politician."

The others felt that Bercow particularly enjoyed the argy-bargy of debate rather than being too entrenched on the issues themselves. "He was relatively right-wing, but then again we all were", says Crosbie. "He was never extreme about anything. With John, it was less about policies and more about engaging with other ideas and opinions.[90]" It's interesting that at a time when Bercow was still in the Monday Club, others within the Conservative Party felt that he was relatively moderate. It perhaps indicates that politics for Bercow is above all about the debate, and explains how he managed to move so seamlessly from authoritarian to libertarian, and perhaps also why his views later changed again. Alternatively, one might simply take it as evidence of just how right-wing the Tories were at Essex in the 1980s. As the University Senate was told when Speaker Bercow was put forward for his honorary degree in 2010, "At the time he was, to say the least of it, pretty right-wing. Some of his views at the time would have made Margaret Thatcher herself look a trifle wet, even a bit of a wimp."

Inevitably the few active Tories also became firm friends, in part because they were pushed together as they were ostracised by many of the left-wingers on campus, although Bercow did have some other friends outside his Conservative circle. One of those in his group was Stuart Millson, who had some very hard right views indeed and later joined the BNP[91]. Bercow was horrified, with a friend recalling, "Stuart and John were very friendly…but when Milson joined the BNP Bercow didn't want much to do with him."

Bercow spent much of his first year hanging out in Crosbie's flat, which was closer to the university's two bars, library and lecture theatres than his own student halls. In some ways his existence was that of the typical student, spending much of his time in the university bar and having fun with his friends. There was, however, always something different about Bercow, even amongst his Tory friends. Crosbie remembers Bercow as, "Very bookish, quite unusual. He certainly gave the impression that he was very driven and not your average student. He was a bit of an outsider in the social group as he didn't have things in common with students. We'd quote Monty Python and he'd quote Disraeli. He was consumed with his interests.[92]"

Those interests still included regular trips back to London for Monday Club meetings and Bercow was also becoming increasingly active in the national Federation of Conservative Students. Much of his time away from campus was spent with John Carlisle, the MP for Luton West, whom Bercow had come across in the Monday Club. Carlisle was known as the "MP for Pretoria" thanks to his opposition to sanctions against the apartheid regime in South Africa and he was Chair of the Foreign Affairs Committee while Bercow was at the Club. South Africa was a key flashpoint in the 80s and as Carlisle remembers, "It was a very sensitive subject. There were big political divisions, it was headline news and we didn't go to public meetings without demonstrations against us.[93]"

There was significant opposition to Mandela within Conservative circles. It was commonplace for some members of the FCS to wear "Hang Nelson Mandela" T-shirts when Bercow was a leading member of the organisation, although Bercow never wore one or believed in the sentiments expressed. However, Bercow did choose to spend his time with people who believed Mandela was a "terrorist" – a view held by Carlisle and that was also expressed by Margaret Thatcher herself[94].

In general terms, Carlisle says Bercow, "Broadly subscribed to what I was saying. He used to ring me up to say, 'Where are you going next, can I come?' He knew what I was speaking on, my reputation, the opposition we would find... John would never have come on those trips if he hadn't concurred with that view.[95]" Many of Carlisle's engagements were at universities, with inevitable student protests, but Bercow used to give as good as he got. On one occasion in November 1983, Carlisle was due to speak at the Cambridge Union, proposing the motion, "This House Would Tour South Africa". As the party made their way to the Union, they came across the protestors waiting for them and amidst a sea of rotten eggs, Bercow started arguing back. "He loved it", Carlisle recalls, "he was good on his feet and believed in the cause, he genuinely did. He would stand his corner and give his views. He was strong minded with lots of talent.[96]"

Back at Essex, in Bercow's second year, he took over the Chairmanship of the Association in a smooth transition from Crosbie. By that point, there were around one hundred members, a particularly impressive increase as that equated to nearly 10% of the total student body. The Association wanted to increase its power on campus further still and Bercow volunteered to stand to be President of the

Student Union, a particularly hard task given the left-wing support at Essex. He produced a typically robust manifesto, declaring "We need to protect the interests of all students, not just a minority of egotistical political hacks," as well as rallying against those who felt they had a "divine right" to stop people from talking. On the back page, it posed a test as to whether you were a Conservative: "Do you like having fun, drinking, Clint Eastwood movies, making money, playing sport? Do you never wear sandals, men's earrings, dope pouches, Palestinian scarves, Oxfam coats?"

Incredibly, in the first round Bercow came out with the highest number of votes, comfortably beating the Labour candidate, Maria Debono, into second place by more than 100 votes. Unfortunately for Bercow, however, the Union used the alternative vote system. When the disparate left-wing candidates were knocked out one by one, their second or third preferences inevitably went to Debono, who edged past Bercow to take the presidency. Nonetheless, the Tories must have had little hope of actually winning. Coming so close was a significant victory and a sign of how far the Association had come.

The constant battles with the left naturally made Bercow something of a target. As one fellow student says, "Bercow was well known and well despised by most of the student activists, partly because he seemed to go out of his way to say things that he knew would annoy them…[But] he may have been abrasive as a student, but he wasn't entirely a prat." For Bercow, winding up the left-wingers was very much his *raison d'etre*, although as Crosbie says, "the left-wing tolerated John because they appreciated his intellect and because he was more than happy to engage in debate he got their respect, because he was [prepared to] stand up in front of 200 people with 190 screaming at him, intimidating him.[97]" Alison Murphy, who recalls Bercow as a political adversary rather than a friend, says, "He was the best speaker at the university and a courageous one as it was a very left-leaning student union. I once bumped into him late at night, as he was putting up posters of Margaret Thatcher. We agreed to disagree, and despite all his very right-wing rhetoric he came across as a libertarian who liked the cut and thrust of debate."

Despite Bercow's confidence, he often found it a nerve-wracking experience facing such tough crowds, and he would sometimes throw up with nerves just before a big speech. His worries were understandable, for it was not uncommon for local lefties to come to the Student Union to pick a fight. That Bercow was prepared to face up to that risk and make his point regardless is certainly to be commended.

Nonetheless, despite the affection of some on the left, the attacks on Bercow were often very personal. With Bercow still suffering from persistent acne, one left-winger cruelly stuck a squashed pizza to the notice board of the student union with the tag, "Portrait of John Bercow[98]". There were other confrontations in the student union, too. One night, Bercow had been involved in heated discussions with a set of left-wingers and a feminist who was part of the group was getting particularly worked up by Bercow's arguments. In the middle of the conversation she finally decided she'd had enough and emptied her pint over Bercow's head.

Bercow liked to hold set-piece events and used his contacts to arrange for a number of prominent political figures to speak to the Association. One particular coup was organising for Cecil Parkinson, the former Chairman of the Conservative Party, to come to Essex. Significant protests accompanied Parkinson's arrival and he and Bercow were forced to make their way inside through an underground car park, being jostled and abused by the crowds as they went. It seems that matters went from bad to worse. A fabled version of events is that the notoriously scruffy Bercow bought a new suit for the occasion. "First he tried to put his hands in his pockets, and scuffled about for a bit before he realised they were still sewn up. [Then] when he reached out to shake Parkinson's hand it became clear that the Burton's label was still attached to the sleeve.[99]" Other speakers included Teddy Taylor, a prominent Monday Clubber and MP for Southend who was later duped into an interview with Sacha Baron-Cohen's Ali G, which culminated in a serious discussion (on Taylor's part at least), about the effects of European integration on Dutch pornography. When Baron-Cohen suggested that Swedes were "easier and less frigid" than English women, Taylor didn't miss a beat, replying, "Southend-on-Sea is the place with the loveliest girls".

However, a lot of the staff were concerned by Bercow's activities.

For Prof Anthony Barker, Bercow's practice of inviting speakers like Parkinson and Taylor to Essex risked the university's reputation. Barker feels that Bercow was, "In effect challenging them to ban the meeting…his purpose was if they banned the meeting he'd be on to the [newspapers] at once, damning the University for suppressing free speech. The Dean wasn't quite that daft and realised that it would be better for the meeting to proceed[100]."

Incredibly, despite spending so much time on political activity away from the university and most of his time on campus involved with university politics, Bercow still had an excellent reputation amongst many of the academics in the government department. Prof. Anthony King says of Bercow that, "When he was a student here, he was very right-wing, pretty stroppy, and very good[101]." Barker, who taught Bercow British politics in his first year at Essex, remembers him as an exceptional student. "Bercow was in a class of his own," he told me. "I had a handful of outstanding students, but the thing about John was that he didn't just produce a 1st class essay and exam scripts on the basis of what was necessary, he went far further. He produced six or seven thousand words which would have been printable and publishable in the way that it was presented, rather than two to three thousand words [that everyone else did]. It was the volume and industry, combined with great ability." Such was Bercow's prowess that Barker felt the marking guidelines wouldn't let him go far enough. "We weren't supposed to go above 75 at Essex and I thought 'that's not fair. If the other students get 70 or 75 he should get 85 or 90'. He was the only student I ever gave such marks to".

Bercow's academic ability set him apart, both metaphorically and literally, from the other students. Barker remembers that Bercow always sat on his own, away from the rest of the group in tutorials. However, Bercow was a surprisingly calm influence. "He was clearly quite different from the other students in his knowledge and capacity to express himself, but he came and participated courteously. He said his piece on the discussion and would let others speak.[102]" Having under-performed at school, it seems that Bercow had finally found his niche. For his dissertation, he chose to write about Edmund Burke and his political philosophy, producing an excellent piece of work. And despite all his student politics, Bercow still managed to score a first in his final exams. He was, says King, "An outstanding student, who richly deserved the first-class degree that he got[103]."

When Bercow was elected Speaker, the Lib Dem MP Bob Russell, the Member for Colchester and another Essex graduate, told the House of Commons, to laughter, that, "The University of Essex is proud of you.[104]" An honorary degree soon followed in 2010 for one of the university's most prominent alumni. But it is Bercow, more than the university, who should be grateful. On campus, he finally excelled, both academically and politically, and being at Essex allowed him to take a vital step towards national politics. Without Essex, there would have been no Federation of Conservative Students. And without the FCS, Bercow might not have made it as a politician at all.

8

The National Stage

"A pocket Cicero"

John Bercow was never meant to be the Chairman of the Federation of Conservative Students. If everything had gone to plan, he would have been just another committee member, subsumed in the organisation and far removed from the limelight. Instead, circumstances conspired in his favour and he soon became a very public figure as the organisation entered some extremely troubled waters.

The FCS was not your standard student movement – it was radicalised and highly controversial. Its meetings had a rough and tumble feel to them and the typical FCS member was far removed from the stereotypical Tory, with the movement reaching out to working and middle class Tories, to the typical Basildon man who powered Margaret Thatcher to three election victories. Most people there would wear jeans, which was thought hugely significant and subversive at the time, and as one delegate at an FCS conference put it, "It had a very different atmosphere to it, both in the appearance and the make up of the people there – and there was also a large proportion of women. There was lots of excitement about where we were in politics, we were part of a Thatcherite revolution rolling back the frontiers of the state...we saw ourselves as the vanguard of her thinking and everyone loved Margaret Thatcher."

This viewpoint was at odds with that of more traditional Tories and it was no surprise that it found particular favour amongst students from less privileged backgrounds – usually those who were from state schools and were non-Oxbridge educated. As the senior FCS hack Mark MacGregor said when the Tory Party Chairman, John Gummer, temporarily suspended funding for the organisation after its notorious

Loughborough conference in 1985 – where FCS members were described as "Tory Louts on the Rampage[105]", even though only £14 worth of damage was caused[106] – "Our supporters are from working class backgrounds and the party establishment seems to feel that we don't quite fit in.[107]" For Bercow – educated at a comprehensive and then Essex – the FCS was a natural home.

As well as taking the battle to the left, The FCS was also fighting it out internally, with ongoing tensions between a number of factions. The controlling and most radical grouping was the "Sounds" – libertarians who took on the tactics of the radical left and made them their own in the pursuit of a far-reaching agenda of libertarianism. It certainly wasn't all that unusual to hear a sound FCS hack arguing for the legalisation of all drugs; proposing the abolition of the law against incest; or advocating the privatisation of the road system. Although Bercow never advocated these most barmy ideas, he did find his home amongst the sound faction.

The sounds were closely followed in terms of popularity if not campaigning zeal by the "wets", the more traditional Tory grouping who broadly followed One Nation Conservative ideas – although many wet views were to the right of current Conservative Party policy in a number of areas. But, at the time, there was a very real ideological conflict and just as wet Conservative MPs were finding themselves increasingly outnumbered by Thatcherites in the Cabinet, so the sounds were very much in the ascendancy in the FCS – even if their views were more extreme than those of many Thatcherite MPs.

As Bercow's friends at Essex – and all other good Monty Python fans – might have known, wherever there is political action, there are "Splitters". The FCS was no different and it had its own minority faction made up of Tory authoritarians. It was called the "2.10 group" – named after the room at an FCS conference where the authoritarians had held their first meeting – or, alternatively the "Dorset Group". To everyone else, however, they were known simply as the "shits" and they had a relatively limited reach.

It was an exciting time both nationally and in the FCS itself and it's easy to see how students could have become so obsessed with FCS activities. In the past, Conservative students might have held dinners, arranged meetings to hear MPs speak or have gone on trips to Parliament. These events remained part of the overall FCS repertoire in the early 1980s, but the students went far further than before, taking on a real campaigning zeal. For example, during the miners' strike, when Bercow was on the FCS national committee, more than a hundred Conservative students met at a service station on the M1 in the middle of the night. They piled into minibuses with posters and buckets of paint and spread out across Yorkshire to get to work. By the morning, a range of towns had been plastered with posters declaring, "Stop Scargill's fascist thugs – national ballot now". It was the type of guerrilla warfare that seemed so un-Conservative to Central Office but which made life in the FCS so appealing.

The situation in Northern Ireland also captured the imagination of the FCS, often to the detriment of its relations with the party high command. The FCS ran a "Loyal Ulster, British Forever" campaign and was, as one member put it, "Very hardcore Unionist with an Orange subculture", with the IRA at the top of the FCS hate list. In fact, the organisation had its own taste of republican terrorism when Edgar Graham, a leading Ulster Unionist and former FCS member, was shot dead at Queens' University in Belfast in 1983, aged just 29. He was widely regarded as a rising star, with the then leader of the Ulster Unionists, James Molyneaux – who, coincidentally, had proposed Bercow in his unsuccessful Monday Club Executive election – saying that, "Had Mr Graham not been murdered he would have become the leader of our party, such was his calibre[108]". The FCS high command did not forget the death of their friend and colleague.

Then in 1984 the IRA bombed the Grand Hotel in Brighton during the Conservative Party conference, killing five people, including the MP Sir Anthony Berry, with Margaret Thatcher only narrowly avoiding injury in the blast. Her bathroom was destroyed by the force of the bomb but the main part of her hotel room, where she was working on her speech for conference the following morning, was largely untouched. Margaret Tebbit, the wife of Norman Tebbit, who was for so long was the darling of the FCS, suffered severe spinal injuries and was paralysed in the attack.

Against this backdrop, the FCS took a resolute line on Northern

Ireland and it wasn't unusual for members of the Federation to address Orange Orders across the UK. Then, in 1985, came a defining moment for Northern Ireland and the FCS's relationship with the Province. The Anglo-Irish Agreement was signed by the UK and Irish governments, giving an advisory role on the governance of Northern Ireland to the Republic for the first time. The agreement faced virulent opposition from the Unionist parties, many of whom saw it as selling out to the same terrorists who had bombed the Grand Hotel just a year earlier. All of Northern Ireland's Unionist MPs resigned, causing by-elections which they used as a platform to campaign against the agreement. The Thatcher government stood firm against the opposition and it was passed in Parliament with the Labour Party's support. The majority of 426 was the largest during the whole of Thatcher's time as Prime Minister.

The FCS, meanwhile, were having none of it. The committee mobilised and organised a trip across to Northern Ireland to campaign alongside Unionist politicians, including Enoch Powell, who was then the Ulster Unionist member for South Down. Tebbit, as Party Chairman, did his best to block the visit, but he was famously told, "Sorry Norman, the tickets are booked", and the trip went ahead regardless. It was to be one of a number of occasions when the FCS went too far for Tebbit's liking, with serious implications later on for Bercow and his career. But in this instance, Bercow, who was on the FCS National Committee, was noticeable by his absence. One of those who went to Northern Ireland recalls, "He conspicuously had some prior engagement which prevented him from going. But everyone knew the reason he wasn't there was for careerist, 'I want to stay with the party' reasons." Another says, "It was a big thing to do but students were allowed to disagree."

It certainly wasn't the only time when Unionism made life uncomfortable for Bercow, On another occasion, he was sent to address a heavily loyalist Orange Order in Glasgow. His speech was arranged by Mark Dingwall, an FCS member who came from a council estate in Glasgow and who later edited a Glasgow Rangers fanzine. At the time, Dingwall freely admitted having contact with legal Loyalist paramilitaries but rejected violent activity[109]. The atmosphere was highly intimidating especially for a small man from north London in a room full of uncompromising Glaswegians. Bercow was so nervous that he ran out the back of the Orange Hall and vomited on the ground, before going back in and giving the speech.

More worryingly, in allying itself with various Orange Orders, some members of the FCS also seemed to subscribe to some of their less palatable practices, including the promotion of sectarianism. It was common practice for sectarian songs to be sung at FCS events. One of the favourites was 'No Pope of Rome':

> "Oh no Pope of Rome,
> No Chapels to sadden my eyes,
> No nuns or no priests,
> No rosary beads,
> Every day is the Twelfth of July"

Also controversial – and sung by some in the FCS – was 'Here lies a soldier of the UVF', which glorified those who had died fighting for an illegal paramilitary group, responsible for the killing of many civilians.

As his attitude to the trip to Northern Ireland shows, Bercow was never interested in the most hardcore Orange undercurrent in the FCS. What's more, he made a point of denouncing one member who used the phrase, "The murdering papist minority", at an FCS conference. However, although it is not clear that Bercow ever personally sang such songs, he was around a number of fellow FCS members who were regularly singing them, including at the Scarborough Orange Hall immediately after he was eventually elected as FCS Chairman in 1986. Likewise, at that same conference, when a vote was held by a show of hands, a large number of delegates started humming another Orangemen's song, 'The Sash', until the hall was filled with the tune of that loyalist refrain. Singing sectarian songs was so common amongst the FCS that it seems implausible that Bercow was unaware of what was going on. It's clear that such behaviour is totally unacceptable and Bercow now must surely cringe at the thought of what some of the members of the FCS were doing under his watch.

Back in early 1985, however, the heady heights of the

Chairmanship still seemed an unlikely destination for Bercow. Much of what happened in the organisation was controlled by a few influential members at the top and not all of them were convinced by his suitability. "I thought he was creepy," one colleague recalls. "Some others thought he was marvellous because he had this gift of oratory, but I thought it out of date and it made my stomach churn." A friend from the time says that the only things that stood out were that Bercow was "always very unfashionably dressed with a shabby jacket," and that he was a great mimic of Enoch Powell and Tony Benn and would often pick up on people's mannerisms. Another fellow member says that he was, "A weird character and always very disorganised" – hardly a ringing endorsement; while Oonagh Moulton, another FCS aficionado says, "Bercow always carried a briefcase to conferences, as if he thought himself more important than us. We regarded him as funny, a caricature and you wouldn't find him attractive. He was more in the background and then jumped to prominence.[110]"

But the man who mattered most was MacGregor, who surprised a lot of the FCS leaders by taking Bercow under his wing and propelling him up through the ranks of the organisation. At the Loughborough conference, MacGregor ran for Chairman and put Bercow on his slate for the FCS's National Executive, with both being elected comfortably. As his profile rose, Bercow became a regular feature on the platform at FCS conferences. At Loughborough he gave a bombastic and popular speech, described by one delegate as an "ultra-ranting address. Bercow was pandering to the crowd. He would sniff out the mood and then say it in a more verbally vivid way than anyone else". Such was his oratory that was even referred to as a "pocket Cicero" by the future Conservative MP Paul Goodman at one FCS meeting, but, even at this stage, it still looked unlikely that Bercow would ever become leader. Many of his fellow committee members remained unconvinced by both his organisational ability and the conviction of his beliefs. Moreover, the biggest obstacle in his way was MacGregor himself, who was considering running for the leadership again in 1986, thereby blocking Bercow from making his own bid for power.

However, as with much of student politics, not everything went to plan. MacGregor's deputy, David Hoile, also had his sights on the

Chairmanship and he began undermining MacGregor amongst the FCS Committee. Realising that he was losing ground, MacGregor needed someone to take his place. He and his friends refused to accept Hoile, not only because he'd been actively campaigning against MacGregor but also because his hard line views on foreign affairs made many uncomfortable. The senior members of the sound faction, including MacGregor, saw Bercow as the ideal solution. He was on the executive, was articulate and he might be able to win. What's more, Bercow was a comparative moderate – although he was a definite right-winger, at around that time other members of the organisation were setting up the Committee for a Free Nicaragua, which was later addressed by a leader of the Nicaraguan Contras; and amongst some of the rank and file members there was continued support for the legalisation of incest, as well as the appearance of the notorious "Hang Nelson Mandela" T-shirts. As the FCS had alienated the Tory Party's high command with both their radical policies and some very public rebellions like the trip to Northern Ireland, a more moderate approach was desired. "Bercow opposed the loony stuff," a friend told me. "He had his eyes set on a political career and he realised the FCS didn't look good to the party." That he would be unlikely to pick a fight with Central Office was certainly in Bercow's favour – although some of those who backed Bercow for this reason were to regret it by the end of his year in office.

Once Bercow had been anointed by the small cabal as the chosen successor, the next task was to win him the support of the sound faction. A few years earlier, in-fighting among the right-wing of the FCS had split the vote and allowed Goodman, a wet candidate, to win. After that debacle, a caucus system had emerged, whereby the sound faction voted amongst themselves to decide who would be put forward as Chairman. Every year, Thatcherite FCS representatives from each region of the country were sent to a special meeting to make the decision.

In 1986, although MacGregor and his friends were backing Bercow, Hoile was also winning a lot of support and the race was too close to call. On the day of the caucus, disaster struck for the Bercow camp when one of their supporters, Mike Simmonds, who lived in Leeds, didn't turn up, thinking the ballot was the following day. His vote was potentially crucial, so various frantic phone calls were made and MacGregor adjourned the caucus to give Simmonds enough time to drive down to London. To play for time, the meeting was moved from central London to the flat that MacGregor shared with another FCS hack, Russell Walters, in Tooting Bec.

The apartment was infamous amongst FCS members for the legendary parties that were held there, including one where all three emergency services were called on the same night. That particular gathering had an "Orange" theme to mark July 12th and the guests had a raucous time, enjoying themselves in the swimming pool at the back of the block of flats until the early hours of the morning, variously drinking alcohol, having sex or chanting political slogans. They were so loud that the police came to give them a warning to keep the noise down; during the evening gatecrashers set fire to an entry 'phone and the fire brigade were called; and then, the next morning, as the guests were finally making their way home, probably a little bit the worse for wear, two of them fell into a hole in the front garden and the partygoers dialled 999 to fetch an ambulance. It was this final incident that saved the hosts: when their landlord wanted to know what had been going on, it was pointed out to him that thanks to a hole in his driveway, someone had been injured. They got away with the other indiscretions.

Soon the twenty or so delegates were gathered at MacGregor's but still there was no sign of Simmonds. The Bercow side desperately began filibustering, making overly long speeches, raising points of order and generally trying to slow down the meeting in any way they could, but they were running out of steam. Almost at the exact moment when the vote couldn't be put off any longer, Simmonds finally walked through the door. The vote was held and Bercow defeated Hoile – by a majority of one.

For some, though, the fallout didn't end there. One of the delegates that day was William Beggs, a student at Teeside Polytechnic and a regional FCS Chairman. He was a fervent Hoile supporter and was extremely angry when Bercow won the sounds' nomination. Luckily for Bercow, Beggs's anger focused on MacGregor – the man he saw as the true architect of Hoile's downfall. Bizarrely, Beggs began a campaign of psychological terror against MacGregor, calling him up over and over again in the middle of the night and whispering his name down the phone. Then – if it were possible – Beggs's behaviour became even more sinister. He enjoyed children's lullabies and would ring MacGregor up in the night to eerily sing "The Runaway Train goes down the track" down the line at him.

Only later did MacGregor realise what a lucky escape he'd had. That same William Beggs was convicted in 2001 of sexually assaulting and murdering an eighteen year old man. The victim's head was discovered on a beach near Troon, in Scotland, and his arms and legs were found 60 miles away in Loch Lomond. At his trial, it was revealed that Beggs had previously been found guilty of the murder of a Newcastle barman who was found on the North York Moors with his throat slashed, but the conviction had been overturned on a technicality at appeal. That first murder took place just a few months after the caucus and the ensuing phone calls to MacGregor. A series of chilling sexual assaults followed and police say that Beggs carried all the hallmarks of a serial killer[111]. It certainly gives a new dimension to the usual back-stabbing that goes on in student politics.

Once Bercow had won the sound faction's nomination, serial killers aside, it was all plain sailing. The official election itself took place at the FCS's annual conference, held in 1986 in Scarborough, where he was being opposed by the wets' Mark Francois, later a Tory MP. The annual gatherings were like mini party conferences – around three to four hundred people would gather in the conference room, with the national committee on the stage and various people making speeches to the crowd. The influence that such student conferences had is hard to believe today. The national media covered the proceedings, with Jim Naughtie, now the presenter of the *Today* programme, being one of those despatched to an FCS conference in the 1980s.

If anything, an FCS meeting was like a Marxist rally with a right-wing ideology. Delegates called each other "comrade" and the attitudes of many people there were summed up by Mark Dingwall, in the speech he gave before being elected to the national committee. "I'm proud to be an admirer of Derek Hatton and the Leninist discipline. If you vote for me you'll be voting for the tendency that puts its principles before expediency.[112]" The FCS members might have despised what Leninism said, but they drew much from it in terms of organisational zeal.

The 1986 conference was typical FCS – videos of orange marches were prizes in the raffle, there were calls from some delegates for incest to be legalised, and some members sang songs glorifying the Yorkshire Ripper. There was also a defiant nod towards Central Office a year on from the controversial Loughborough conference, which had seen Gummer threaten those involved with ten-year expulsions from the Conservative Party. In one of his last acts as Chairman, Mark MacGregor said, "None of this has happened. The named individuals are back here, your national officers are still in charge of a growing and vibrant organisation… I believe we have triumphed, comrades, we are back and we are back for good.[113]"

Bercow himself may have been uncomfortable with this line of argument, although he knew he might have to hold his tongue to win the Chairmanship. He didn't go in for the most extreme policies and some of his colleagues had doubts about the conviction of his beliefs. As one told me, "I never believed that he was a believer. The whole libertarian side were obsessed with contemporary libertarian writers but he showed no interest in the theory. He would always go over the top and ham it up, but he gave vague speeches and always stuck to safe water and went on about Edmund Burke. He would never talk about legalising drugs or prostitution or ever say anything remotely dangerous." This might not come as a surprise when you remember that just a few years earlier Bercow was a Monday Club member, which would have put him more in line with the "shits". No wonder he wasn't the most fervent believer in the libertarian line.

However, Bercow was never in danger of losing because the right was united behind him. The message was very much "vote the slate, vote Bercow", and vote Bercow they did, as he beat Francois by 197 votes to 123, with the sounds winning all the places on the national committee to boot. The successful faction went off to the Glasgow Rangers Supporters club to celebrate, where some FCS members would sing those infamous loyalist songs. There, John Bercow could reflect on a remarkable rise to prominence. The pompous boy who had been written off by his peers was now the man in charge. Soon it would become clear that he would bow to nobody; and many of those who helped him to climb the greasy pole – and who celebrated with him that night – were left cursing their choice.

9

Shutdown

"Guilty"

John Bercow's time as FCS Chairman can be summed up by one word – "guilty". It was that stark headline on the front cover of a magazine that was to prove the catalyst for bringing down the whole organisation. And it was the verdict given of John Bercow by his peers and friends on the FCS national committee, who felt betrayed by his actions as the FCS was taken away from them right under their noses.

But, at first, there was no sign of the turmoil to come. Bercow happily worked away in the FCS office in party headquarters, and it seemed that he would be able to fulfil his mandate of bringing the FCS closer to the party high command. The relationship between the two had been badly damaged by the continuing militant tendencies of the Federation, which were a constant source of embarrassment for the party, but under Bercow's leadership there were a number of potentially promising signs for cooperation with Central Office. Bercow was instinctively less extreme than your average FCS hack and, in any regard, the Party Chairman, Norman Tebbit, was particularly well-liked amongst FCS members, who regarded themselves as Tebbitists more than Thatcherites. They subscribed to his uncompromising tactics in taking on the left and his belief in Conservatism being powered along by hard-working individuals. No wonder that at the Tory Party Conference in 1985, the FCS rounded up the most attractive set of girls it could find and decked them out with T-shirts that spelt out, when read in a line, "Tebbit is Magic".

The pair had an excellent working relationship and, as Bercow had ambitions to become a politician, there was no way that he would alienate a senior figure just for the hell of it. The stand-off with Tebbit back in 1985 over the Anglo-Irish Agreement had proved that it might not all be plain sailing, but with Bercow as Chairman the FCS looked – at least for a time – as if it might move back towards the mainstream of the party. Bercow was also on good terms with Jeffrey Archer, who was then Deputy Chairman of the Party, and they used to play squash and tennis together. "A lot of people thought it was good because we wanted someone with our beliefs who'd succeed in getting selected as a Tory MP to advance these policies,[114]" says Harry Phibbs, another members of the FCS National Committee.

Bercow relished his new job and he took to the role with his typical enthusiasm, travelling up and down the country giving speeches to various Conservative groups. The first key meeting came when the FCS leadership were invited to meet Mrs Thatcher at 10 Downing Street. It was reported that Bercow and his comrades urged Mrs Thatcher to "stand firm in her opposition to sanctions on South Africa [and] called for the abolition of the University Grants Committee as a prelude to the privatisation of Universities coupled with the introduction of student loans.[115]" However, Phibbs, who was part of the delegation, recalls that, "Bercow was anxious to reassure her that he was not unduly wild in his views, mentioning the need to win consensus for reform. Mistake. "We are a party of conviction," Thatcher told him firmly.[116]"

Meanwhile, Bercow showed no sign of losing his confrontational attitude to political opponents – despite the heavy chains of office. Just a couple of weeks after winning the FCS election, he had already started picking fights. Vicky Phillips, who later became the Labour Party's Women's Officer, had been elected as leader of the notoriously left-wing NUS, but Bercow was not one to offer an olive branch. "Congratulations," he wrote in a letter to her. "I very much look forward to waging political warfare against you. If you are a product of the Phil Woolas [the previous year's NUS President] school of political practice, I shall especially relish the experience.[117]"

Bercow didn't just use his considerable oratorical talents against members of the Labour Party. As Chair of the FCS he had the right to go along to the rival Young Conservatives conference, where a motion was being put forward condemning the idea of a poll tax. The levy had been approved in a Green Paper, entitled 'Paying for Local Government', which had been produced by the Adam Smith Institute, the economically liberal think-tank much favoured by the FCS. Unsurprisingly, the FCS were all for the idea, but the Young Conservatives liked the idea of the poll tax about as much as they liked the FCS. The case against it was being put by the YCs' Chairman Nick Robinson, now the BBC's Political Editor, who in those days was an active participant in student politics before taking a step back from the front line in the interests of BBC impartiality. Bercow could scarcely have disagreed with him more, but, undaunted by being in enemy territory, he argued his case with all the vigour and aggressiveness that you'd expect. It was, as one observer called it, a "full and frank exchange of views".

Nonetheless, the first signs of discontent soon began to spring up amongst the sound faction, with some of them worrying that Bercow was putting his own success ahead of the needs of their hardcore libertarian beliefs. One says that they found an, "Overwhelming impression of an opportunist, not someone whose principle motivation was ideological politics. It was first and foremost about self-projection: John Bercow only cares about John Bercow". Another colleague was suspicious because it, "Was clear he was a chancer. I didn't trust him".

Bercow's problem was that it would have been almost impossible to please the most right-wing FCS hacks without alienating the party; and while he was attempting to build bridges, others set about burning them in spectacular fashion. Simon Morgan, the chairman of the Scottish section of the FCS, organised a conference for September 1986 – described as "100% against the party[118]" – to protest at the signing of the Anglo-Irish Accord, while other committee members let it be known that they were intending to return to Northern Ireland to attend another rally against the Thatcher government's position. Just because Bercow didn't want to pick a fight with the people who could put him on the candidates list, it didn't mean that the rest of the libertarian faction had lost any of the radical tendencies.

Nonetheless, it is likely that, all other things being equal, Bercow would have muddled through to the end of the year. There would have been a few good speeches, a couple of minor controversies and a handful of puff pieces in the newspaper diary pages. Like any chairman, he would have pleased some and angered others. But, then, Harry Phibbs published the summer edition of *New Agenda*, a magazine he founded and edited. Like the rest of the FCS, *New Agenda* was generally outrageous, belligerent and right-wing in equal measure. That summer edition included a leader article on apartheid South Africa entitled: 'SANCTIONS: Why Blacks say No', arguing that "Apartheid is an inherently socialist system based on an array of bureaucratic regulations which restrict economic freedom and individual liberty. The answer is to reduce the role of the state and to allow the free market to operate". It also featured a poster from a "Soviet Front" organisation which called for the release of "jailed terrorist leader Nelson Mandela." Other articles included a piece on "The Great Unmentionable – race"; another arguing that the Conservative Party must use "Dialectical phenomenology" in its view of the world; an interview with the leader of the Angolan rebel group UNITA; and an article by Jeffrey Archer. And yet, one FCS member told me, "New Agenda was the sensible magazine".

But the true powder keg was the front cover. It featured Harold Macmillan, the former Conservative Prime Minister, with the word "GUILTY" splashed across the page. Inside, Phibbs interviewed Count Nikolai Tolstoy, the author of *The Minister and the Massacres*, who claimed that Macmillan had sent 40,000 Cossacks based in Italy to their deaths by handing them back to the Soviet Union after the Second World War. Many of the sounds didn't much like Macmillan – he was a champion of Keynesian economics and they regarded him as "essentially socialist" – and as one committee member said, "All this stuff about Macmillan is just schmaltz. He's a former prime minister and an old guy, but he was responsible for many of the sufferings which the British people endure today.[119]"

The reaction from Central Office was furious. *New Agenda* carried both the official Conservative Party logo and also the Party's Central Office address in Smith Square. To make it worse, Tebbit was in the middle of the first holiday he and his wife had been able to take since the Brighton bomb. Michael Dobbs, Tebbit's chief of staff, was forced to interrupt his boss's break to ask him to deal with the crisis.

Tebbit swung into action and personally ordered all 3,000 copies of the magazine to be pulped and threatened an injunction if Phibbs didn't comply. For him, the article was, "A disgraceful attack on a distinguished former Prime Minister.[120]" Typically defiant, Phibbs said the publication of the article was "perfectly justified" and went into overdrive, rushing out 2,000 copies in a number of days, saying, "The magazine has gone around the country. There is nothing anybody can do about that[121]". In response, Tebbit employed the lawyer Peter Carter-Ruck and applied for the injunction – which the court awarded on August 19th. Phibbs came back fighting, saying that, "As far as I am concerned, *New Agenda* is no longer the property of Tory Central Office. It is an independent publication, which does not receive party money but is funded by subscriptions, advertisements and donations. I will be taking legal advice and intend to battle against this all the way.[122]" Carter-Ruck also sued for libel, misrepresentation and breach of contract – although it was widely believed that the actions would be shelved if Phibbs gave way. Looking back, Phibbs tells me, "It was only really a question of whether it was worth having a row about. I thought it was and most people were pretty supportive. But others felt that as Tebbit was the Chair of the Party, the idea of alienating him was a great mistake. I was so worked up about the substance of the article that I didn't care, it was about moral indignation about people being sent to be killed. With Macmillan, it transcended the fact that he was a wet, it wasn't about political considerations."

Bercow, meanwhile, was stuck between a rock and a hard place. He had Norman Tebbit and Jeffrey Archer breathing down his neck to condemn the article, while opinion was split amongst the sounds. "It seems to be the case that if Phibbs gets the chop all will be well," said one. "Otherwise, the FCS is on the line, and the party will cut off its funds.[123]" But there were still many others amongst the libertarian faction who supported Phibbs and wanted Bercow to stand by him.

In the end, Bercow went with the party and condemned Phibbs for not following the proper procedures. Although his decision may not have been within the tradition of the campaigning libertarian right, given that the FCS couldn't keep going without Central Office funding, he made a mature and pragmatic choice. However, the strength of

Bercow's response managed to alienate a number of the sounds, as he gave a series of interviews roundly condemning Phibbs. In one he said, "Mr Phibbs cannot claim to have published the issue with FCS approval. He flagrantly violated the rules that all party publications have to be scrutinised before distribution. I was not consulted about the publication in advance.[124]" He also called on Phibbs to, "Cease his posturing[125]" and called an emergency committee meeting to dismiss him. As one of Bercow's sound friends told me, "Bercow had been given a mandate to improve relations with the party, and Phibbs had gone over the top, so Bercow was probably right to distance himself from Phibbs. But when we heard him on the radio laying into Phibbs, there was this huge sense of bewilderment." Others felt he should have taken greater account of the motives behind the article, and Phibbs says that when he tried to make the moral case for printing it, Bercow's "eyes would just glaze over; he wouldn't care about it at all[126]".

It was becoming clear that the row was escalating so quickly that it could end up costing Phibbs his future in the party if he didn't make some conciliatory moves. Behind the scenes, he met with Michael Dobbs to thrash out a deal. Phibbs agreed to resign as the editor of the magazine, apologised unreservedly to Tebbit and promised to retrieve as many copies of *New Agenda* as he could. "While I stand by my personal position on the substance of the Tolstoy interview, I recognise that it was wrong to include the interview, without permission, in an official party publication and in the face of clear legal advice as to its potential consequences for the Conservative Party," he said, in a statement agreed by his and Tebbit's lawyers. "I intend to produce a new magazine under a new title but this will be entirely independent of the Conservative Party.[127]" As expected, Central Office then dropped the writs that had been issued against Phibbs and Annagh Graphical, the magazine's printing firm.

But despite the agreement, Bercow remained isolated. He was keen for Phibbs to resign from the FCS executive as well, but the sounds rallied round to block Bercow and the proposed emergency meeting was cancelled[128]. What's more, Phibbs returned to *New Agenda* just days later as its deputy editor, whilst simultaneously offering a prize of Count Tolstoy's book that made the original allegations against

Macmillan for whoever came up with the best name for his new, independent magazine. Such activity must have been deeply embarrassing for Bercow.

That, however, was by no means the end of the matter. The FCS held half-yearly conferences in preparation for each new academic year and by the time the delegates arrived in Leicester in the autumn, events were moving against Bercow. Sensing that he had lost the support of his faction, Bercow offered his resignation to Tebbit in a meeting at Central Office[129], but it was refused. The sounds wanted to see the back of Bercow and were still not satisfied, so they arranged what was effectively a court martial to examine Bercow's perceived "disloyalty". He was called in to explain himself in front of his fellow officers, national committee members and regional chairman, but the outcome was obvious from the start. Bercow was censured, by a majority of 16 to 1 and deposed as the leader of the sound faction, to be replaced by a triumvirate of other sound members, including – to rub salt into the wounds – Harry Phibbs. Then, Count Tolstoy spoke on a platform at a fringe event, accompanied by two members of the executive, including Phibbs[130].

Amidst the *New Agenda* trouble, Bercow was also failing to control the other excesses of the FCS. Some sounds made public their plans to visit Washington to see members of the right-wing pressure group, The Heritage Foundation; David Hoile took a delegation to join the Nicaraguan Contras on armed patrol, followed by a visit to the UNITA group in Angola; and a policy document called for the Foreign Office, and the Commonwealth, to be wound up[131]. When the Chilean dictator General Pinochet was wounded in an assassination attempt, members of the FCS sent him a get well card – a move described by Bercow as, "Utterly stupid.[132]"

The position was quickly becoming unsustainable and Tebbit came to the conclusion that the FCS had gone too far, too often. His solution was to shut down the organisation for good. Bercow was a potential ally thanks to the excellent relationship between the pair, with the Party Chairman even saying at Conference that year that he hoped that Bercow would one day become a Conservative Chancellor[133]. Tebbit's plan – with which Bercow concurred – was to replace the FCS with the

"Conservative Collegiate Forum", a tame organisation with a mandate to look solely at areas relating to Higher Education. It was to be led by Peter Morrison, a deputy Chairman of the Party, thereby stripping the student group of its autonomy. Bercow himself was to be one of the committee members, in the hope of giving the CCF a sense of legitimacy and helping to assuage the feelings of the former FCS hacks. In essence, Tebbit had offered Bercow a choice: he could go along with the plans and stay in with the party, or fight to save the FCS but be cast out. The stakes were high for Bercow and for a second time he sided with Tebbit over some of his friends in the sound faction.

In the middle of this, just as Bercow became engulfed in the most significant crisis of his short political life, another life came to an end all too soon. On 31st October 1986, Charlie Bercow, who was just 66, died after a sudden heart attack. This crushing news must have been all the more heartbreaking as it fell on Bercow to fulfil the formalities – no easy task for a young man in his early twenties. It was Bercow who had to sign the form entering his father's death onto the register. Charlie was buried at the Jewish cemetery in Cheshunt, near London. At a moment of such dramatic turmoil within the FCS, student politics was very much put into perspective by Charlie's unexpected death.

One other consequence of Charlie's untimely death was that Bercow suddenly became a well-off young man, although it was money that meant nothing compared to the loss of a father and that Bercow would have foregone without a thought if only his father could have still been alive. Charlie was not a poor man and he left a total of £68,173.46 in his estate, which worked out at £63,271.57 after tax, divided equally between John and Alison. At today's prices, that would be the equivalent of around £130,000 each – not an insignificant sum.

The FCS row rumbled on and Bercow had to return to duty, even in the most difficult of months, in order to deal with the growing crisis. In November, it was announced that all funding would be immediately cut from the FCS. Its members – apart from Bercow – were banned from using Central Office and in time the organisation would be officially closed. It was also announced that Bercow would keep his sabbatical salary until his anticipated year of office ran out[134]. The sounds were apoplectic and many of them were caught completely unawares. As one says, "The first anyone knew about it was when it was all announced. People were absolutely furious. Our attitude was that, yes, some of the kids were unruly but it was a genuinely popular movement with 15,000 members." Bercow, however, was unrepentant, saying, "It took a fair degree of incompetence on behalf of some members of the FCS to alienate the most sympathetic chairman we've ever had.[135]" He then fanned the flames by going on to Radio 4 and turning on his former colleagues: "The difficulty has arisen by virtue of the fact that a lot of extremely good activists are at local level and some of the trouble-makers have unfortunately been at the very top[136]". He accused "A minority of recalcitrant individuals" of being more interested in grabbing power than campaigning[137].

Much of the anger was directed at Bercow's behind-the-scenes manoeuvres. One FCS member said that, "We would have been fine with closing the FCS if he had levelled with us in private. The people behind him thought they could control him, but in Central Office he ditched them to suck up to the bigger fish". In fairness to Bercow, it seems unlikely that he could have done anything once Tebbit had made up his mind. The organisation had become a consistent embarrassment to the party and with an election coming up in 1987, the FCS had become too much of a risk. But other members felt that Bercow could have argued for some kind of compromise – or even that if he had taken a firm stand, he could have made it too problematic for the FCS to be shut down at all. However, in truth, it seems that the FCS was doomed. The party controlled its purse strings and, therefore, its future.

Much as Bercow knew which side his bread was buttered, he couldn't afford to completely jettison his old allies from the FCS, as many of them were personal as well as political friends. Even during the tumultuous months after the *New Agenda* controversy, Bercow and the rest of the sounds had continued to meet every Friday night in the dive bar of the St. Stephen's Tavern in Westminster. The week after the demise of the FCS was announced, everyone gathered there as usual. As Bercow walked in, a deadly silence fell across the room and he was forced to awkwardly take a seat at the back, largely ignored by the sounds. Harry Phibbs walked over to Bercow's table and announced, "John, I feel the need to inform you, as of now our friendship is at an end[138]", although some of his friends took pity on him and joined him at his table. Later that night, Bercow went back to MacGregor and Walters' flat and he disconsolately sought his friends' advice as to what to do next.

Many of the FCS felt betrayed, but they understood his dilemma. Under pressure from senior politicians who could potentially ruin his career, Bercow was in a no-win situation and a number of friendships, including with MacGregor, have lasted despite Bercow's "sell-out". But for those like Phibbs, Bercow's actions had been unforgivable. More worryingly, for other FCS members there in the dive bar that night, a pattern of self-interested behaviour was being set. As one put it, "How much can you take from someone that you call a friend?"

Bercow's time as FCS Chairman has been hugely influential in his career, not just because of the public exposure and profile it gave him, but also because it allowed him to come into the fold. The boy who wanted to belong was finally one of them. In that sense, the Chairmanship allowed Bercow to also put his more extreme views from his Monday Club days behind him. While he was by no means a moderate, he had become a die-hard Thatcherite – which in the 1980s simply meant being fully behind the direction and leadership of the party. It's no surprise that a number of the main protagonists in the FCS never became MPs, despite their best efforts; Bercow chose a different path and the rewards speak for themselves.

10

Holding his Council

"He was terribly, terribly ambitious"

John Bercow was always an ambitious young man. He had made his way to the top of the Federation of Conservative Students, but he knew that greater things awaited. He was a big fish in a small pond, and the next step was to prove himself in the real, grown-up world of proper politics. The question for most student politicians was: what would come next? Bercow's opportunity presented itself in the form of Lambeth Council.

In the 1980s, Lambeth was a training ground for future MPs, filled with young guns like Peter Mandelson who cut their teeth on the Council's numerous political controversies. Most famously, the Labour leader of the Council, Ted Knight, had refused to set rates in protest at the cuts to public spending instigated by the Thatcher government, driving the Council to the brink of bankruptcy.[139] For Bercow, the chance to take on the so-called "loony left" would have been irresistible. While local politics rarely makes the front pages these days, in the 1980s the goings on at Lambeth were often in the headlines. Serving on Lambeth council would do no harm to Bercow's already bulging contacts book, whilst giving him more credibility when he applied to run for a seat in Parliament.

Bercow decided to move to Lambeth ahead of his run on the Council and by the time of the election on Thursday, 8th May 1986, he was living in the borough at 41, Tooting Bec Gardens, where he was to live for a number of years.[140] However, his flat in Tooting Bec Gardens was not the site of his first appearance on the electoral roll in Lambeth.

The annual records show that Bercow was put down as living at 60 Hopton Road on the roll that was in force from 16th February 1986 to

15th February 1987. The property was actually owned by Teresa Gorman, who in 1987 became MP for Billericay, replacing Bercow's old Monday Club friend Harvey Proctor. Mrs Gorman was well-known as a maverick MP who stood out for having tattooed eyebrows – she shaved hers off when she was a teenager and they never grew back. At the time, both Bercow and Gorman were active in the Tory Party and a number of FCS members were friendly with her. Marc Glendening, a friend of Bercow's and another former FCS chairman, worked as her researcher.

60 Hopton Road was later to become a real thorn in Gorman's side as her career progressed. In fact, it was a key part of the investigation into her dealings that resulted in her being given a one month suspension from the House of Commons in 2000. The house was large, with four storeys and a small garden with, it has to be said, plenty of room for extra people to live there. At today's prices, it would cost well over half a million pounds – quite possibly more – and it was well-placed between Streatham Common and Tooting Bec Common in the Conservative-supporting part of Lambeth.

Mrs Gorman and her husband James had bought the house in the 1960s and she claimed they lived there as their matrimonial home "until shortly before I was elected to Parliament in 1987[141]." James Gorman, who was seriously ill at the time of the investigation into his wife's affairs in 1999, told Richard Sturt, of Mowll & Mowll Solicitors, that "He continued to live at 60 Hopton Road and use it as his UK home. He also took in his nephew and a man called Roy. From time to time other people stayed there.[142]" There was no mention of John Bercow, although the report into Mrs Gorman's affairs notes that he was on the electoral register in 1986[143]. Elizabeth Filkin, The Parliamentary Commissioner for Standards, criticised much of Mrs Gorman's evidence and called it "seriously misleading[144]".

However, in Bercow's case, nobody seems to have any recollection of him residing at the property at the time. One close friend of Bercow's in the mid 1980s explained to me, "He never lived there – he never spent a night in his life there." Another friend who knew Bercow in the year immediately before he stood for election confirmed the same story to me. "He never did live there. He was round at my flat all the time and he lived with his mother". Penny Garcev, a neighbour who lived next door at number 62 and who also gave evidence to the investigation into Mrs Gorman's affairs, told me: "He has never lived next door, it is incorrect. There is no question of John Bercow living next door." Mrs Garcev's husband confirmed that he had never seen Bercow at 60 Hopton Road either. As for Gorman herself, she says, "He definitely never lived there, never."

If Bercow did not live there, then the electoral roll would have to have been based on incorrect information, and there is other compelling evidence that the roll that year was not accurate. Glendening was also listed as a voter at 60 Hopton Road in 1986, although he never lived at the property either.

However, there is no suggestion of wrongdoing, as nobody can help who puts them on the electoral roll – and it was not Bercow's fault that somebody else must have registered him as living at 60 Hopton Road. It is, however, clear that neither Gorman or Glendening was the one to register Bercow, either and there is no suggestion of wrongdoing on their part. Nonetheless, it shows that in the world of Conservative politics in the 1980s, there were mysterious forces at work.

If Bercow didn't live at Hopton Road, he must have had some other connection with the borough. The fact that he lived in Tooting Bec Gardens would only have been sufficient if he had lived in the borough for twelve months, although Bercow was not registered as a voter in Tooting Bec Gardens on the roll that closed on 10th October 1985. The system was certainly inefficient and perhaps unfair. Why should someone who lived in the borough at the time of an election – but who had not lived there in time to go on the electoral register and did not meet the other qualifying conditions – be refused the chance to stand? As Bercow said in 2001, when the Commons finally voted to allow entries on the electoral roll all year round, the changes were "common sense" as the old rules were "arcane and unnecessary[145]". But, right or wrong, that was the law in 1986. Fortunately for Bercow, however, he satisfied another one of the conditions and was able to stand.

★★★

Once Bercow decided to run for council, his next steps were simple. Even in Lambeth, where council politics was making national headlines, there was little competition for places. After all, being a councillor involved spending large amounts of time in committee meetings and only a true politics-lover or genuine altruist would have found the prospect an appealing one.

There can be little doubt on which side of the divide Bercow lay. As one of his colleagues told me, "He was much more into the bigger issues". Bercow was selected to contest St Leonard's Ward, where the Conservatives were far and away the leading party. Bercow stood there alongside two other Conservatives – Mary Leigh and Hugh Jones – for the three council places. The triumvirate proved an initial success and all three were comfortable victors. Mary Leigh topped the poll with 1,803 votes, but Bercow was only a few behind with 1,753, beating Jones into third. Their nearest rival failed to make it into four figures. However, despite it being a very safe Conservative ward, Bercow took his campaigning duties extremely seriously indeed. Harry Phibbs, who at this time – before the contentious version of *New Agenda* had come out – was still friends with Bercow, recalls, "He asked me to campaign. I said I was going away so I couldn't and he became edgy and indignant. Although he was generally quite an enjoyable conversationalist, he lost his temper with me over that and generally would get very worked up about things.[146]"

The Tories' success in St. Leonards was not replicated elsewhere. Labour easily maintained control of the council, with many of the councillors coming from the "loony left". Linda Bellos, who took over from Knight as leader after the 1986 election, was typical of the tendency. She was Jewish, black and a lesbian and could hardly have been more different from the Conservative members of the council. Even in the 1980s when politics was at its most divisive, there can have been few places where the gap between the two main parties was more pronounced than in Lambeth.

Bercow was far from alone in vigorously opposing everything that the Labour councillors stood for. The 1986 election had seen an influx of so-called "Young Turks", a bunch of ambitious Thatcherites who wanted to take the fight to Bellos and her allies. But most of Bercow's politicking ended up being in vain as the Labour majority proved too solid, despite his best efforts. He'd put forward a motion having a dig at Labour, but Bellos would come back with her own, anti-Tory amendment, which would pass instead. The battle lines were clearly drawn between liberterianism on the one hand and central provision on the other, with a bit of class warfare chucked in for good effect, but the Labour armoury was too strong. Even so, there were hours of political to and fro along the way, with grandstanding and belligerent speeches from both sides. Bercow loved it.

It didn't take long for him to start making an impact, either. By September 1986, just four months after being elected, he was already facing a potential ban by NALGO – The National Association of Local Government Officers – which would have made him unable to circulate papers or send mail, in retaliation for Bercow's decision to help break up a meeting of the Women's Rights Committee. Bercow had insisted on going to the meeting to prove a point and he only made matters worse by mimicking a Labour Councillor's accent – it was meant in jest but was taken by some as a "classist attack". Bercow was having none of it, retorting: "This is the sort of bullshit you get from the left... If NALGO try to stop services to me I think they'll find themselves up against the Local Government Act. As for classism, well, they call me a young upstart, so I suppose that counts as ageism.[147]"

After his bombastic start Bercow quickly set about getting his teeth into another project – but this time he was attacking his own side. Mary Leigh, a solicitor who was head of the Conservative group and another St. Leonard's councillor, wasn't popular amongst the Young Turks. She and Bercow had got on well enough when they contested St. Leonard's ward together, and Bercow even introduced her to his father shortly before his death. However, she recalls, "I offended him mortally by giving an interview on a subject he thought that he should have given the interview on, as he said it was his portfolio. From there our relationship went downhill. He told me off quite roundly – he rang me up and said, "How dare you?". He was like that; he had enormous potential which I could see, but I thought it was flawed.[148]"

The Young Turks set about overhauling the Conservative group to give themselves control and to get Mary Leigh out. In part, they were driven by ideology and in part by a belief that the Conservative group wasn't dynamic enough. Graham Pycock, who was then a Tory councillor, recalls, "John at that time was seen as very much on the Thatcherite right-wing. He took a resolute line and that was the upcoming line in the party. Mary Leigh wouldn't like to call herself a wet, but she would see herself as a traditionalist and less hard-line.[149]" Part of the problem lay in the divide between the professional politician class of councillors who saw Lambeth as a stepping stone to Parliament and the older members of the council, who didn't take well to Bercow and his thrusting style. As Pycock remembers, "Bercow's view was that we weren't hard edged and attacking enough, that we were like pussycats compared to the Marxist approach[150]".

The Young Turks began putting their plot into action, working the phones and speaking regularly to various members of the grouping to try to win their support. But it made life very uncomfortable for some of the older councillors. "I don't like intrigue," Pycock told me. "I made it clear to my own party members that I would resign if matters didn't improve". Another colleague recalls, "I thought he [Bercow] was just being a naughty little troublemaker. He decided to depose the leadership just for the hell of it. However, I was rather glad he was there in a way, because there were some awfully limp old things who sat on our benches, at least Bercow was always ready to have a go".

At the annual meeting in September 1987, Bercow helped to put forward a vote of no confidence in Mary Leigh. "He [Bercow] was instrumental,[151]" she recalls. The group was split and Leigh had to use her casting vote to defeat the motion. She then resigned and stood again for the leadership and there was talk that Bercow would run against her. In the end, though, Bercow didn't put himself forward and the Young Turks nominated Hugh Jones. A colleague of Bercow's at that time told me that Bercow wanted to be kingmaker but didn't want to be seen as the spearhead of the attack. Some were a little disappointed, though, thinking that despite Bercow's age he might have done a better job.

For her part, Leigh is quite phlegmatic about the incident. "My main criticism was that he was terribly, terribly ambitious," she says. "He wanted to make a mark, but the one he made wasn't a good one.

He put his personal ambition and likes and dislikes above what was best for the party." However, some years later, after a mutual acquaintance died, Bercow rang Leigh and apologised for his behaviour and the pair have since buried the hatchet. She admits, though, that at the time she "avoided him like the plague[152]".

The incident did damage Bercow amongst the old guard. As one councillor told me, Bercow was "Not someone I would have trusted further than I could throw him." However, the coup certainly helped propel Bercow forwards: in the reorganisation that followed the plot, he emerged as one of the powerhouses in the grouping and became Hugh Jones's deputy leader – one of the youngest in the country to hold such a senior council position.

By all accounts, he was extremely effective in this role. In the set piece debates in the grand council chamber, Bercow would vigorously argue the toss against the Labour majority and he enjoyed the chance to show off his oratory – when there was a big issue to be discussed his friends from the FCS would come down to see him in action. He was certainly worth watching, too, as he was usually very funny and very sharp. As Pycock says, "Most councillors were not at the cutting edge of debating skills or ideological knowledge, but Bercow could joust with people who also saw themselves as career politicians in the national league. You might call it ponderous, but he had a debating style that was outstanding in terms of local government. He could present a cogent set of arguments that left his opponents thrashing around and floored. His views were very sophisticated and his position was always beyond the understanding of a lot of the councillors on both sides. He would have the Labour benches in uproar as he knew exactly what to get them on. He would point out the ideological problems in their position and would quote Marx or Trotsky at them.[153]"

Bercow was also extremely good at being rude to people, including Linda Bellos, on whom he exercised his powers of mimicry, although Bellos was just as rude back to him. He was, "A very, very good ranter," she says. "There was almost foam coming from his mouth. I used to treat him with the contempt he deserved. It was like swatting a fly with the back of my hand. I'd say, "Oh get away little boy" – but he took that with his usual wit and charm – and despite everything he *was* charming, and was a very bright man.[154]" Bercow's comprehensive background also gave him an effective weapon against the left – unlike many of the Conservative councillors, he hadn't had a privileged upbringing and he used his own story as an example of the power of Thatcherism. Bercow was always conscious that he was not a traditional Tory, but a child of the new right, who had to work to make something of himself. If anything, it made his arguments all the more compelling.

Bercow's rudeness also extended to his own side. John Pinniger, the Monday Clubber with whom Bercow had fallen out some years before, was another Tory Councillor. Their relationship was still frosty and during a meeting in the group room Bercow said to him, "Of course I'm much more articulate than you[155]". Tempers flared with others, too. One day, Bercow wound up another member of the group so much that he chased Bercow round the room, threatening violence against him.

For all the political posturing, there were serious matters of both political practicality and principle being debated on the council. Lambeth was one of the first councils to introduce racial placement as a formal policy for children in council care and Bercow was violently opposed to it. Despite speaking well, the Labour majority again prevailed. Later, representatives of Sinn Fein were invited to council meetings and again Bercow led the line against this. He also continued to support the poll tax and, despite the reservations of some Tories on the council, he gave a number of tubthumping speeches strongly in favour of its introduction.

His time on Lambeth Council was typical Bercow: he both enlivened and exasperated in equal measure. He may not have made many friends outside of his cabal of Young Turks, but he did win the grudging respect of some of his opponents and most of his own side. The chamber provided an excellent forum to practise his speaking and Lambeth proved a good training ground. Ultimately, though, the council was only ever a stepping stone, and when he stood down as a councillor, his horizons were much broader. It was a formative time, but just one step on the road to what he saw as a far more glittering prize; a seat in Parliament.

11

Unwinnable

"We didn't have a cat in hell's chance"

1987 was election year. Whenever individual voters get to cast their ballots, the normal political ebb and flow comes to a halt as MPs go about gaining the approval of the very people that many of them will have wilfully ignored for the past four or five years. For an aspiring politician, getting into position for an election is vital. Most MPs will tell you that you need to fight at least one unwinnable seat before you'll be considered for a constituency where you have a decent shot of winning, so making sure you have the experience under your belt is key.

For someone as ambitious and as well-connected as Bercow, it was obvious that he would run if it was at all possible. So it was that, while Bercow was busy both on Lambeth Council and in student politics, he applied to be a candidate for the next General Election.

The timing was perfect for Bercow. It seemed almost certain that Thatcher would go to the country at some point in 1987 – she was still riding high in the polls, despite having been in office for nearly eight years, with unemployment finally dipping below the three million mark. That meant that if Bercow was selected for a seat, he'd have the chance to get a no-hoper out of the way at the age of 24, clearing the path for a serious campaign in his late twenties. He was just about old enough to have the credibility required to go for a selection; any younger and he might seem too young, but Conservative associations in unwinnable seats were used to taking on candidates who were only a couple of years out of university. What's more, a 1987 election would suit Bercow as there would be a short campaign. There's nothing worse for a young politico than having to traipse across the country every weekend for three years to and from a constituency where there's more chance of a monkey being elected than a Conservative. (A perfect example is Hartlepool, where H'Angus the monkey, Hartlepool United FC's mascot, was elected as Mayor, but there has been no Conservative MP in the last 45 years. H'Angus – better known as Stuart Drummond – is still the Mayor, having won re-election twice, although the monkey suit has been dropped. The club, though, are still known as the 'Monkey Hangers' but fortunately for Drummond the last (and only) hanging took place, somewhat apocryphally, during the Napoleonic Wars).

The election also fitted in very well with Bercow's broader plans. His term of office as the Chairman of the FCS, which later turned into a role on the Conservative Collegiate Forum, ran out in the summer of 1987. Working for a Tory body meant that he would have ample time to go off and fight a seat; and the campaign would bolster his CV as he looked for a job later in 1987. Convenience was, however, never the driving motive. Bercow knew he wanted to be an MP and there was little that he would allow to stand in his way.

By the spring of 1987 an election in the next few months was looking like a certainty and many of the 'unwinnable' seats began advertising for candidates to put their names forward. Amongst them was Motherwell South, in Scotland, and Bercow put in his application. Motherwell would hardly seem like a natural fit for a boy from north London. For one thing, the English often don't go down too well in Scottish constituencies. Moreover, the town was renowned for its heavy industry, with the Ravenscraig steel plants casting a long shadow over the area. At the time there were concerns about the future of the steel works as other heavy industries around the country began to falter. Motherwell was a small town with around 30,000 inhabitants and, with nearly 12,000 jobs relying on the works[156], the future of Ravenscraig was of paramount importance to the people there. Again, Bercow had little experience of dealing with workers or their problems and he was long gone from Motherwell by the time the Ravenscraig works closed in the early 1990s.

The seat was, in the words of a local, "a jungle as far as socialists are concerned". In other words, it was completely unwinnable. Although the Conservatives were in second place, at the previous election in 1983 the Tory candidate had won just 20% of the vote, with the sitting Labour MP, Jeremy Bray, taking over 50%. It's interesting to note, though, that Bray was an English academic, perhaps showing that the people of Motherwell were happy to give their vote to an Englishman when he stood for the "right" party.

The selection procedure could scarcely have proved any easier for Bercow. Bob Burgess, who was Chairman of the constituency association, recalls that the local party found it hard to source good candidates. "There were 2 people [under consideration]. What happens is they've got to be put forward to us from Central Office and in the lower ranks as us you'd maybe be offered two. We don't have that luxury where you've got people falling over themselves to try to become MP for Motherwell.[157]" Nor was Bercow's background a problem, with Motherwell having proved to be a happy hunting ground for a number of men from south of the border who'd previously tried their luck there as the Tory candidate.

There were only about forty members in the whole association and five of them sat on the interview panel. Bercow's time on the FCS paid dividends, with Burgess remembering that, "We were quite impressed in what we'd heard about him before. We heard he was a good speaker and up-and-coming politician.[158]" Bercow didn't disappoint when it came to his interview. For Burgess, what stood out was, "Just his total Toryism at that point. He was great on Margaret Thatcher... There was a freshness about him. He just sold you with his 'let's have a go at it' attitude". Nor was Bercow's age a worry. "He came across as young," Burgess recalls, "but there was no naivety about him. He was very well-versed and grounded and we didn't have any problems whatsoever with him. When someone comes and he's got 'it', you know he's got it. Where he's gone since hasn't surprised me at all.[159]"

With Bercow happily ensconced as the candidate, all that was needed was for there to be an election. He didn't have to wait long and Thatcher finally took the plunge on May 11th, after a positive set of local election results. With just a month before the General Election itself on June 11th, there was precious little time to make much of a difference, particularly when Bercow had a 12,000 majority to overhaul.

The Conservative campaign nationally focused on lower taxes, a strong economy and being firm on defence. Labour's policies included nuclear disarmament – which led to a famous gaffe from its leader Neil Kinnock, who said that in the event of a Soviet invasion Britain would defend itself by "guerrilla" fighting. The Conservatives responded with an ad campaign depicting Labour's defence 'policy': a British soldier with his hands in the air, captioned 'Surrender'. Bercow was a huge fan of the poster. But Labour was beginning to become more professional and was moving away from its disastrous years under Michael Foot. Critically, although the party did not really expect to win the election, 1987 sowed the first seeds of New Labour. A certain Peter Mandelson was put in charge of the campaign and the party's red flag symbol was dropped in favour of the red rose.

As the arguments were played out on the national stage, Bercow took up his own, very local, battle. He moved to Wishaw, a small town next to Motherwell, where he set up home for the duration of the campaign as a paying guest in a family house. Another of the rooms was taken by Gary Mond, who was also standing for the Tory Party in the neighbouring seat of Hamilton. Mond remembers, "It was an ordinary three bedroom house. We had a bedroom each and the lady there had a couple of children. It was like being billeted, like being evacuated kids.[160]"

There was plenty of fun to be had. Mond was also English and facing an equally Herculanean task – or in his words, "we didn't have a cat in hell's chance[161]" – so he and Bercow had plenty in common when it came to comparing notes about the campaign. Mond says he "got on very, very well" with Bercow and the two became firm friends. "He's a very nice guy and a good friend", Mond told me. Inevitably, as two English boys stuck up in Scotland, there was plenty of comedy to go alongside the serious business of politics. On one occasion, Mond filled up their car with diesel instead of petrol and a mile down the road it conked out, with Bercow laughing uncontrollably in the passenger seat.

The pair were joined north of the border by Bernard Jenkin – now a Conservative MP – who was fighting Glasgow Central, and Jenkin's wife Anne, ennobled in 2010 and a former girlfriend of the film writer Richard Curtis. Michael Ancram, the future Party Chairman who was then the MP for Edinburgh South, hosted a number of drinks parties for the Scottish candidates and there was a real ex-pat feeling amongst the young hopefuls. Liam Fox, the future Secretary of State for Defence, was also another unsuccessful first-time candidate in Roxburgh and Berwickshire. Even amongst such an over-achieving group, Bercow still made quite the impact. Mond recalls, "His oratory and political knowledge were second to none. I was absolutely certain that he would go a long way. He was always fanatical and very devoted to politics.[162]"

There was also a lot of hard work to be done and Bercow had to do much of the leg-work himself as there were very few resources available in such a hopeless seat. As Burgess recalls, "When it came to putting money on the campaign we didn't have it. Financially we could only give him a minimum push.[163]" The local Tories could only afford to put out one leaflet, whereas Bercow's opponents would have had three or four. Mond says, "I remember John being hard at work sorting out his posters. There was nobody to help him[164]". His attitude also went down very well with the local association. Burgess says that he was "Definitely the most popular in the association that we've had in all the campaigns we've run. He was flamboyant and...he was such a small guy but I couldn't believe it, he made you feel like you could do something. He had that leadership and I admired him very much[165]".

Much of the day to day work involved knocking on doors and, despite the empathy gap between Bercow and Motherwell South's steel workers, he was surprisingly popular. They did see him as different, of course, with many a householder coming away describing Bercow as having "boules in his mouth", a saying up in Motherwell that means you're quite posh (think of Eliza Doolittle in *My Fair Lady* having elocution lessons with a load of marbles being put into her mouth and you'll get the idea). However, despite those boules, Bercow came across well. "He spoke to you at your level," says Burgess. "There wasn't an aloofness about him[166]". He also managed to tap into local concerns, a skill that has stayed with him to this day. The leaflet put out in his name said, "Conservatives recognise the crucial importance of the Scottish steel industry and have twice stopped the closure of Ravenscraig. We agree with the shop stewards that privatisation is not the issue here. Ravenscraig is now profitable and there is no question of it being closed." This text was accompanied by a beaming picture of a windswept Bercow outside the Ravenscraig plant, giving a thumbs up, which rather unfortunately made him look like a hitchhiker.

There's no doubt, though, that the policies being put forward by the government were not popular in Motherwell – but Bercow was a whole-hearted supporter of them. Mond recalls that, "We were right-wing Conservatives. John was a mainstream Thatcherite and had long since resigned from the Monday Club. He was very nervous about wet influences. He was a Eurosceptic, very much in favour of the free market, low taxes and privatisation.[167]" However, the nature of the seat meant that for much of the campaign Bercow was shielded from some of the more pitched battles that he'd have been used to at university and on Lambeth Council. There were two hustings meetings between the candidates, but both passed off relatively peacefully. As Bercow has found subsequently, when the sitting MP has a huge majority, it's much easier for the candidates to get on nicely.

When polling day came on June 11th, it was, as expected, a night of triumph for the Conservatives on a national level. Mrs Thatcher won a majority of over one hundred, winning four million votes more than the Labour Party. Enoch Powell, standing as an Ulster Unionist, lost his seat in South Down to the SDLP, despite a pact between the various unionist parties who were still smarting from the Anglo-Irish Agreement.

Up in Motherwell, it was a very different story and a more disappointing night for Bercow. The Scottish Nationalists were able to make significant inroads into the Conservative vote and they leapfrogged the Tories into second place. Bercow only managed to finish third, with 5,702 votes and a 14.5% share of the vote, down from 20.0% in 1983. The decline of the Conservatives was a trend seen throughout Scotland, with the party's support down 7% from 1979, losing three seats in the process, including a defeat for Michael Ancram in Edinburgh South. Within ten years, the party would be wiped out in

Scotland, with no seats at all, and even now there is only one Conservative MP north of the border.

At the count in the local sports centre, the relatively peaceful co-existence between the parties was also dramatically shattered. When the result was announced at around 1 o' clock in the morning, the winning candidate, Bray, gave a victory speech that passed without incident. Soon it was Bercow's turn. Speaking to a crowd of hundreds, but with just a handful of Tories in the room, he began his speech. It was obvious from the start that he wasn't going to pull any punches. Bercow gleefully pointed out that Mrs Thatcher was on her way to victory across the country and started extolling her virtues to the crowd. "Margaret Thatcher had really gotten herself a bad press up here and everybody hated her," recalls Burgess. "He [Bercow] sang her praises all the way[168]." Bercow was laying it on thick, the booing started and the crowd began to become even more agitated. Eventually, some of the Labour supporters could stand it no more and in anger they grabbed their chairs and started throwing them onto the stage at Bercow. As if oblivious to the uproar, he carried on giving his speech. "John wasn't fazed at all," says Burgess. "He just took it in his stride, they had to rip the mic from him.[169]"

However unpopular his speech was with the Labour Party, it went down a treat with the local Conservatives. Burgess says that it was, "Absolutely brilliant, it really was. With John the night of the election was unbelievable, it was a high you couldn't get any other way. It makes it worthwhile when you get that as it gets you away from the boring situation you normally have. John just ripped it – I couldn't believe somebody could get up and talk like that.[170]"

The Tories had lost the battle but won the war. The national victory was what mattered and the Motherwell Conservatives were well used to losing. Bercow accompanied the hardy souls from the Association back to the house of Councillor John Thompson, where they had a much-needed cup of tea, before turning in for the night. It was the last time that any of them saw him in Motherwell.

Those six weeks were a brilliant experience for Bercow, and as he has said, "I was bloodied by it. I got the experience of fighting in a tough territory[171]". More pertinently, it also showed for the first time his knack of winning over constituency associations. It may well be argued that it's only those who get to know him away from the frenetic atmosphere of Westminster who discover the real John Bercow; or perhaps, as Anthony Barker found, Bercow was just very good at charming the blue rinse brigade.

Even more important, however, was that Bercow had ticked a vital box by becoming a Tory candidate. With his unwinnable seat out of the way, a whole world of possibilities was open to him and the ultimate prize – a seat in the House of Commons – was potentially just a few years away.

12

A Working Man

"No John, you can't go there, they'll kill you"

Politically, everything was going right for John Bercow. He'd fought a seat and impressed the locals; he was making a name for himself on Lambeth Council; and the Conservatives were still in power. But as he made the journey back from Motherwell to London, he must have wondered what on earth he was going to do with his life. His time in student politics was coming to an end and he needed to get a job. There was, of course, a financial need, but for Bercow there was another motivation altogether. It was always obvious to those around him that Bercow wanted to become a politician and any alternative career would only be a holding measure until he could find a safe seat. The choice of job was therefore extremely important, as selection committees were more impressed by some careers than others. For an aspiring politician, any career path inevitably has to be picked with prospective local associations in mind. Going back to being a tennis coach was never a real option – remembering the reaction of the Monday Club members who sneered at it – and Bercow had in any case moved on. With a degree behind him, a whole set of options was available.

The one job that did really appeal to Bercow was in the law and he now says, "My only major regret is that I would have liked to have been a barrister…[I wish I had known that] short-term debt shouldn't have stopped me qualifying for the bar and practising at it.[172]" Unfortunately, despite his inheritance from his father, Bercow felt the significant financial outlay required in converting to law and then taking his bar exams was prohibitive.

Bercow turned to another one of his Conservative contacts, Sir Peter Morrison, the MP for Chester and later Margaret Thatcher's

Parliamentary Private Secretary. Morrison's career faltered as Mrs Thatcher lost power and he misjudged the degree of the rebellion against her, with Alan Clark claiming in his diaries to have found Morrison asleep at one of the crucial moments as her premiership crumbled around her. Back when Bercow was running the FCS, Morrison was a Deputy Chairman of the Party and had been particularly critical of the Federation, disliking its indiscipline and considering the way in which the FCS members dressed to be far too casual for his taste. However, like most of the party high command he was on good terms with Bercow personally.

Fortunately for Bercow, Morrison was also a very successful businessman away from politics, with plenty of contacts in the City, and he was able to put Bercow in touch with a friend at Hambros, the merchant bank. Bercow applied for a job as a credit analyst, was successful, and his new career began in the summer of 1987. It was not, however, to be a happy time for Bercow as he didn't enjoy the job at all. While he was an extremely able young man, maths was hardly his strong suit and sitting in a bank all day did not play to his strengths. Lacking client interaction and without the opportunity to put his oratorical skills to good use, he soon became disillusioned. Gary Mond, who stayed in touch with him after they both returned to London, says that, simply, Bercow "just wasn't cut out[173]" for life as a big city banker. Bercow soldiered on for less than eleven months before finally deciding to call it a day. Although it may have been a disappointment to have given up so soon, it was clear that he would be both happier and more successful doing something else.

In almost everything else Bercow has ever done, he has stood out, a small glowing beacon illuminating the interest of those around him. Whether he was loved or loathed, people knew him. At Hambros, however, the experience was very different. Despite repeated and extensive attempts, this author has been unable to track down anyone who remembers Bercow, even amongst those who would have worked alongside him. A typical example is James Thomson, who was a director in the Commercial Banking Department, which worked closely with the credit analysts who were part of the parallel General Banking Department. Thomson told me that despite working at the bank for the whole time when Bercow was there, "The curious thing is that I have absolutely no recall of a John Bercow".

The solution lay in the world of political lobbying. A successful government lobbyist needs an excellent contacts book, a good political nose and suitable communication skills – three assets that Bercow had in abundance. He applied for a job at Rowland Sallingbury Casey (RSC), a public affairs company, and was accepted for the role, starting work later in 1988. RSC was part of the American Rowland Group and was later subsumed by Saatchi & Saatchi, the advertising agency set up by Maurice and Charles Saatchi, which had created the celebrated "Labour isn't working" poster for the 1979 election, helping Mrs Thatcher to victory over Jim Callaghan.

Lobbying is a huge industry, now estimated to be worth around £2 billion every year. Although it is low on the radar of the general public outside Westminster, lobbyists are a highly powerful network wielding huge influence – power that many in Parliament believe is dispropor-tionate and unfair. Back in the late 1980s when Bercow started working in the industry, it was undoubtedly less controversial, in part at least because lobbying was perhaps less professional and the industry was much smaller. However, political affairs workers would still try to bend the ear of MPs and Bercow's contacts within the Conservative Party would have been very useful to him in performing the job. It's no surprise that when the party in Government changes, the lobbying industry has to respond by bringing in public affairs operators with good access to those who make the decisions. With Mrs Thatcher in the middle of her third term in power, the presence of an arch-Tory like Bercow would have been very useful indeed to RSC. As one senior member of the team who worked with Bercow told me, "We'd all deal with anybody, but it was a Conservative government so when he was there [the people were] mostly Conservatives as they were more useful to the Conservative clients."

Bercow's Thatcherism put him on common ground with the other workers at RSC. "The Conservative Party gave us a bond," one told me. "We talked a lot about politics and Bercow was very good natured." However, even in this Conservative environment, Bercow's political views still came across as somewhat extreme. "He surprised me, he was so right-wing," says one colleague, who was also a Conservative Party member. "He was very anti-European and thought I should never be in the Conservative Party at all."

The company was based on Whitfield Street in Central London, with around one hundred people in the PR section and fifteen or so in the public affairs arm. Within this small group, Bercow progressed well. A colleague remembers that he was, "Very competent, we had a satisfactory working relationship and I always liked him." Munir Samji, who was then the Chief Financial Officer of the advertising arm of Saatchi & Saatchi, recalls that Bercow was, "Unassuming and a really nice guy.[174]" Another colleague is equally effusive in her opinion of him: "He's a lovely guy and I've not got a bad word to say about him," she told me.

Bercow's main work involved meeting MPs and briefing clients, putting together documents and creating strategies with political objectives for a wide group of big businesses that included Rupert Murdoch's News International. Bercow enjoyed the work and the role was a natural fit for him. He was rewarded with a series of promotions, becoming an account executive, although his progression was perceived in the office as, "pretty good, but not staggering".

But however hard he worked at his PR career, it was clear that it was always a second choice, as his experience in Motherwell in 1987 had only strengthened his already burgeoning ambition to become an MP. Bercow continued his politicking on Lambeth Council and he was an ever-present in Conservative circles, with right-leaning lobbyists like him forming part of a broad group of politicos that included MPs, advisers, researchers and journalists of a Conservative persuasion.

However, with the ultimate prize of a seat in the Commons still to be won, there were important decisions to be made. There was little respite for the aspiring candidate and by late 1988 – just a few months after joining RSC – the selection process for what turned out to be the 1992 General Election had started to come to life. With his status as an up-and-coming Conservative by now well-entrenched and with the campaign in Scotland under his belt, Bercow was well-placed to have another shot at being selected. He was, however, somewhat cautious and the usually ebullient young man seemed to shrink back from taking the risks needed to get into Parliament. As Gary Mond recalls, "John at the time didn't think that he would get a safe seat for [the next election] so he went for a marginal seat. He underestimated his own abilities.[175]"

Part of the problem for Bercow was that he felt the selections were coming too early. He had only turned 26 in January 1989 and at that time most of the safe seats were going to people in their 30s or early 40s. However, there were plenty of signs that Bercow might well have done better. Bernard Jenkin, who had stood in another unwinnable Scottish seat in 1987, was just four years older than Bercow and ended up being selected for the safe Tory seat of Colchester North for the upcoming poll. And although he was young, Bercow would be 29 by the time of the 1992 election. William Hague was only 27 when he won his place in Parliament in 1989 and Matthew Taylor had taken Truro for the Liberals in 1987 at the age of just 24. With as precocious a talent as Bercow's, a safe seat could well have been a possibility. As Mond says, "He could have waited a year…held out and ended up getting into Parliament[176]".

Instead, not wanting to end up without a constituency, Bercow decided to target a Labour seat where he could try to unseat his opponent. "The Conservatives were still riding high", Mond says, "and there was even the chance at the time that he might have won[177]". However, it seems likely that Bercow was putting a long-term plan into action. If he managed to impress again in 1992, this time in a more high-profile, marginal seat, he would be very well placed to make a tilt for a solidly safe seat at the election after that.

If proof were needed, however, that Bercow might well have made it into Parliament in 1992, it comes from the ease with which he was eventually selected. One of the first applications he made was to Bristol South, a Labour seat held by Dawn Primarolo, who was known by the local Tories as "the Red Dawn" and later became Tony Blair's Paymaster-General, before becoming Deputy Speaker. Primarolo had won the seat by only 1400 votes in the 1987 election and so on paper she seemed vulnerable, but locals felt that the Tories had hit something of a high water mark – even in the Tory landslide of 1983 Primarolo's predecessor had won by 4,000 votes. As local committee member Iris

Gillard says, "I don't think that it was a winnable seat at that stage.[178]" Cora Stephenson, who later became Bercow's agent, agrees: "We didn't stand a chance of getting him in really, because it was an old die-hard Labour area.[179]"

Bercow was called for a first interview down in Bristol, where there was a shortlist of around twenty. He had been to the area before – when he spoke at a meeting of the Bristol University Conservative Association in October 1986, just four days before his father died suddenly. It had been quite a day, with protests taking place beforehand, although these could scarcely have come as a surprise, as Bercow had chosen to share a platform with two teachers who had faced disciplinary action after expressing controversial views on race.

The first round went well and Bercow breezed onto a shortlist of three, with the final to be held at the house of the local MEP. Around thirty members turned up, ready to vote in a secret ballot to decide who their candidate would be. First off, each of the finalists had to give a speech to the audience. "I got the impression John was always going to win," says Stephenson. "He was outstanding. I think one of the things that came across was that he was so sure of himself. With some young speakers you worry whereas with John you sat back and you listened because he was quite confident.[180]"

Next up was a question and answer session. Gillard says, "He was an expert at that. That is where he excels, because he can tell you what you didn't want to know, but is full of information you might want to know.[181]" Stephenson says that the committee were also particularly impressed by his knowledge of the local area. "His great strength was the fact that he had obviously researched the constituency because one of the things the committee sets out to do is to see how ignorant they are on a specific subject, but John had done his homework.[182]" The local members voted and Bercow was the comfortable winner. On the day it was a successful outcome, but in hindsight his victory might be viewed as a double-edged sword, as it tied him down to a marginal seat many years before the next election.

There was also one other, more pressing problem. Cora Stephenson noticed that Bercow had a hole in one of his shoes. "I thought, 'that means he walks a lot, so he doesn't drive'.[183]" For an agent, a candidate who doesn't have a licence is a nightmare as he will constantly need someone to ferry him across the constituency. After Bercow was adopted, Stephenson confronted him; he admitted he couldn't drive and valiantly promised to take lessons.

The embarrassment didn't end there, though. Bercow worked away at his driving and eventually passed his test, ringing up the local association in great excitement to tell them the good news. Stephenson suggested a celebratory lunch at her house and Bercow agreed to drive down from London the next day to meet her and some of the other Bristol Tories. Richard Eddy, the chairman of the Association, arrived a little early and the members stood talking in Stephenson's sitting room, waiting with some anticipation for their candidate to turn up. At last, the doorbell went and there was Bercow, looking pale and flustered. The novice driver confessed that as he'd pulled up, he had smashed into the side of the car parked out the front of the house, which it soon turned out belonged to none other than Eddy. "You can imagine what a start it was for the poor fellow on his first proper trip![184]" says Stephenson.

For the next three years Bercow would come down to Bristol almost every weekend. Unlike Motherwell, where he had a short, sharp shock, standing in Bristol involved a really significant time commitment for quite a chunk of his life. With his job up in London during the week, and his ongoing commitment to Lambeth Council until 1991 on top of that, Bercow had very little spare time outside of work and politics. This only increased his focus on his political ambitions and hindered his social life outside of the political world. He also had to get used to making the long journey back and forth from Bristol, spending hours on the train from Paddington or in the car, with his driving thankfully much improved.

He stayed with various members of the local association at weekends. Stephenson says, "He never had a problem finding a bed because he was so well liked and so willing. If you have someone who you can see is working his socks off, you'll help in any way that you can.[185]" One of the first weekends was spent at Iris Gillard's home. "The first time he came I nearly had a heart attack," she says. "He enjoyed his breakfast, and then he said 'thank you very much Iris, I've got to go and get canvassing'. And I said, 'But what about the dishes?' He was quite shocked. And I said, 'Well, don't you take them out into the kitchen?' It just showed you: his mother obviously had ruined him. She's a nice woman too.[186]"

It does seem that Bercow was a little lost without the maternal touch. Around this time, friends recall going over to his flat in Tooting Bec Gardens and being overpowered by a truly disgusting smell. "Bercow was not a champion of personal hygiene," one recalls, "but this was a step beyond." As Bercow's mates stood around shouting, "Jesus, what's that smell?" and the like, one brave soul ventured on to find the source of the odour. He followed his nose to Bercow's bedroom where, to his disgust, he found a plate under Bercow's bed, topped by an unidentifiable foodstuff which had been completely obscured by mould. "It had clearly been rotting under the bed for god knows how long," the friend told me. "It was horrifying."

Once he became a little more house trained, Bercow became very popular indeed with the local association in Bristol; and they were impressed with his dedication to the campaign and to the community. Bercow was always out canvassing and knocking on doors and he wasn't afraid to venture out into the rougher parts of the constituency, including Hartcliffe, a socially deprived area full of run-down estates which had seen rioting in 1992. "He could get responses from tough people. That was part of his charm and part of his charisma,[187]" says Gillard. "People said, 'No John, you can't go there, they'll kill you,'" remembers Stephenson. "But he insisted. He turned into a star there. People were staggered that this very well spoken, little man was in this area where there were great big bruisers. He'd go in and chat and had a lot of support there.[188]"

The three year period as Bristol's candidate helped to raise Bercow's profile in the local area and he offered himself as an alternative source of advice if his constituents didn't want to talk to "Red Dawn". He was also a big help to the party internally, turning up at fundraisers and whipping up the local members into as close as you can get to a frenzy in Bristol Conservative Association. One starring occasion was at the monthly lunch club, when Geoffrey Howe, who was then the Foreign Secretary, was due to speak but had to pull out at the last minute. Philip Stephenson, who organised the event, remembers that, "John got on the train from Paddington expecting to be a guest. I met him off the train and said, 'You're speaking'. He had quite a big audience as people were expecting to see [Howe], but John survived, he did very well and people were charmed.[189]"

Invariably at these events Bercow would be accompanied by one of a number of girls whose task it was to hang off his arm for the evening. On one occasion, the Cabinet Minister Chris Patten was so taken with the beauty of Bercow's latest female friend that he asked, "Is she the raffle prize?[190]" It's at this point in the story that the most controversial figure in Bercow's life makes her appearance. The winning ticket was none other than Sally Bercow – or Sally Illman as she was then, although she was just one of a number of "stunning" girls to come with Bercow to the local functions. Sally and Bercow had met at Conservative Party Students' Conference in 1989 (although much more of that later). The intense, initial period of their relationship coincided with his first year as Bristol's candidate and she was a semi-regular visitor with him. Not everyone was convinced, though. As one local Tory told me, she "didn't go down very well...they thought she was a bit brash." Nonetheless, Sally put in a lot of leg work for Bercow and ended up calling herself his "communications manager[191]" while he was a candidate – not the last time that she would end up working for her romantic partner.

More importantly for Bercow, at this time Sally was a very willing campaigner for the Conservative cause. When they finally married many years later, Sally was a rather risky weapon to deploy as she had become a devoted supporter of New Labour – and so was, perhaps, not the best person to be selling a Conservative candidate, however good she thought he was personally. But back in the late 1980s, the former Marlborough girl was blue all through – and in some ways almost as devoted a Conservative as her future husband. In that respect at least, when Bercow was running for Bristol, Sally appeared to tick all the boxes of a perfect political wife.

Sally certainly did make quite the impression on the local Conservatives and she was able to call on her contacts in Bristol South when she needed a ticket to Tory Party Conference. In 1993, when

Illman made what one rag called, "a rousing speech in defence of press freedom[192]" to the Tory faithful, she could only do so with Bristol South's help. She had failed to obtain a conference pass through her local association, so she turned to Bercow's old friends back in Bristol to help her make it to conference. Showing off her right-wing credentials – just four years before she "came out" as a New Labourite – Illman explained that it was "all to do with the Tory entrepreneurial spirit. There's a free market in conference passes too.[193]"

Another frequent visitor was Bercow's mother Brenda, who was still playing a very active part in his life. Gillard remembers that she used to come down to support Bercow but would still "lecture" him on what he should be doing – as any good mother would, of course. "She was I suppose very enthusiastic about her son...she certainly gave a lot of support[194]."

Bercow's political views were by and large unchanged from his FCS days and he remained a mainstream Thatcherite. Some members of the Bristol association thought that he was "a bit right-wing" but nobody seemed to find this particularly problematic. At the Tory Party Conference in 1989, Bercow gave an interview to the BBC and it's easy to tell that it's the same man who appeared on *Question Time* ten years before. For one thing, Bercow's acne was still visible and he had a spot above his eyebrow. As serious as ever, he told the BBC in that same engaging manner: "I believe we know we've got the policies right and there can be no question of flinching from that. We have a record of taking tough and necessary decisions, we now need to effectively explain and articulate our policies to the country and I'm sure the Prime Minister will do that." When asked about the Labour Party, Bercow was just as combative. "We will be identifying and exploiting the weaknesses of our opponents," he said. "It's important to understand Neil Kinnock has got off virtually scot free with a rehash of old policies presented in a politically sexy fashion but which fundamentally represent no change from the past. He's not going to get away with it any longer."

As Bercow continued his work in Bristol, events at Westminster began to take a dramatic turn. Geoffrey Howe, whose verbal jousts had previously been likened to being "savaged by a dead sheep[195]", delivered a devastating resignation speech in November 1990. Talking about Mrs Thatcher's stance towards the European single currency, he told the Commons: "It's rather like sending your opening batsmen to the crease only for them to find, the moment the first balls are bowled, that their bats have been broken before the game by the team captain." The wicket then became even stickier, with Michael Heseltine challenging the Prime Minister's leadership, sparking a leadership ballot.

Although Sally had always been impressed by Heseltine, Bercow himself was still an arch-Thatcherite and was appalled at the prospect of Maggie being thrown out. He soon rallied to the cause and began drumming up support for her in the leadership election. One current Conservative MP remembers, "His dedication to Margaret Thatcher was such that I can distinctly remember he faxed virtually everybody on the candidates list [of prospective MPs] insisting that we should declare our support more for Margaret Thatcher. That was just a classic, classic case of John."

It was the first, but certainly not the last time that Bercow backed the wrong horse in a leadership contest. Mrs Thatcher failed to beat Heseltine by the required margin and then, on November 22nd 1990, the Iron Lady was finally broken. Her Cabinet told her she would lose in the second round of voting and she resigned. Within five days, John Major was Prime Minister.

Despite Bercow's misgivings about Mrs Thatcher's removal, Major's appointment helped to reignite his campaign in Bristol. Two weeks before she quit, the Tories were 16 points behind Labour in the polls, but Major soon took a 12% lead. Bercow often pointed out that Bristol South was the "13th most marginal seat in the country[196]", and a national lead in the polls made a victory in Bristol a possibility. Even so, these improved poll ratings were not all good news for Bercow. However much he wanted to be an MP, to be elected in a marginal constituency would inevitably consign him to a precarious and ultimately short-lived existence in the Commons.

Nonetheless, Bercow continued the hard work over the next eighteen months in the lead up to the 1992 Election, incessantly pounding the streets to spread the Conservative gospel. The local

Tories were impressed, with Cora Stephenson finding him to be, "A wonderful candidate. Nothing was ever too much trouble; he would go anywhere at the drop of a hat[197]". He was also starting to be talked about as one of the next generation of leading Conservative MPs; and he raised eyebrows and his profile by telling former Prime Minister Edward Heath at the 1991 Party Conference that his views on Europe were "irritating, not to say obnoxious[198]". Bercow freely admitted at the time that he was interested in high office, remarking that "anyone who says they're not is a liar, [199]" and it was to be very many years and some bruising political confrontations later before Bercow would finally decide that a front bench post was not for him.

When John Major finally called the election in March 1992, Bercow and his helpers upped the pressure on "Red Dawn". Michael Heseltine, who was by then back in the Cabinet, came to Bristol's Grand Hotel to launch the Tories' campaign across the city, accompanied by the Health Secretary William Waldegrave. Nationally the polls were very tight indeed, with most predicting either a hung Parliament or a slim Labour majority. It was all to play for – but that meant Bercow was very unlikely to succeed in unseating Primarolo.

Undaunted by the unfavourable polls, Bercow was determined to win support in any way he could and the local Tories purchased a very old Bedford mini-van to use as a rather humble battle bus gathering up votes across the constituency. There was one problem, however: the bus was red. That colour just wasn't acceptable for a Tory candidate, so Bercow set about doing something about it. He was staying with Cora Stephenson during the campaign and she was having some renovation work done at her house. Such were Bercow's powers of persuasion that he convinced the builders to give up their lunch hour to help the cause. Soon they found a tin of paint and by early afternoon the van had a brand new colour – it was, of course, true blue.

Another unlikely source of support came from the local radio personality Eric Gadd, who went by the name of "Captain Courage" and presented a Saturday morning programme for kids. He was so taken with Bercow that he volunteered to drive the minibus for the whole of the campaign. "We had the most tremendous fun with him," says Stephenson. "People's spirits were on top notch; the bus was permanently filled with people wanting to help. It had never been known in the history of Bristol South. People were desperate to help John[200]". Bercow's time in the FCS also came in handy, as he was able to persuade the students at Bristol University to muck in. They came campaigning, dropping in leaflets and knocking on doors with him. However, inevitably the flip side of the FCS reared its ugly head as Bercow was dogged by rumours – and in some cases outright lies – about his time in the organisation.[201]

Inevitably not everyone was persuaded by the Tory campaign, but – faced with this resistance – Bercow wasn't afraid to speak his mind. On more than one occasion the Tory delegation would knock on a door and ask a woman which way she intended to vote. "Ooh I don't know, I'll have to ask my husband," she'd say. Bercow would have none of it. "What about the women who fought for the vote?" he'd ask in reply.

As voting day neared, things were looking as dark for the Tories across the UK as they did in Bristol. With Labour ahead in the polls, the party held its now infamous rally in Sheffield. The contrast to John Major, standing on his upturned soapbox, could scarcely have been more marked. In what looked more like a victory rally, Neil Kinnock was introduced as the country's next Prime Minister and repeatedly shouted "We're alright!" at the crowd. But Labour were not all right and the famous Tory poster depicting Labour's "£1,000 tax bombshell" – produced by Saatchi & Saatchi, the parent company of Bercow's PR firm – was helping to turn voters back towards the Tories. Still, though, the polls put Labour in the lead. Even on election day, April 9th, Labour were ahead. Expectations were low in Bristol as Bercow worked tirelessly throughout the day in the final push, marking the culmination of three very long years.

Having thrown everything into the campaign, as the voting stations closed the Bristol Tories gathered for the count at a local secondary school. Despite some unfavourable exit polls, it was soon evident that Major was on course to win a famous victory as he took fourteen million votes, the largest ever popular vote for one party, beating Labour by 8%. In Bristol, the Conservatives celebrated the good news, but when the results there were finally announced, Bercow had to face up to yet another disappointing personal performance. As in

Motherwell, his fared worse than the Tories' average result across the UK: Primarolo had easily beaten him into second place, the 1,400 majority from five years previously becoming a comfortable 9,000 vote margin. What's more, the Tories' share of the vote fell by nearly 6%.

Some comfort can be had from the fact that, as in Motherwell, the decline was part of a wider trend. No Conservative in Bristol South has managed to come close to Bercow's percentage of the vote in any election since and in 2010 the Tory candidate came third, despite the party's national success. In that sense, Bercow's poor performance can be put down to factors beyond his control. However, having worked his socks off for more than three years, it must have been very disheartening to still do so badly. Bercow might not have expected to win, but he would have wanted to keep the swing down as much as possible. Nevertheless, the members of the Association are clear that there was little more that he could have done. Stephenson's opinion is that, "He was wonderful, he was loved desperately by everybody[202]"; for Gillard, "John Bercow was one of the best candidates we've ever had[203]"; and for local Tory Derek Fey, "He was a good candidate. We thought he was very genuine.[204]"

13

The Special Adviser

"Stormy day after stormy day"

As the Conservative Party celebrated its unexpected victory in the 1992 election, the reality was much more mundane for John Bercow. He had a number of dreams to realise, but for now he had to get back to the day job at RSC. The good news was that Major's win had kept up the demand for Tories in political PR, so there was no chance of Bercow being shunted out of a job in favour of a wave of lobbyists with Labour contacts.

There was also the added enticement of the chance to work for a new division created by the Saatchi brothers, rather grandly called "Saatchi Government Communications Worldwide", which straddled the PR division of the Rowland Group and the Saatchi ad agency. John Maples, a former Treasury Minister who had lost his seat at the election, was put in charge of the project. A host of other high-profile names were brought on board, including Steve Hilton, subsequently David Cameron's Director of Strategy, who had been working at Central Office during the 1992 campaign. Whilst Bercow continued his work at Rowland, he also spent time on the new Saatchi gig, advising the Conservative government and a host of foreign administrations and political parties.

Although his heart might have been in Westminster, Bercow continued to do extremely well in his work for RSC. However, Bercow's colleagues knew full well that he didn't want to stay in public affairs forever. Peter Rae was his boss in the immediate aftermath of the 1992 election. "It was obvious he wanted to be in Parliament," he says. "He was a very earnest and serious young man[205]". Bercow continued to go to Party Conference and again made headlines there, with a spirited attack on Michael Portillo's detractors at the 1992 gathering. With his usual panache, and a nod to Heseltine and Thatcher, Bercow told Conference that Labour feared "a minister with the moral courage and self-confidence to eat them alive – before breakfast, before lunch, before tea and, yes, before dinner as well." He asked, "Who better to slaughter Europe's sacred cows than this prize bull-fighter? And who better than he to tell federalist conspirators what they need to hear: no, no, no and no![206]" It was one of the earliest signs that Bercow was hinging his own fortunes on those of Portillo, a man who would prove to be a political guiding light for Bercow for many years.

Bercow's ability and competence were evident as he moved into his early thirties. Rae recalls him as an, "Exceptionally bright and a very quick witted chap, a very personable chap. He stood out because he was one of the most articulate people I've ever met, and a very effective public speaker and a very good communicator. He was a very popular member of staff. [207]" Bercow was well known for his love of the English language and he used to give training in presentation skills to other members of the RSC team. Public speaking lessons with Bercow were also offered to clients as part of the RSC service. In an industry where people live or die by how they put themselves across, it's a measure of just how effective Bercow was that others wanted to learn from him. On a day-to-day basis in the office he would also try to make sure that people used the highest standards of both spoken and written English, correcting them, "But not in a heavy-handed way[208]", according to Rae. It seems that some of Bercow's interests had not changed since his school days, but his tact had.

Bercow's ability was recognised in January 1994, when he was promoted to the board of the Rowland Company. As a lobbyist, the title was all-important for his business card, but the role didn't involve any significant responsibility in running the company. In fact, at Rowland, in a company of around eighty people, there were almost twenty employees on the board. Bercow was, however, finding his feet financially and someone in his sort of job at that time would have been earning the equivalent of around £40,000 or £50,000 now[209] – a pretty decent salary for a man of thirty, although still far less than a successful banker at Hambros.

As Bercow made a success of his public affairs career, his future wife Sally, who says he was still "chasing" her on and off over this period[210], was also forging ahead in the PR and advertising industry, providing them with yet another common bond. Over the years she worked for a number of firms including Masius, Countrywide Communications, Anderson and Lembke, GGT Direct Advertising and CST Intelligence, becoming a senior consultant[211].

However, Sally ran into trouble back in 1994 when she applied for a job at Consolidated Communications. She had included her time at Oxford on her CV, even though she had left without finishing her degree as her party lifestyle took its toll. Oddly, she listed her initial success in her theology exams, even though these were "mods" – exams which do not count towards a final degree result. Sally insists that she was not disingenuous, arguing that she had listed the real dates of her time in Oxford, 1988-90. "Anyone could work out that that is two years and not three. Nor did the CV say that she completed her degree,[212]" her spokesman has argued.

But her boss was not happy. On discovering the confusion, the head of the firm, Alistair Gornall had a stand up row with Sally, accusing her of lying, and she was fired.[213] However, she claims that the pair fell out because the job was in public relations, not, as she believed it would be, advertising – and she says she wanted to leave in any case. Either way, she was able to bounce back quickly enough, becoming an account director at City Financial Marketing soon afterwards.

There were no such difficulties for her future husband. But despite being on such a successful trajectory, Bercow decided to leave behind RSC and the PR world to become a government special adviser (Spad) little more than a year after his promotion to the board. By quitting lobbying, Bercow turned his back on an industry where he could have made it to the very top. His boss, Peter Rae, told me:

"John would have achieved great things, whether he remained as a lobbyist or he became a general business consultant. He was exceptionally bright with a wide knowledge of current affairs not just in the political sphere. People like that don't grow on trees in the PR industry. He could have ended up as the MD or Chief Executive of one of the big PR companies. He had the leadership ability that would have helped to coalesce a team underneath him and he would have been very successful at it. He had the gravitas; the intellect; the presence; and when he spoke, he spoke sense."

Despite such promise, it's clear that Bercow's interests always lay with politics. Why else would he have worked away campaigning, almost every weekend, in Bristol, alongside a full-time job? Nonetheless, the choice to leave when he did – and to do so to become a special adviser – is in some ways an odd one.

Bercow had of course decided to continue working for RSC after the 1992 election. Back then, an up-and-coming Tory like him would have been in with a good shot of getting a job as a special adviser and he would have been an able candidate. Time-wise, it would have made more sense, as a special adviser cannot also be a Prospective Parliamentary Candidate. By the time Bercow left RSC in 1995, a General Election was a maximum of only two years away, meaning that he was giving himself a very limited shelf life in the job. If he were selected – and Bercow was soon looking in earnest for a seat – he would need to resign from his new job. Having stuck at public affairs for eight years, it seems a strange moment to jump when a chance of being selected for a safe seat was so tantalisingly close.

Perhaps Bercow was merely concerned that he needed something else on his CV to beef up his chances of being selected in one of the plum seats. Just as he may have underestimated his own abilities before the 1992 election, so, too, he might have been unduly worried about his chances in 1997. Given his total focus on becoming an MP, it is likely that Bercow would have done whatever it took to finally make it into Parliament. If that meant a few quick job changes in succession, then it was a price he was happy to pay.

Once again, Bercow set to work on his network of contacts. He was on good terms with Lord (Malcolm) Pearson, a businessman who had made a fortune in the insurance industry and who later led UKIP in 2009-10. At that time, however, Pearson sat in the Lords as a Conservative. Luckily for Bercow, Pearson had been the closest friend of Jonathan Aitken, the newly appointed Chief Secretary to the Treasury, for forty years.

Aitken recounts that, "Malcolm Pearson called me up and said, 'I know you'll appoint a special adviser. I think you might have to have a look at John Bercow'[214]". Pearson told Aitken that he came highly recommended by Julian Lewis, who is still Bercow's closest friend and was then the Deputy Director of the Conservative Research Department at Central Office. But Pearson also warned, "He might be a bit too right-wing even for you![215]"

If Bercow might have been a little too far to the right of the party for Aitken's liking, his saving grace was that he was a hardened Eurosceptic. Aitken was one of the leading campaigners against further European integration and he wanted his adviser to share those views. "I had a feeling of a need for balance in the Cabinet and indeed the Treasury between the strongly pro-European view personified by Ken Clarke [the Chancellor] and Heseltine, a feeling that Eurosceptics were in large parts underrepresented in the Cabinet...I wouldn't have hired a Europhile enthusiast.[216]"

Aitken decided to give him a chance and Bercow seized the opportunity when he came for interview. He arrived at the Chief Secretary's room in the Treasury, where he was ushered in to meet the interview panel which included Aitken and his private secretary. Aitken asked Bercow about his track record, and Bercow gave a frank account of the dust-ups in the FCS, although his prospective boss was impressed in any case. "He interviewed well, he was the best candidate," he says. "John was clearly an astute political operator and he understood quite a bit about the media, the political currents of the time.[217]"

But it wasn't just Aitken who needed to be won over. Next up was the Chancellor himself. "I was very wary of him," Clarke recalls, "Because John would not deny it, he was on the extreme right-wing of politics when I first encountered him. Jonathan had to persuade me that it was a good idea to have John at the Treasury. I had a meeting with John to talk to the guy, see whether I could really be persuaded he should come in. John was perfectly straightforward – I think I slightly read the riot act to him...he had to be loyal and he had to be discreet. He gave me his solemn undertaking that he would behave himself. He absolutely kept to his word, I did not have the slightest trouble with him at all, I increasingly got on well with him, there's no doubt that he's extremely bright, he's extremely able and I was pleasantly surprised.[218]"

Bercow finally started work in March 1995 – and it was immediately clear that his was an important role. Aitken was in charge of the expenditure round, negotiating the budget for each government department and then dealing with ministers who were unhappy after the Budget itself had been announced by the Chancellor. It was a particularly challenging job as the Chief Secretary often has to battle against a minister who outranks him in Cabinet and who wants to safeguard his department's money. Then there was the immense difficulty of selling cuts in government expenditure to the general public at a time when the Tory Party under John Major was starting to become seriously unpopular with the country at large. As his special adviser, Bercow had to be Aitken's political eyes and ears.

Bercow's job was varied and very hands on. He drafted political press releases, wrote speeches, went to meetings with senior Treasury figures and dealt with interview requests that were passed on by the Treasury press department. However, the role of a special adviser was much less high-profile than it is today and somewhat more nebulous; and the special advisers themselves were less well-known to the public.

Once again, Bercow made an astonishingly strong impact in a short space of time. As Aitken told me: "I remember my first appearance as Chief Secretary on the *Today* programme – this was considered an important debut for me and the setting of the government's policy of cutting expenditure. I remember he briefed me particularly well on what the questions would be. He had thought out the angles well and he showed shrewd political antennae."

Bercow was also progressing well in his speech-writing and Aitken remembers him working particularly hard on a speech addressing Britain's economic future in Europe. "Looking to the future, do we need European trade?" wrote Bercow. "Britain's future is as a world trading nation.[219]" Julian Lewis, who was still working at Central Office, was also a continuing help to Bercow, sending him a dossier on the BBC ahead of a speech by Aitken that attacked the Corporation for turning into the "Blair Broadcasting Corporation."

However, others who were closely involved with the Aitken camp have a far less positive recollection of Bercow's abilities. Patrick Robertson, a PR guru who later represented General Pinochet, was tasked with helping Aitken's image. "I remember being very dismissive about [Bercow]," he told me. "He didn't have a strategic mind; a tactical mind. The material he produced was very verbose with not enough full stops in it. He never briefed particularly well, he would jump on the issue of the day and make a loud noise of it. He was not an articulate character, not an incisive thinker."

More surprisingly, the public image of Bercow as something of a hard-line head banger was also much more tempered in private. He was often involved in policy discussions but noticeably tried to stand up for the underdog. "He would always say, 'That would really hurt the hard up' or, 'That would really hurt the unmarried mothers'[220]", says Aitken. Clarke agrees: "I certainly didn't have [from Bercow] any of the outrageous opinions that I was half expecting. He was perfectly mainstream politically, there was never a moment's trouble.[221]"

Robertson, too, saw little of the adversarial fire that had come to define Bercow for so long. "[I would say] 'John back off' and he was like a caterpillar being touched by a pin prick, he's not a guy for confrontation. His manner is softly softly. There was no way he was going to win an argument with me. Some Spads throw their weight around to establish position and protect their turf; John wasn't even like that.[222]" For the first time, then, there are signs that behind the more extreme exterior, there were the stirrings of the social conscience that played such an important part in Bercow's political career as he moved from right to left in the Tory Party.

Bercow muddled along in the job for a few weeks, but then everything changed on April 10th 1995. Up till that point, Aitken had been progressing well in his cabinet role and the *Mail on Sunday* had even run a headline saying:

"HESELTINE IS TOO OLD
CLARKE IS TOO CAVALIER
AND PORTILLO IS TOO RIDICULOUS.
So who will succeed John Major?

STEP FORWARD JONATHAN AITKEN
... The only Cabinet minister who hasn't a single enemy.[223]"

But a whiff of scandal managed to get in the way of such lofty predictions. On that day in April, the *Guardian* ran a story headlined: "AITKEN 'TRIED TO ARRANGE GIRLS' FOR SAUDI FRIENDS", following up on an inside page with, "AITKEN CONNECTION TO SECOND ARMS DEALER DISCLOSED" and "NEW LIGHT SHED ON WHO PAID WHAT AT THE RITZ IN PARIS".

Although Aitken was not an arms dealer and not a pimp, the story unleashed the vultures who soon began to circle ominously around his political career. Worryingly for Aitken, he had allowed a hotel bill at The Ritz in Paris to be paid for by an old friend, Said Ayas, an associate of Prince Mohammed of Saudi Arabia.[224] Aitken heard about the article whilst he was in Switzerland and it was there that he began to write his now infamous "Sword of Truth" speech. He returned to his home in Westminster where he was joined by Bercow, Robertson and the MP Alan Duncan, before making his way to the Treasury, where he tried out the address on a number of officials including Bercow. Then, Aitken made the short trip to Conservative Central Office in Smith Square to deliver the speech, although there were so many journalists along the route that Bercow was tasked with clearing a path for Aitken, his wife and daughter through the crowd. Once inside, Aitken addressed the cameras, calling the allegations "wicked lies" and saying he wanted to start a fight "to cut out the cancer of bent and twisted journalism in our country with the simple sword of truth and the trusty shield of British fair play." Despite newspaper reports at the time, and although Bercow did often write speeches for Aitken, both Robertson and Aitken himself are adamant that Bercow did not write that most famous Aitken speech of all[225].

The Sword of Truth speech did little to dispel the allegations and rumours swirling around Aitken, and Bercow's job had suddenly morphed into one where he had to advise a Minister under intense pressure. That same evening, Granada broadcast a *World in Action* programme entitled "Jonathan of Arabia", with more allegations against Aitken. The stories – true or false – just kept on coming, and Robertson recalls that there was "one scandal after another[226]". Aitken issued a writ against the *Guardian* and Bercow put out a press release saying that the Minister would also be suing Granada[227].

Aitken was hanging on, but they were grim times, although Bercow had no knowledge that Aitken's denial of hospitality at the Ritz was untrue. "John couldn't possibly have known what happened in the Ritz," Aitken told me. As Aitken's political adviser, Bercow was under a lot of stress, but he didn't let it distract him from the job. "The magnitude of the bombardment was mega, there was stormy day after stormy day. He, in human terms, could see the wretched minister sinking under the weight and he was very loyal. I thought he was a very nice man and a very kind man. I remember him for his human kindness. [228]"

By June, Aitken began to realise it would be increasingly difficult for him to stay on as a Minister and prepare for his libel action at the same time. Meanwhile, there were rumblings that a Sunday newspaper was digging into Aitken's private life from fifteen years beforehand. Robertson had been trying to find out what the tabloids were planning and attempted to fax Aitken, telling him the *Sunday Mirror* had, "Some pretty dreadful stuff, far worse than any extra-marital affair[229]". Unfortunately Robertson pressed the wrong digit and sent that fax to a London arts producer who passed it on to the press.

As matters went from bad to worse, it seemed that Aitken had to go. But events got in the way, as John Major, who was also struggling badly but for different reasons, decided to face down backbench dissent by calling a leadership election, telling his detractors to, "Put up or shut up". Aitken decided to resign soon after, but delayed the announcement until after the ballot on July 4th. In the event, Major easily defeated his only challenger, John Redwood. The next day, Aitken resigned.

As a postscript, it is well known that Aitken perjured himself in his libel action against the *Guardian* by claiming his wife had settled the Ritz Hotel bill. The libel trial subsequently collapsed and Aitken was convicted of perjury and sent to prison, going bankrupt in the process. However, despite such a fall from grace, and the potential political ramifications of maintaining contact with a disgraced ex-politician, Bercow remained loyal. Aitken says that Bercow, "Stayed in touch, which not everybody did. He wrote to me in prison and one of the first social invitations I received after prison was when he invited me to his wedding.[230]" Amidst much of the abuse hurled at Bercow by his former colleagues on the Tory benches in recent years, it is worth noting that Bercow will remain loyal where he thinks it right, despite the potential political impact.

For Bercow, the fall of Aitken was a catastrophic event. He had ditched his successful PR career but had ended up becoming an appendage to a Ministerial career which nosedived with considerable speed. More worryingly, the fate of a special adviser is often linked with that of his Minister, so when Aitken resigned, Bercow also lost his job.

However, Bercow managed to turn the situation around with remarkable speed and he was back in gainful employment within a couple of months. Much of this was thanks to the Conservative MP Peter Ainsworth, who had worked with Bercow when he was Aitken's Parliamentary Private Secretary. "I, like everyone else, had heard of John Bercow as a firebrand right-wing lunatic," says Ainsworth. "But it turned out he was quiet and studiously courteous and very efficient.[231]" Ainsworth was transferred to be PPS to Virginia Bottomley, the former Health Secretary who had recently been demoted to the National Heritage brief and was, coincidentally, another alumnus of Essex University.

Bottomley needed a Spad and Ainworth suggested she consider Bercow for the job. However, the process was still a difficult one and Bercow and the other candidates had to submit a 750 word "tabloid style" article singing the praises of the National Lottery, which fell within Bottomley's brief. Bercow put his PR expertise to work and duly delivered; he made the final shortlist of ten and was called in for interview.

Bottomley and Bercow were never a natural fit and she was known as an arch wet, holding a position on the opposite wing of the party to Bercow, so Ainsworth's reassurances that Bercow was much more measured in private were a key to his selection. Also in Bercow's favour was that he was, as he puts it, "The Jewboy son of a taxi driver". Bottomley was reportedly frustrated at the well-heeled middle class girls that turned up for interview. "They are all far too like you and me," she told Ainsworth, "I think we need a contrast.[232]" Bercow was much more rough and ready and provided the *je ne sais quoi* that Bottomley wanted. John Major also had his part to play in Bercow's appointment: a few weeks previously he had issued a decree banning workers from Central Office from taking up special adviser roles, fearing a brain drain from party HQ with an election only 18 months away. As Bercow had never worked in Central Office, he was in the clear, whereas a number of able young Tories were barred from applying.

So it was that Bercow won through and was appointed as Bottomley's Spad in late August 1995. "He was grateful, but not particularly so," says Ainsworth. "[But] I wouldn't have helped him if I hadn't respected his ability[233]." However, in some quarters the appointment was greeted with much amazement. The *Guardian* commented, "No one at Westminster can imagine why the soaking-wet Mrs Bottomley would appoint a bumptious, abrasive libertarian free-marketeer like Mr Bercow, who is said to have both the far-right politics and physical stature of Alan Duncan, but without the attendant personal charm.[234]" Ken Clarke recalls, "John still had the reputation of being slightly to the right of Norman Tebbit. I remember being amused that my old friend Virginia Bottomley had got him on the payroll, and in fact Virginia had her leg pulled about having John Bercow as her special adviser.[235]"

Compared to working with Aitken, the challenges with Bottomley were much more straightforward. Not only was she not facing crisis after crisis, but the Heritage brief was also less demanding in terms of policy and ministerial horse trading. Once again, those around Bercow remember him as being surprisingly reserved in terms of his politics. Gone was the small man who would always take the unpopular corner and fight for it. "In all the time I worked with John Bercow he never expressed a political opinion," says Ainsworth. "What had happened to this firebrand with strong ideological opinions I don't know.[236]"

However, although – to the surprise of many – Bercow and

Bottomley managed to rub along quite nicely in ideological terms, the discord speculated about in the press was soon to come to fruition. Despite coming through such a stringent interview process and having been chosen from a large field, Bercow and Bottomley never really gelled. Part of the problem was that Bottomley was very demanding of her advisers. Ainsworth recalls that, "She asked 110% attention at all times and needed him on a 24 hour basis all year round. It was not an easy job for anyone and it was hard for John. His mind seemed elsewhere.[237]"

Bercow had never made any great secret of his ambitions – and it was perfectly obvious to anyone who knew him well that he was desperate to be selected for the 1997 election. Aitken had been quite happy with this, and he told me, "I very much encouraged him in getting a seat…I understood totally that he was an ambitious young man who wanted to move on to be a proper politician himself, putting in for seats."

However, to Bottomley it seemed that Bercow's priorities were all wrong, as the departmental remit seemed to come second to his search for a seat. In part, this may have been because the selection process was reaching something of a crescendo in late 1995 and early 1996, when Bercow was working for her. More awkward was that Bercow was applying for the same seats as Bottomley's husband Peter and the two came up against each other on at least one occasion. Bercow was not one to desist, though, just because he was up against his boss's husband. "How many people would do that?" says his friend Kevin Bell. "Other people would say 'oh I'm not going to' but he just gets through it. It's brilliant in many ways, you need people who just get on and do things.[238]"

Then, when Bercow was finally selected in February 1996, he left Bottomley, just six months after he'd joined her. Given that he had only been appointed as her Spad eighteen months before a General Election, she might well have hoped that he would see the job through to the end. Things did not end well, and Ainsworth says, "Virginia is vitriolic about him. She is no fan. She still bitches on about him. He didn't give her the attention she wanted. She felt it disloyal to her personally.[239]"

However, by this time, the National Heritage department was no longer Bercow's priority. In early 1996 a lifelong ambition was about to be realised. The process that had begun in Motherwell some ten years earlier – or perhaps, some might say, over twenty years beforehand in his primary school elections, was about to conclude. But, as with most things in the life of John Bercow, the path did not run smoothly – and he only made it over the finish line thanks to an incredible, flamboyant touch that showed just how much he wanted the prize awaiting him.

14

Flying to Victory

"The best £1,000 I've ever spent"

The operation was military in its precision. The first appointment was nearly over. Outside, a chauffeur-driven car was waiting with its engine running. The young man answered the last question, thanked his audience and a few seconds later rushed out of the door. It was 7.35pm and the race against the clock was on. He and his entourage jumped in the car and moments later it sped away through the Surrey countryside, covering the few miles to Blackbushe airport in just fifteen minutes.

A Twin Squirrel helicopter was waiting there for the young man and his helpers as they rushed from the vehicle. The changeover took just a few minutes as they donned their earmuffs and secured their seatbelts. Moments later, the chopper was ready for take off. Up it went into the winter darkness, skirting its way round central London to make its way north.

Meanwhile in Finmere, near Buckingham, the next part of the plan was being put into action. Time was running out. Two cars had been parked with their headlights on and their indicators flashing, marking out a landing spot for the helicopter. There was no room for error if the young man was to make it to his next, all-important meeting.

At 8.25pm, the helicopter made its way back down to earth and the small group dashed out into the darkness as quickly as they could, jumping into one of the waiting cars and driving on...towards a local school, for a Conservative Party selection meeting.

John Bercow, accompanied by his friend Julian Lewis and his then girlfriend Louise Cumber – he was in a definite "off" period from Sally at this point – had made it from Surrey to Buckingham just in time. He addressed the local members, won the vote and became the candidate for that ultra-safe Tory seat, all but securing the coveted place in the House of Commons. Those final hours might sound like an excerpt from a bad novel, but they also marked the final chapter in a long and gruelling process.

***

After his experiences in Motherwell and Bristol South, there was never any question that Bercow would have another go at becoming an MP. This time, though, the Commons was within his grasp. Having fought an unwinnable and then a marginal, he didn't want to miss out for a third time. "He was only focused on absolutely safe seats[240]", says Gary Mond.

The process was stressful – as it is for any prospective MP who is so close to a golden ticket to the House of Commons – but Bercow did better than most. In fact, he applied to fewer than ten seats this time around – all of them solidly Conservative – before he was selected. But the road was a hard one and Bercow might have thought that he was set to be dogged by continued bad luck that would stop him ever making it into the Commons. The line between a successful selection followed by an illustrious career and total failure can be a matter of a couple of votes from little old ladies in a rural backwater. Many of the candidates on the list at the same time as Bercow who came within a whisker of a safe seat have never found their way into the Commons; for others it would be more than a decade before they'd have another decent shot. The stakes were high and the margins of error were small.

An early failure came in North Wiltshire, where Bercow made it to the last twenty but no further. The selection committee had been impressed by his CV but were put off by the way he spoke: everything he said was absolutely word perfect, which they felt showed a lack of the common touch. As Bercow often writes out the words for his speeches in full – as if he is writing an essay – before memorising the whole thing, he can come across to some people as rather stilted and just a bit too over the top. But, no matter: it is rare for any candidate to be selected straight away and there were plenty more seats out there for the taking.

Soon, though, the bad luck set in. One particularly frustrating experience came in the final round of the north-east Bedfordshire selection in October 1995, when Bercow had initially seemed to be one of the frontrunners. But then the Attorney-General, Sir Nicholas Lyell, lost a selection in his own, neighbouring seat and the Tory high command mobilised behind him to help him retain his place in the Commons. Bercow did have an ally in his old Monday Club friend John Carlisle, whose constituency was also in Bedfordshire, but that was nothing compared to effort being made to help his opponent: "They were ringing round and bus-loading people in to hold the seat for Lyell,[241]" Carlisle recalls. On the night, Bercow put in an excellent performance and against the odds it soon became clear that he would push Lyell very close. But in the end it wasn't quite enough and Lyell took the nomination – and the guaranteed place in the Commons – by just four votes. Whilst the result might have been frustrating, it would nonetheless have been a big confidence boost. Having previously stood in two urban areas, this was one of Bercow's first forays into a high Tory, rural seat. It seemed that despite being a Jewish boy from north London, his charm still held sway. "It was really a victory," says Carlisle, notwithstanding the result. "He was unknown to them and it was a traditional Tory country seat.[242]"

Bercow also came very close in West Worthing, a new seat with a notional majority of around 20,000 for the incoming Conservative MP. Inevitably, though, it was the scene of another bitter battle centred on the neighbouring MP, Michael Stephen, who had narrowly been selected for the new constituency without an open contest. Party officials then took legal advice and re-opened the selection to outsiders. Bercow was one of those who applied and made the final six, but came up against the rather awkward obstacle of his boss's husband, Peter Bottomley. Bercow didn't make the final three but Bottomley went on to win the selection, no doubt making for an interesting conversation when Bercow went to work the next morning.

Although he was getting very close, these were nervous times and his failure to be selected was soon attracting attention. For the commentator Peter Riddell, the problem was that Bercow was too right-wing for the more casual members of local associations. "Shortlists [are] chosen by a small group of committed activists, but the final decision lies with the wider party membership, which is generally less ideological,[243]" he wrote. However, bad luck seemed to be as important a factor. With boundary changes freeing up a large number of MPs with marginal seats to have a go somewhere safer, Bercow had seemed to find himself in the middle of a number of particularly fraught struggles.

However, Bercow's resolve did not waver and he put his nerves aside to continue the search undaunted. Soon, he was called for a first round interview in Buckingham and this time he made it down to the last three, with a final selection meeting scheduled for the evening of February 7th. Meanwhile, he also applied to Surrey Heath, yet another very safe seat, where his CV did the trick once again and he was placed on the preliminary shortlist of six. But then he received some very bad news – the committee wanted to see him on the same evening, February 7th.

Bercow despaired as there seemed no way of combining the two meetings, which were to be held eighty miles apart and at around the same time. On a good day, it would take him two hours to make the drive, but on a Wednesday evening the traffic made the journey time much more unpredictable. A train was no good, either, for by the time Bercow got back into London, changed stations and jumped on a train to Buckingham, it would be even slower than driving and just as unpredictable.

The only option seemed to be to turn down one of the seats. But that was a huge wrench – both were solid blue constituencies and any aspiring politician would have given his right arm to be selected in either; and Bercow was aware that time was running out as the list of good places still waiting to select a candidate was dwindling fast. Buckingham was the logical preference if he had to choose – he was in the final round – but there were no guarantees. Bercow was at a loss and he turned to his old agent from Bristol, Cora Stephenson, for advice. "Cora, I'm in a terrible state," he told her. "I don't know what to do. I've got two interviews and I can't do them both.[244]" It was Stephenson who then came up with the brilliant idea of hiring a helicopter.

The committee at Surrey Heath allowed Bercow to go up first and Buckingham said he could go last, giving him a decent shot of making it between the two in time. But even with the chopper, it was going to be very close and there was always the chance that the weather would be too bad to fly. That would leave Bercow stuck in Surrey, a couple of hours by car away from his final round. But the gods were smiling that night and the plan went without a hitch. "It was just like the French Resistance," said Julian Lewis, "Dropping out of the sky to win the day.[245]"

Of course as Bercow and his entourage swept into the room in triumph, the real battle – the selection itself – lay ahead. He was up against two impressive figures, the banker Howard Flight and another rising star, David Rutley, but neither could compete with Bercow's sheer flamboyance that night. "We thought that Howard had done a pretty good speech," recalls Flight's wife Christabel, "and Bercow was incredibly late. Suddenly this helicopter arrives and out pops Bercow and that was it, we knew we'd lost, it wouldn't have mattered what he'd said, if he'd talked about chocolate elephants, he'd won it.[246]" Bercow rushed up on stage and was soon regaling the local members with his tale of adventure across the country to be with them. "Just because I am a little chap," he said, clearly not letting his diminutive size stand in his way, "It doesn't mean I haven't got a big ambition.[247]"

Soon afterwards, the Buckingham Conservatives voted. It was close, but it was the helicopter "wot won it" and Bercow was selected as the candidate to fight the next General Election – in a seat with a Conservative majority of nearly 20,000. Barring some unforeseen disaster, it meant that Bercow was, at last, on his way into Parliament. No wonder that, thinking of his dash across the country to be there that night, he turned to Lewis and said, "Julian, this is the best £1,000 I have ever spent[248]."

In becoming a candidate, Bercow was effectively forced to resign as Bottomley's special adviser. Out of a job and with a lot more time on his hands, he resolved to work hard in Buckingham to get to know the local area and its voters. Given the humiliation of the Conservatives that followed in the 1997 election, as one supposedly safe seat after another fell to Labour, Bercow was right not to take anything for granted – although the size of the majority meant that if Bercow was to be wiped out then most of the Parliamentary Party would most likely have gone with him.

But much as Bercow enjoyed working for his soon-to-be constituents, he had to pay the bills. Just months after leaving public affairs, he was looking for a route back into the industry. He turned to James Gray, who had been a special adviser at the same time as Bercow and who had also been selected as a candidate for the 1997 election. Like Bercow, Gray had had to give up his political job and had returned to the world of PR, becoming a director of Westminster Strategy. Bercow was a logical person to take on as a consultant: he knew how government worked; he was well connected in the Tory Party; and he had significant experience in PR. Gray offered Bercow two days' work a week, which he accepted. It was his fourth job in around twelve months and he knew that it was merely passing time until he could take up a fifth role – as an MP.

Nonetheless, Bercow was as effective as ever as a political consultant. Working from Westminster Strategy's office in Dean's Yard, he advised clients on how they should approach the lame duck Tory government and the strategy they should take towards Labour. Despite Bercow's talents, he was still relatively old fashioned and much preferred to scribble away at his desk rather than use a computer. "John was a prolix," says Gray. "He wrote everything and handed it in to his secretary...in longhand with a huge sprawl.[249]"

That left five days a week for Bercow to spend in Buckingham and he soon made as much of an impression there as he had done in Motherwell and Bristol. "He was a slick operator," says his opponent, the Labour councillor Robert Lehmann. "He was a great speaker. He can stand and talk off the cuff very effectively. He got into community events well and would get to know the key movers and shakers.[250]" When John Major finally called a General Election, Bercow swung into action once more. He had lost none of his fire and he spent much of the time campaigning against New Labour and attacking their policies, with a particularly strong line against the introduction of a minimum wage, but the campaign was friendly enough as he knew he was on the winning ticket. The key to the country's future was not in Buckingham, but elsewhere.

Another important part of the Bercow team in Buckingham was Sally – although by this time Bercow's future wife had completely turned her back on what he might call her "former party." Despite having spoken at the Conservative Party Conference in 1993 – and having been so keen to do so that she had called in favours to get hold of a conference pass – Sally had performed a startling U-turn. It was more dramatic than any change that her husband has ever performed, as in the space of just four years she changed her allegiance from Tory to Tony. By 1997 Sally had become a whole-hearted devotee of the New Labour cause, eschewing the Conservative Party in which she had found her home, first at Oxford and later as she made her career in advertising and PR. For the first time, she had to practice the art of supporting Bercow, for whom she cared deeply, even though he was a Conservative, whilst also backing the party which seemingly stood for everything Bercow despised. It was a difficult balancing act to which she soon became accustomed.

On 1st May 1997, Sally got her wish, as Tony Blair swept to power in a landslide, with the Tories losing more than half their seats in Parliament. The Conservatives had known they were in for a beating, as the country was tired of the party after 18 years in power. Major's personal ratings were astonishingly low, while the public had lost confidence in the Tories' ability to manage the economy after the ERM debacle. However, the scale of the defeat still surprised many. But, in Buckingham, one of the truest blue constituencies in the country held firm, and Bercow cantered to victory with 50% of the vote. At last, it was John Bercow, MP.

15

A House of Commons Man

"My behaviour was spectacularly bad"

The first session of John Bercow's first Parliament began on May 7th 1997 and Bercow had to fulfil his first task in the Commons by taking the oath of loyalty. For most MPs this was a moment of some pride but essentially an administrative task. For Bercow, however, it was a matter of some importance. He told James Gray, who was also new to the Commons, that the order of seniority in the House was determined by the time and date at which they took their oath. This was crucial when it came to choosing the Father of the House – the longest-serving member – as the date of the oath was a tie-breaker when two MPs had been first elected in the same year. Bercow wanted to be as near to the front as possible. "John's ambitions were in a particular direction," says Gray. "Frankly, good luck to him[251]". The most senior MPs went first, starting with the Speaker and followed by the Father of the House, Ted Heath, and then Tony Blair. New MPs went last, so Bercow had to wait till the next day to have his go. Despite his best efforts, he wasn't first among the new intake, but he was in the first forty out of 253 new MPs to take the oath.

Once the formalities were over, the most immediate concern was the Conservative leadership contest that had been triggered by John Major's resignation immediately after the election defeat. As with so much of Conservative politics during the 1990s, it seemed that the party was looking inwards instead of out. The leadership election presented something of a dilemma for Bercow. His preferred choice would have been Michael Portillo, as he had been a keen supporter of his for some time. But Portillo had been famously dumped from the

Commons by the voters of Enfield Southgate and so was not in the contest. The other candidates from the right – Michael Howard, Peter Lilley and John Redwood – and the more centrist William Hague, were all doing their best to win support from Portillo's supporters. The final contender, Ken Clarke, was too pro-European and too wet for Bercow to consider as a realistic possibility – at least back in 1997.

In the end, Bercow plumped for Peter Lilley, joined by a number of others including his old FCS friend Nick Gibb and Ann Widdecombe. Lilley, who had been Major's Social Security Secretary, was a traditional right-winger and his politics sat well with Bercow at a time when he was still very much on the right. However, the rather unfortunate habit that Bercow had picked up when Mrs Thatcher resigned of backing the wrong horse seemed to have stuck. Lilley was never considered likely to win and so it proved: in the first round he came fourth out of five, only spared the wooden spoon by Michael Howard, who had been badly damaged by Widdecombe's comment that there was "something of the night" about him.

Lilley and Howard threw their support behind Hague and suddenly the young Yorkshireman was the favourite to become leader. But even so, Bercow was having none of it. Within hours he was on *Newsnight* declaring his support for Redwood, who had come third in the first round, saying his choice had always been between Redwood and Lilley. "I'm sorry that Peter wasn't more successful, but I think John...is upright, direct, capable, has leadership quality...he's got a grasp, he's got a grip, he can win.[252]" Bercow was sticking to his ideological guns, as Redwood's politics were far closer to his than Hague's. But it was also a politically dangerous move as Bercow was doing a very good job of opposing the man who was most likely to win. As Cecil Parkinson said in a warning letter to Bercow, "Take a water can with you as you march into the wilderness.[253]"

As the contest rumbled on, the curse of Bercow struck again. Redwood came a distant third, well behind Hague and Clarke, and Bercow had to choose – yet again – which candidate he'd back ahead of the final round. However, he refused to reveal which way he would go and his reticence did not go down well with his new colleagues. Alan Duncan, who was supporting Hague, furiously told him, "You know

you're a new MP. A vote for Clarke might not play well in your constituency[254]." Bercow had backed two of the candidates to stand, but
it was William Hague, the man whom he had never publicly supported,
who triumphed.

While the Tories were concentrating on picking a leader, politics as
usual was continuing, too. The new Labour government was already
beginning to put into train a number of new measures, giving independence to the Bank of England and signing the Social Chapter –
hardly a welcome development for a Eurosceptic like Bercow. As issues
cropped up in the Commons, Bercow was beginning to put his
significant debating and public speaking experience into action – and it
was as if he had finally come home when he took his place on the green
benches. In fact, long before Bercow had even made his maiden speech,
he was already making a name for himself by his continued presence
in the chamber and a seemingly endless desire to barrack the
government's MPs. It is quite telling that the first time Bercow
received a mention in Hansard for contributing to a debate was when
the Deputy Speaker felt the need to tick him off, saying "he had better
be silent[255]". Just a few weeks into the new Parliament the commen-
tariat had already begun to notice his behaviour: "The David Shaw [a
former Tory MP] memorial award (for long periods of sullen silence,
punctuated by bouts of rancorous barracking) went to tiny John
Bercow,[256]" wrote one.

Soon it was time for Bercow to make his first – official – speech in
the Commons. At 12.38pm on 4th July one of the most divisive MPs of
our time began to speak, with his mother Brenda sitting proudly in the
gallery above. In a short, centre-right tour de force, Bercow noted that
Enoch Powell was "One of the most memorable parliamentarians of
modern times[257]"; told the House that Buckingham was noted for its
grammar school[258]; and said that Margaret Thatcher was "the world's
greatest living statesman[259]". Then, despite mentioning that "it is
normal to make non-controversial maiden speeches,[260]" Bercow was
anything but non-controversial as he went on the attack. He ripped
into the Labour government's budget, calling it, "The most breathtaking act of betrayal visited on an electorate by an incoming Government
in living memory[261]"; and he laid into Harriet Harman – then the

Social Security Secretary, sniping, "She is practised in the art of defending the indefensible and that it comes as no special surprise to me to see that she has been willing to do that on this occasion.[262]" Little did he know that as he made his way to the Speaker's chair many years later, it would be his friendship with Harman that would help propel him on his way.

Throughout his first Parliament, Bercow was making noise from the backbenches: he contributed a number of skilful speeches as well as a significant degree of catcalling. Looking back, Bercow is contrite about his behaviour. "I've issued a fair number of [mea culpas] over the years," he said in 2010. "I think they can scarcely be overdone. In the early years…I think this was Bercow 'mark one'… [from] 1997 it probably lasted till about 2002, my behaviour was spectacularly bad. I mean not just sort of bad but bad on an industrial scale.[263]" He was certainly very eager to speak whenever he got the chance and, as James Gray recalls, "There was a wooden bench below [where he was sitting]. He would kick it as he stood up and lean right forward. It was designed to make sure he got called and it was quite successful[264]". At that time, Bercow was described as, "By some distance the most strenuous questioner in the House, leaping to his feet in the brief lull between speeches like a junior subaltern whose commanding officer has just entered the room. He does this a lot and while he is waiting for the critical moment he tenses in his place like an athlete waiting for a gun, his arms poised on the seatback, ready to propel him upright… I don't often speculate on the lower limbs of opposition members, but every time I watch Mr Bercow going for the burn I can't help thinking that he must have thighs like a Tour de France cyclist.[265]"

When he spoke, he took no prisoners; and the attacks certainly did not end with Harriet Harman. Soon after his maiden speech, Bercow tabled an Early Day Motion criticising the Labour peer Lord Simon for failing to declare a significant number of shares in BP.[266] He also called on him to resign, although Simon held on. Next in line was Tony Blair, who was embroiled in controversy over the £1m donation from Formula 1 boss Bernie Ecclestone, which the Labour Party later returned. Bercow asked a typically searching question at PMQs and Blair swiped back, pointing out that Bercow's last job had been with

Jonathan Aitken[267]. Although the allegation was incorrect (Bercow had of course worked in two other jobs in between) the jeers from the Labour benches seemed to give the fight to Blair on points. Bercow got his revenge, of sorts, later in 1997, when he was ranked as the fifth best looking male MP in *The Unofficial Book of Political Lists*, pushing Blair down to sixth[268]. The result must have proved all the more heartening as Bercow was still without a wife. Having never been a particularly special hit with the ladies, it seemed that Bercow was getting on well as an MP in more ways than one.

Bercow was making quite an impact and, at least to begin with, the impression amongst his colleagues was a pretty good one. For Ken Clarke, "He became one of the most effective people in the chamber. John, from the word go, was very keen on being in the chamber. He was a very big speaker.[269]" A former senior Shadow Cabinet member told me, "I remember a conversation with Virginia Bottomley. I was singing his praises and she said 'he's just a total careerist'. I was very surprised as my initial impression was very favourable. I always found his speaking style rather impressive." John Redwood was equally enamoured, telling me, "John has always been someone who takes politics seriously. He loves and values Parliament. Lots want to be ministers rather than love Parliament and that's what I liked about John. He was articulate and capable". For Howard Flight, Bercow was "the best orator of the '97 intake,[270]" but perhaps the most startling comparison comes from another Conservative MP who simply said, "He reminds me of Churchill in the chamber" – quite the compliment, albeit perhaps a little over the top.

Bercow was very keen indeed on making a name for himself as a go-to-guy for broadcasters and he soon began to make regular appearances on television and radio. Dan Kelly was a producer on the BBC Radio 4 programme *The Midnight Hour*, on which Bercow appeared a number of times. Kelly remembers him as determined and motivated politician. "He was keen to come on air and always wanted to be very well briefed about what the other guests were going to say – remember [the programme] was going out at midnight – but I don't deride him for that. He prepared himself very, very carefully. He was clearly very ambitious and took himself very seriously.[271]"

So if his profile was rising, the John Bercow that people began to get to know was ferocious and opinionated. A Conservative MP says, "What I remember of the 1997 intake was the two backbench MPs who were the most personally rude and ferocious towards Labour and the Labour ministers – I mean really personal and nasty – were Shaun Woodward and John Bercow." The huge irony is that Woodward later crossed the floor to join Labour and Bercow became perhaps the most unpopular Conservative MP amongst his own side. But back then, there was no let up. Bercow would sit there, sledging his opponents like Shane Warne during the Ashes. "That's just pathetic!" he would shout; or, "God, his rhetoric is so boring!", "Useless, useless!", or just simply, "Hopeless!272"

Labour's MPs were ready to fight back, of course. But Bercow was by then well-used to being on the receiving end of what he saw as leftist posturing and he deliberately set about winding up the other side. "I'm often heckled in the chamber," he said at the time, "but some of the intellectual retards on the Labour benches are so low-calibre they don't distract me for a second. The common one I get is 'Stand up!', because I'm short. I'm not amused by it; it's not even funny. Once, when a woman called out: 'You're offensive!', I just replied: 'Correction: we both are; only I'm trying to be, but you can't help it'.273" Nor was it just MPs who found Bercow to be abrasive. As he said, "Whenever I get a letter saying, 'Dear Arsehole, I saw you on TV and thought what a little prat you are', I only reply if they're constituents.274"

Bercow was also standing out amongst the group of new MPs for his unique choice of language. Then as now, he spoke slowly, often using arcane words and odd turns of phrase, as if he were in an Evelyn Waugh novel, and when he passed other MPs in the corridor he would holler, "Great man, great man" at them, apparently in all seriousness. One MP joked that his florid speaking style was such that if Bercow was meeting a friend for a cup of tea, "He could never say 'It's great to see you.' Instead he would say, 'It gives me inestimable pleasure to meet you for the finest condiments created by Mrs Twinings.'" A serving Minister who has known Bercow throughout his time in the Commons told me, "It seems like he goes to bed with a dictionary and thesaurus, he can't say things in a normal way." A former Conservative MP agrees, "His style of speaking is very affected. I thought it was silly, but then he's Speaker and I'm not." Bercow certainly knew that he spoke rather differently to everyone else – after all, at Westminster Strategy, his colleagues used to regularly bellow "INDEED" at him in a deep voice, mocking Bercow's very serious manner and tone. However, just as when he was a teenager, Bercow loved his oratory and he was not going to change it merely because it raised a few eyebrows. "He takes a pride in it," the former MP told me. "But it's a bit of a joke in Parliament."

However, it was not just how he spoke, but also his seemingly superhuman memory that set Bercow apart. He could dredge up endless lists of facts and figures from his head at will. "It is as if he has a screen in front of him," says John Redwood. "He will remember complete quotations with column references from Hansard.[275]" Sir Peter Viggers, the MP now best known for his floating duck island, told me, "He can list exact numbers of, for example, unemployment figures from five or ten years ago, it is uncanny.[276]"

Bercow's linguistically anomalous style coupled with this exceptional memory made for quite a combination when it came to giving speeches. As David Cameron proved with his Party Conference speech in 2005 that won him the leadership, speaking without notes is often a real crowd pleaser. It had worked for Bercow at his selection in Buckingham and it was to make him stand out in the Commons, too. An MP remembers, "When he was making a speech it was unnerving because he would talk for fifteen minutes and would simply memorise it". Listening to Bercow, however, was like taking a bite of Parliamentary marmite. For some, he was supremely confident and witty – an opinion that most of the local associations he visited over the years seemed to share. However, for many MPs, his speaking was laboured and over the top. Peter Ainsworth says, "There was something slightly strange about his talent to speak completely off the cuff in paragraphs. It was not quite normal.[277]" Bercow's photographic memory allowed him to write his speeches or questions out in full, memorising them and regurgitating them, so that, as one MP told me, "His speaking manner is written English." It was no surprise that at an awards ceremony a few years into his first Parliament, Bercow was seen mouthing the words along to one of his speeches as it was played on a television screen to the audience.

The Commons seemed to be the most important thing in Bercow's life and he now admits that his passion for Parliament engulfed him. "In my first Parliament I was so utterly thrilled to have got into the House – and you'll think 'God, what a muppet, what an anorak'. I was delighted to be sitting in the chamber at two in the morning, debating matters late at night with [the Tory MP] Eric Forth.[278]" It seemed that whereas other men in their late thirties might have been at home with a wife and kids, Bercow found his comfort in the Commons. He and Forth so enjoyed being there that they even devised a system to allow them to keep debates going for longer, well into the night. Once Forth had been on his feet for about forty minutes, Bercow would ask him to give way. With mock reluctance, Forth would agree; Bercow would make a short point, and then, nicely refreshed, Forth would start up again. Bercow says, "We thought that this phenomenon – "in-flight refuelling" we used to call it – was the most enormous fun and I was quite convinced that I was at my best at 2 o'clock in the morning. There is a difference between *thinking* you're at your best at 2 o'clock in the morning and *being* at your best at 2 o'clock in the morning.[279]"

On one occasion, on the day before the "celebrations" to mark Labour's first 1,000 days in office, party poopers Bercow and Forth managed to keep a debate going for more than thirty hours, meaning that PMQs scheduled for day 1,000 never took place. Thanks to them, the party was cancelled. Then, as one of the Conservative members of a committee examining Labour's proposed minimum wage, Bercow went even further. He was still a staunch opponent of the measure, asking in the Commons why waiting staff should be paid the minimum wage when they also receive gratuities, declaring to the Trade Minister Ian McCartney, "My goodness, I often give waiters a £5 tip." McCartney – a former chef – drew on his experience in the trade to reply, "Listen son, pompous idiots like you got a damn sight more than soup in their soup.[280]" In the committee stage, with the Tories trying to block the bill, Bercow and chums slowed down the process so that only one clause out of fifty-three had been examined after six sessions.

Bercow indignantly said, "I would challenge anybody to identify a single example of filibustering,[281]" but Labour were having none of it. They forced an all-night session, which lasted over twenty-six hours, and the bill went through.

As Bercow now admits, it was only later, after he married, that he began to question whether a system of debating at any and every hour could stop MPs from "being rounded people who live normal lives.[282]" But at the time his obsession with Parliament was absolute and his dedication to the job was such that he undoubtedly had his lonely moments. He very much wanted to have a serious girlfriend, get married and have a family; and without such comforts to go home to at night it must have been a somewhat sad existence at times. The House of Commons both took him away from normality and also filled the gaps that existed in his life. It was his poison and his cure – and this fact did not go unnoticed amongst the other MPs. As Bercow was rolling out one of his famous lists – this time in a Commons debate on sport – the Labour MP Stephen Pound shouted from the backbenches – very cruelly – "Personally, I'd rather have a sex life.[283]"

Nonetheless, the people of Buckingham were getting very good value from their representative. Bercow was always in the Commons, attacking on all fronts, and he was perhaps the hardest working of any backbench MP. He was still a very solid, mainstream Conservative and – despite his continuing friendship with the Blair-supporting Sally – there was no sign at all of the conversion that was to come. The Bercow of old – who argued against the single currency, complained about bureaucracy and found constant fault with both the Blair government and the backbenchers on the Labour side – was still very much in existence. He had strived for years to be an MP and, now he was finally in the Commons, the Bercow juggernaut showed no sign of slowing just yet.

16

The Shadow Minister

"A difficult person to have at a higher level"

The Conservatives' General Election defeat in 1997 had been cataclysmic. The party had been wiped out and a rump of only 165 MPs was left to pick up a pieces. But in adversity there is opportunity and with a large number of Shadow Ministerial roles to fill, anyone with talent stood out. In their depleted state, the Tories did not have enough political ammunition to allow the most effective performers to stay on the backbenches for long. For a young gun like Bercow, there was the chance to make the step up in double-quick time.

It's easy to forget that amongst all of the posturing, the bluster and the late night sittings, Bercow was very able indeed. He was clever, quick and at ease when attacking the other side. All of those characteristics made him a natural fit for a junior role on the Shadow front bench, even if he was perhaps a little too raw in his enthusiasm. The shame was that, on occasion, his talent was obscured by that energy, the slightly too over the top attitude that made him a little bit of a caricature. Behind that exterior, the substance was there. As one senior MP at the time told me, "He was an obvious person to be on the front bench." In fact, Bercow had previously been offered the chance to become an unofficial Parliamentary Private Secretary to the Shadow Cabinet member Francis Maude, although he had turned it down as he wanted to spend more time speaking in the Commons.

So it was that when Hague reshuffled his team in June 1999 – having managed to make very little impact on Blair's huge lead in the polls – Bercow received the call. He was not alone amongst the 1997 intake – Sean Woodward and Howard Flight were both elevated alongside him – but there was a recognition, nonetheless, that he had done very well in his first two years. He had stood out – and seemingly in the right way. Bercow accepted, but only on the condition that he could continue speaking from the backbenches in the Commons on matters outside his brief.

His reward for his love of Parliament was an excuse to spend even more time, if that were possible, in Westminster, in his new role as a spokesman on Education and Employment under Theresa May. That combined position allowed him to attack the government's New Deal proposals aimed at helping people into work and to continue his interest in grammar schools.

The schools issue was clearly important to him, as Buckingham was a grammar school area and Bercow had seen at first hand the strength of the emotions involved. He strongly opposed plans to ballot parents on whether a school should retain its grammar status, calling it "egalitarian hooliganism[284]" and arguing that, "The ballot regulations have almost as many holes as a packet of Polo mints.[285]" Bercow's support for grammar schools is not shared by his wife Sally, who says that academic selection "entrenches privilege.[286]" It seems very unlikely indeed that Bercow will be able to send his children to one of the grammar schools that he fought so hard to save, as Sally has said, in her usual forthright manner, "I don't even want to send the children to the grammars in John's constituency.[287]" In a case of history repeating itself, the younger Bercows, like their father, will most likely end up at a non-selective school even though they have a home in an area that boasts a grammar school. But Bercow's personal zealousness over grammar schools in the late 90s does nonetheless perhaps reflect the angst of his early years, started by the decision of his primary school headmaster not to allow him to go to the local grammar. The chance to go to a grammar school – the very thing Bercow wanted to preserve – was exactly what he had been denied.

Nonetheless, what is striking is that even at what seems to be the peak of the right-wing yearnings of Bercow as an MP, there were the first signs of a schism beginning to open up between his liberal social stance and his right-wing views on just about everything else. Bercow bore the standard for the right with the same ferocity of tone of old on schooling, Europe and the like, but there were signs that he was starting to soften elsewhere. One of the earliest examples was when he made a point of questioning the Sport Minister Tony Banks about the underrepresentation of Asians in the England cricket team[288] – which would have been a dodgy line to take with some of his former companions on the Monday Club's Repatriation Committee.

Then, as the new millennium arrived, there was the clearest sign yet that his political "journey" – as many contestants on the *X-Factor* might call it – had begun. Bizarrely, Bercow's new-found liberalism came in the same week that he spoke out against his leader William Hague over the sacking of John Redwood from the Shadow Cabinet. Hours after the decision was made public, Bercow addressed a meeting of the right-wing 92 group, which Hague attended, with Bercow telling Hague that he had made the wrong decision[289]. In doing so, Bercow was standing up for the party's arch-libertarian and standard-bearer for the right, thereby bolstering his "soundness" on economic policy.

Within days however, Bercow was invoking the anger of many on his own side by dropping his opposition to equalising the age of consent for homosexuals to 16. He stunned the Commons by saying, "I have changed my mind... The words 'I was wrong' do not readily trip off my tongue, but that is what I believe. I think I was mistaken to vote for the status quo last time, and I intend to vote for the Bill, for reform and, I think, for progress.[290]" It was a touchy subject for Bercow as he was still unmarried – and inevitably there would be untrue whispers about his sexuality – but he stuck to his guns. "There is no evidence that the present law reduces the incidence of homosexual activity, minimises the spread of infection, increases the protection available to young people – none of these things is achieved by the present law,[291]" he told the Commons. He explained his change of heart, saying, "I have been reading, I have been listening, I have been conversing with people who know something about this subject both in my constituency and elsewhere.[292]"

This was a baby step, rather than a wholehearted conversion. The right-wing fire was still there, as he told the House, "I couldn't give a tinker's cuss for the European Court of Human Rights and I view the persona and activities of Mr Peter Tatchell as repugnant." He also explicitly backed Section 28, saying "It has a valuable effect, and it would be a mistake to dispense with it.[293]" What's more, a number of dyed-in-the-wool right-wingers had been in favour of gay rights – including, perhaps most notably in Bercow's life, Harvey Proctor from the Monday Club (although his own homosexuality must clearly have played a part). As such, there was no indication that just because Bercow was suddenly liberal on this one point, that the moment marked a Damascene conversion. The greater influence at this stage came from Michael Portillo, who had returned to the Commons and had been made Shadow Chancellor. Like Bercow, he changed his mind to support an equalised age of consent – although Bercow, courageously, announced his own switch before Portillo went public. Nonetheless, having admired Portillo for many years, his backing would certainly have strengthened his resolve.

But Bercow's decision to support lowering the age of consent came as a great shock to many who knew him, and it was an important landmark. It was the first occasion on which he really had to face down opposition from his own side, including from his old friend, and the proprietor of 60 Hopton Road, Teresa Gorman. Bercow even felt the need to make an intervention in the debate to tell her, "We've been friends for 15 years and I'm sure we're not going to fall out over this.[294]" Others noticed how momentous the moment was, and the Labour minister Paul Boateng compared Bercow to Shaun Woodward, who had recently defected to Labour – although such was Bercow's everyday right-wingery that Boateng did note that if Bercow switched sides it would "strain the strength of the pillars of the temple.[295]" Bercow was still as rambunctious as ever, saying, "Can I reassure you and my own friends that as I approach my deathbed the last words that will trip off my tongue are almost certainly: 'Vote Conservative'.[296]" In 2000, then, the signs of the coming conversion were there, but the "Bercow Mark I[297]" phase, as he calls it, was still very much in full swing. This was essentially a time of continuity.

More than anything else, Bercow's undoubted love for speaking in the House of Commons chamber remained unabashed despite having spent three years in Parliament. In the Parliamentary session ending in early 2000, Bercow made 76 speeches, beating Forth, who had a mere

57 to his name – into second place. To put Bercow's dedication into its deserved perspective, he made almost twice as many speeches as the MP who came fifth on the list[298].

Moreover, Bercow's early ferocity continued despite his mea culpa over gay rights. He still strove, relentlessly, to wind up the Labour MPs opposite and he could be found laying into a Labour minister with some panache on most of the big issues. When the spiralling costs of the Millennium Dome began to come to light, Bercow was there, urging the ministers responsible to resign or, "do the decent thing…through the tried-and-tested method of a glass of whisky and the use of a revolver.[299]"

However, Bercow's tactics – which made him pretty unpopular amongst some Labour MPs – were also beginning to annoy his own side, too. The Tory Geoffrey Clifton-Brown was so incensed by Bercow's delaying tactics in the Commons that he turned on him in the Smoking Room, calling him an "arrogant bastard". Bercow replied in kind, calling Clifton-Brown "pompous[300]".

But one of the most revealing incidents came during the row over Laura Spence, an A-level student from a state school who had failed to win a place at Oxford. The Chancellor, Gordon Brown, had used her case an example of Oxford's supposed elitism, despite the fact that 22 candidates had applied for just 5 places and that Spence later admitted she was "a bit upset when I came out of the interview because I knew I hadn't done as well as I thought I could have[301]". For Bercow, this was a highly sensitive subject. Like Spence, he was a comprehensive student and, having been forced to find his own way in life, the Labour government's position really lit a fuse. Bercow turned on Tony Blair, whom he accused of "pontificating" on the issue, saying, "He surrounds himself with a public school clique. He himself is the product of the Scottish Eton, of Oxbridge, of the Bar, and we all know there is nothing ordinary about this Prime Minister.[302]" The attack speaks volumes. Encapsulated in that one little riposte is much of what made Bercow the outsider. He wasn't a public schoolboy, he hadn't been to Oxbridge and he hadn't been able to go to the bar.

The fact that he had made his own way in life was nonetheless the source of much pride. As he argued, "The Tory front bench has got an enormous number of people in it who went through the state sector, who are meritocrats, who've got on purely on merit.[303]" He was talking about William Hague and he was, of course, talking about himself. For Bercow and others in the Tory Party who came from comprehensives, it was fairly bewildering and also hypocritical to be berated on equality issues by those with more privilege than them.

The incident provides an insight into much of what was going on in the Tory Party at the time. It was essentially split between the grafters – like Hague, Bercow and his friend, the grammar school boy Julian Lewis – and the old-school, "clubbable" Tories, many of whom had reservations about "oikish" upstarts like Lewis and Bercow. Bercow was railing against Blair's privilege, but it also showed the divide between old and new Tories. The FCS, with its radical attitudes and casual clothing, had been a symptom of Thatcherism, of the Norman Tebbit "on yer bike" philosophy, which had been followed by two leaders, in Major and Hague, with very normal backgrounds. Bercow was very much of this school of thought. As the party began to change in the years after 2000, so the pendulum between working class and middle or even upper class Tories began to move back; and Bercow's refrain of calling Blair a toff has since been taken up by Labour to attack what they say is the privileged background enjoyed by Cameron, Osborne and other leading Conservatives. Inevitably, these shifts would cause tension.

As these issues bubbled under the surface, Bercow kept up his constant attacks on the Labour Party. But the next target for this metaphorical battering ram was not another MP. Instead, a physical battering took place as Bercow came up against a door in the House of Commons. In June 2000, Bercow found out at late notice that he would have to go up against Shaun Woodward on a BBC radio programme later that evening. Wanting to be as fully briefed as possible, he was desperate to get his hands on a dossier that the Tories had compiled on the "turncoat". Convinced it was in the Tory Whips' office, which was locked, Bercow quickly sent for some guards to come and open the door for him. The problem was that when they arrived, they seemed to have the keys for almost every other room in Parliament, but not for the one Bercow wanted. He was desperate for the briefing and asked the guards to try to force their way in. They obliged and tried to ram the door open with their shoulders, but only succeeded in smashing it up. Bercow was forced to apologise, saying, "It was unfortunate and accidental and I was terribly sorry...the damage was not intentional.[304]" To make it even worse, the document wasn't even in there once the door had been forced open, and Bercow had to pay the £1,000 repair bill. If the helicopter to Buckingham had been the best £1,000 he'd spent, then this was arguably the worst.

This incident does give an insight into Bercow's sheer focus and determination. It was easy to dismiss most of his interventions in the Commons as over the top, as bluster and merely a way of causing trouble. But behind a veneer that was often ridiculous lay a real ambition.

Labour made hay out of the debacle, of course. In a Commons debate on violence in football, Jack Straw spoke of, "our fellow citizens engaged in appalling drunken violence on the streets of Belgium. These people have disgraced the nation and our national game.[305]"

"Like John Bercow,[306]" a Labour MP cried from the backbenches.

Then, to heap misfortune upon the piles of misfortune already suffered, Bercow had yet another run in with a Parliamentary door, although this time totally by accident. He was walking along with the Labour MP Lindsay Hoyle, who had been ribbing him about the initial door incident. As they continued along the corridor, Bercow burst through a door, pushing it wide open with gusto, unaware that there was a painter on the other side, whom he knocked clean to the ground. "I do seem to have a problem with doors," a rueful Bercow admitted. "I just didn't see him.[307]"

As Parliament moved towards recess in the summer of 2000, fate stepped in. The wings of a butterfly began to flap as the Speaker, Betty Boothroyd, announced that she intended to step down that year. There was, however, still no real indication that Bercow was interested in becoming Speaker at that point. He did argue the toss over the procedural requirements for choosing Boothroyd's successor, as he was strongly in favour of a secret ballot, but this intervention owed more to his taking an interest in a huge range of matters before the Commons than any personal goal. Bercow was a Commons man and this was a

Commons matter, so he got involved as he always did, but there was no sign that his ambition extended to being Speaker quite yet.

In any case, Bercow was progressing very nicely indeed within the Conservative Party and so there was no need to be looking at the Speaker's chair when promotion was in the offing. After just a year in the education and employment brief, he was promoted to Shadow Home Office minister, in July 2000. Whilst Bercow was pleased with the leg up the political ladder, that joy was not shared by those on the other side of the Commons. His Monday Club past really came back to haunt him as the Liberal Democrats and Labour piled in to criticise his appointment. They pointed out that Bercow would have a say on the Tories' immigration policy and dredged up his minutes from the Club's Repatriation Committee. "John Bercow's appointment to look after the civil liberties of the nation is dangerous and very worrying[308]," said the Lib Dems' Simon Hughes. Bercow's retort was that it was "breathtaking tripe and stupid", pointing out that, "Senior members of the Labour frontbench were also card-carrying members of CND until recently.[309]"

The Home Affairs brief was a vast and important one and Bercow worked under the direction of the twinkle-toed Shadow Home Secretary Ann Widdecombe. "He was a good debater, calm and fluent," she told me. "He would work very hard and he was therefore very useful." Widdecombe used to give her junior Shadows considerable freedom, allowing them to make frequent appearances at the despatch box – where Bercow was in his element.

Nonetheless, despite his new responsibilities, it did not take Bercow long before he started making some very serious waves. The trouble started with an article by Cherie Blair in the *Telegraph* praising the European Convention on Human Rights, which was due to be incorporated into British law later in the year. Bercow had long been an avowed critic of the Convention and he was incensed that the Prime Minister's wife had weighed into the argument, even though she wrote using her maiden name and was a human rights barrister.

Bercow decided to respond, although he made sure he received the backing of Conservative Central Office and the Party Chairman Michael Ancram first. He went thundering into attack, making perhaps the strongest and most personal assault on a sitting Prime Minister's wife by an MP in recent history. Bercow said that Cherie was an, "Unaccountable cross between First Lady and Lady Macbeth," who was:

"Breaking the long-standing convention that prime ministers' spouses do not push their own political agendas. It is unclear whether Cherie's end goal is to be Lord Chancellor or whether she is happy to direct policy from behind the throne... She forgets that in Britain we already have a First Lady: the Queen. If the Blairs bothered to look at their soulmates the Clintons, they would see that American voters are not impressed by unelected spouses who seek to ram politically correct prejudices down their throats.[310]"

In one sense, the episode was a triumph for Bercow. After all, he had been chosen by Central Office to carry out the very Shakespearian plot against Cherie, and the story was carried across the globe. The reaction from the Labour benches was furious, with many MPs calling for Bercow to resign his position as a Shadow Minister, but he would have expected no less.

However, the attack ultimately proved to be extremely badly judged. Whilst Cherie was never exactly close to the hearts of the British people, Bercow's criticism of her was seen by many as a misogynistic swipe at a successful career woman. Instead of coming across as a defender of the Queen and of proper government, Bercow ended up being painted as a backwards-looking, right-wing politician who was made uncomfortable by the success of a woman. The fact that he was still unmarried can hardly have helped, either. He tried to repair the damage, writing to the *Guardian*, "It is wrong...to say that I am arguing against working women... My own mother has worked for over 40 years,[311]" but it was already too late. Some Tories were none too pleased, either, with Peter Bottomley publicly defending Cherie, while Hague's wife Ffion was reportedly unhappy about Bercow's attack[312].

One can imagine what Sally would have made of it all. She is, after all, a woman who has been particularly outspoken in claiming the right to have her own opinions. "I know you think I should not be here at all, that I should be walking ten paces behind my husband or at home, making cucumber sandwiches,[313]" she told a fringe event at a Labour conference. But her point was clear: "I refuse to accept the argument that just because I am married to the Speaker, I can't have an opinion. There is no constitutional role for a Speaker's wife... I can't help who I am married to.[314]" It is uncanny that the very attacks being made on Sally since Bercow became Speaker – attacks which he has criticised with a passion – follow similar lines to Bercow's broadside at Cherie. Just as Sally points out that she is a modern woman, entitled to her own views and unable to help who she's married to, so Cherie could have said exactly the same. Moreover, Sally has become well known only because of who she's married to, whereas at least Cherie was a leading figure in the legal world in her own right. Moreover, Sally has gone far further in her self-politicisation than Cherie ever did, talking about any and every political topic – including publicly urging Bercow to take particular actions as Speaker. If Bercow was worried about unaccountable spouses, he would surely have to look at his own wife first.

Amidst all the controversy, though, Bercow still had a day job to do on the Shadow Home Office team. At first, it went rather well and Widdecombe recalls that, "John was very pleasant. He knows how to dish out the flattery. I never rowed with him on a personal basis.[315]" But it was not to be long before there were serious disagreements, although these arose, in part, from the strains within Conservatism as a schism in the party became more pronounced. With a possible General Election looming in the spring, the Tory Party Conference in the autumn of 2000 was fraught. Looming over the proceedings was Michael Portillo, back in the Shadow Cabinet and a king over the water from Hague. "Once he [Portillo] returned the party was immediately divided," says a colleague from the Shadow Cabinet. "I did not recognise the Michael Portillo I knew from before[316]".

Portillo was surrounded by a group of so-called "mods" on the socially liberal wing of the party. In part, Bercow's shifting political views were directly following Portillo's and just as both had changed their minds over the gay age of consent, so both men chose the 2000 conference to make a bold rallying cry to the party to change. As before, Bercow went first, giving a quite astonishing speech to a fringe meeting, saying that while the Conservatives had long reached out to white voters, the party had, "created or helped to confirm an impression that at best the Conservative Party was indifferent and at worst was hostile" to black and Asian people. He apologised on behalf of the party, saying "We have not made a significant effort, we have not tried that hard,[317]" and called for more black and Asian Tory MPs. This apology would have been remarkable enough from any Conservative, but coming from Bercow, it was a watershed. The baby steps of gay consent had given way to a giant leap. No longer could you reconcile the new John Bercow with his old Monday Club views – they seemed completely opposed. The very Conservatives who had so angered black and Asian people with their views on immigration – and who Bercow now criticised – were in some cases old friends of his – and back in the 1980s Bercow's own views would have been a total anathema to ethnic minorities; it would have been Bercow himself who was putting them off. With Bercow having cleared the way, Portillo then gave what some thought to be the speech of his life to the conference. He reached out the hand of political friendship to the gay community and to black and Asian voters, urging social tolerance, saying, "We are for all Britons: Black Britons, Asian Britons, White Britons.[318]"

For Widdecombe, the conference was rather less of a success. Her keynote speech called for a "zero tolerance" approach to drugs, proposing fixed-penalties for people caught in possession of cannabis. The speech went down a storm with the delegates in the hall, but the full scale of her mistake was soon to emerge. Under pressure from the media, one shadow minister after another admitted to having smoked cannabis and the policy began to collapse. Zero tolerance itself, however, remained – but not for long. As the splits between the "mods" and the "rockers" became more pronounced, Bercow went on the record to stick the knife into his boss's big idea. It was an incredible attack, signalling for the first time that Bercow was willing to step out of line when he disagreed with those who set party policy. Even more telling is that he did so in order to argue for a liberal stance on drugs, thereby splitting because he was to the left, not the right, of party policy. "The idea that the police should raid every home in the land looking for dope-smokers is transparently absurd," he said. "A vast clampdown is unrealistic. In this country, we police by consent. The police are not interested in launching an all-out war on soft drugs.[319]" Bercow's attack was disloyal to Widdecombe and yet another blow to her political standing. "I had to say [to him], whatever your views, these are mine, they are official policy," she told me. "He was calm and not at all sorry…John is very individualistic, a difficult person to have at a higher level."

What made the whole incident so remarkable was that drugs had never seemed particularly close to Bercow's heart. Back in the FCS, he was not one of the gung-ho libertarians who would have liked to have legalised heroin and LSD – his position had always been much more moderate. If his boss had come out in favour of the euro or against grammar schools, it would have been perfectly understandable for Bercow to issue a public rebuke, however damaging that would be politically. But to do so over drugs seemed so unnecessary.

This, then, is one of the key moments in Bercow's life – as it marks the point when his fledgling Shadow Ministerial career began to stutter. It was far from dead, but many of the seeds of discontent with his behaviour were sown by his reluctance to toe the line. The same weakness that dogged Bercow here would re-emerge again and again, first killing off his front bench career and then helping to almost completely alienate him from his own party.

Bercow carried on speaking his mind, and the furore over zero tolerance did not stop him from criticising his boss yet again. During the passage of a particular piece of legislation through the Commons, Widdeombe recalls, "There was very limited debate time and John led me to believe he shared my view about there not being enough time.[320]" Once the relevant bill had passed, however, Bercow made his objections known to Widdecombe. "He came along with a list of times I could have spoken about it. I was very angry. He implied I'd done nothing; I'd had a dying mother at the time.[321]" Bercow was quite upset by the row and assured Widdecombe that it was not a personal attack, although she did take it personally.

While there was a definite degree of personal conviction in Bercow's decision to go off message, his actions were still part of the wider Conservative fallout from Portillo's conference speech, which had not gone down well with the traditional right-wingers in the party. In late October, at a meeting of the Thatcherite No Turning Back group, Portillo and the Shadow Foreign Secretary Francis Maude were given a dressing down for trying to create a group of "social radicals" within the party. Chief amongst the accusers was Eric Forth, a close associate of both Bercow and Portillo. Bercow himself was at the dinner, but he sided with Portillo rather than Forth. And then, some days later, when Portillo and Maude dramatically announced they were resigning from No Turning Back, Bercow was one of the only MPs to come out to defend their decision. Whilst being careful in his language, Bercow was clear. "I regard Michael Portillo as a formidable force," he said, "and I strongly identify with the message he is trying to put across.[322]"

The autumn of 2000 therefore saw Bercow make a crucial break from his former home in the socially conservative wing of the party. He was still very much of the mainstream in the Tory Party – albeit the new, socially liberal mainstream – but he had become a very different sort of politician to the one who had been elected in 1997. "It wasn't remotely the old John Bercow of FCS days,[323]" says Ken Clarke. Much of that can be put down to Portillo's influence, as well as Bercow's own realisation that the party needed to change if it ever wanted to make it back into government. Most notably, though, Bercow's marriage to Sally was still some way away at this juncture and the two were not a proper couple at the time. At this crucial point at which Bercow's views seemed so fluid, it seems that Sally's influence was relatively minimal.

The other key event in the final months of 2000 was the election of Michael Martin as Speaker. Bercow was none too keen on the choice and he was not afraid to show it publicly: he was one of only eight MPs to vote against Martin when the official vote for Speaker took place. Most other Tories merely contented themselves with abstaining. Bercow was so incensed by Martin's election that he even discussed the issue with Widdecombe, telling her that he wanted to show his displeasure at the choice. "John was very angry but I said, 'No, he is an authority figure'[324]", she recalls. On Martin's first day in the chair some wondered whether the enmity was mutual, as he failed to call Bercow to speak even though he was bobbing up and down like a fish, jumping to his feet whenever he got the chance.

Despite Widdecombe's warnings, the hostility continued, with Bercow becoming part of a guerrilla campaign aimed at belittling the Speaker and generally making his life difficult. During one debate, when Bercow was heard muttering that Gordon Brown was a "con man", Martin demanded he withdraw the comment. Bercow did as he had to, but with palpable sarcasm, saying, "O, readily, Mr Speaker, I withdraw. [325]" It was exactly the sort of behaviour that any Speaker would detest. Even more brazen was a point of order during a session of Prime Minister's Questions. In a sarcastic tone, Bercow asked the Speaker to ensure that Labour MPs stopped chatting to him during debates so the House could have, "The full benefit at all times both of your personal attention and of your intellectual resources,[326]" at which point a fellow Tory piped up, "Like a bus driver![327]" Bercow was once again hammering home his mental superiority and he could scarcely have shown more disregard for the Speaker.

It is now, of course, wholly disingenuous that one of the most vocal critics of the Speaker, the one who refused to accept him as the House of Commons' choice, was Bercow himself. Like many Conservatives he felt that the Speaker had been thrust upon the Tory Party by an unrelenting Labour majority. Betty Boothroyd had been a Labour MP and the Conservatives felt it was their go; not the turn of a dyed-in-the-wool Labourite like Martin. Moreover, as in 2009, the winning Speaker in 2000 beat Sir George Young into second place. Bercow was not happy and he did not want to sit there and take it when a Speaker he disliked ordered him around; he wanted to use his verbal trickery to convey exactly what he thought of the man in the Speaker's chair.

The Commons trundled on towards Christmas as the country prepared for a General Election in 2001, with Labour still well ahead in the polls. By now, Bercow had settled into a socially liberal groove mixed with a dash of traditional Conservatism, voting in favour of allowing research on human embryos but against the fox hunting ban. He was also speaking at almost any given opportunity, so much so that every time he jumped from his seat to try to catch the Speaker's eye, Labour MPs would shout "boing" at the jack in-a-box across the way. Martin, who was barely any warmer in his approach to Bercow, remarked from the chair that, "With the way he jumps up and down it might do damage to the benches. I do not worry about damage to his joints – just about the Benches.[328]" Nonetheless, there were times when even Bercow seemed to tire of the Commons. On one occasion, he found himself drifting off in the middle of a particularly long speech. Suddenly, he awoke with a start: he grabbed a buzzing pager from his pocket and suddenly dissolved into giggles. A helpful colleague had paged him the message: "Wake up![329]"

More importantly for Bercow's career, despite his antics in the chamber he was beginning to be seen as a serious politician: although some colleagues had their reservations, particularly about his perceived disloyalty, many picked him out as a rising star. In fewer than four years in Parliament Bercow had already handled a relatively senior brief with some success and some commentators were beginning to think of him as a future Conservative leader.[330]

He had also won a significant degree of respect for his dedication to the Commons – with the Tories so depleted and so far behind in the polls, Bercow was one of a small number of junior Conservative MPs who had the desire and the dedication to hold the government to account in any meaningful way. While Labour MPs might have loved to wind him up, to poke fun at his size and his love life, they nonetheless recognised that he did at least try to make a contribution to Parliament. When Tony Benn finally left the House of Commons just before the 2001 election, Bercow's tribute to him as "the Parliamentary and political giant of our times,[331]" was well received, as if it came from a standard bearer of the new generation of Parliamentarians to the old.

As Tony Blair called the General Election for 7th June, all the signs were that the result would be very, very bad indeed for the Tories yet again. For Bercow, there were few worries, as the party would have had to have gone into complete meltdown for him to lose Buckingham, with its majority of over 12,000. He was up against Mark Seddon, the Editor of *Tribune* and a local man, but neither candidate was under any illusion as to what the task involved. "I obviously had no hope," Seddon recalls, "So there was little to fear from me. But I thought he was a good person to run against, the debate was fair, there was no bad feeling, no animosity.[332]"

The only note of controversy was when Bercow appeared to go against the party line – yet again – this time over the single currency. Hague had vowed to "save the Pound", but only for the lifetime of the next Parliament, whereas Bercow promised local voters that he would always advocate keeping the Pound. A swift rebuke from Central Office followed, Bercow apologised and the matter was laid to rest. In fact, the most pressing concern for Bercow seemed to be that he was having to spend so much time away from Westminster, the place he loved most, and he admitted that he was getting "withdrawal symptoms[333]" from all that time he spent in the House of Commons.

As June 7th dawned, the outcome was obvious, both nationally and in Buckingham – and Sally Illman was on the right side in both, yet again. The votes cast that day saw Tony Blair re-elected as Prime Minister, with a huge and only slightly reduced majority of 167. As expected, the night was disastrous for the Tories, who won only one more seat than in the nadir of 1997. But in Buckingham the picture was brighter: Bercow was re-elected with a 4% increase in his share of the vote – and for a second time he'd managed to do better than the Conservatives' national average. As expected, the majority was huge – over 13,000.

The result was a testament to Bercow's dedication as a local MP. He was, undoubtedly, very popular with his constituents – like any MP he had his detractors, of course, but the public can spot a hard-working MP when they see one. The average voter would much rather have a jack-in-a-box than an MP who doesn't bother making his way out of the toy cupboard at all.

17

Women

"He was completely clueless"

"ORDER! ORGY![334]", the headline screamed. The news was in: back when John Bercow was a single man, he had been a misogynistic lothario, spending his time carefully planning out how to rack up the next notch on his bedpost. Despite his diminutive size, he appeared to have been a big hit with women. Such was his success that, at a time when he was climbing the FCS's greasy pole, he had been persuaded to pen a how-to guide for other aspiring Casanovas, entitled *The John Bercow guide to understanding women*. It was a vile and sexist publication by any standards, with five categories of "advice" to aspiring young players:

How to pick up drunk girls
How to pick up virgins
How to pick up refined girls
How to get rid of a girl during sex
How to get rid of a girl after sex

The guidance in the pamphlet was pretty crude too, with recommended chat-up lines including, "If you're free later maybe we could go back to your place and name your breasts". The author informed the reader that, "There's nothing more dangerous than an armed hysterical virgin" and that, "Women will settle for anything that breathes and has a credit card". If a man wants to get rid of a girl, he's told to inform her: "Warning: Don't move, I have just broken a test tube filled with the AIDS virus" or "I hate your tits".

The Speaker's office appeared to confirm that Bercow was indeed the author, telling journalists, "This article appeared in a magazine that specialised in being both funny and provocative. It in no way reflects the Speaker's views today.[335]"

There was just one problem: the story wasn't true. Bercow knew it, but apparently his press team didn't. The truth is that the *John Bercow guide to understanding women* was not written by him – far from it – and the pamphlet had reared its rather chauvinistic head before. In fact, Bercow had long become used to denying that he wrote it, telling the *Guardian* way back in 1986, "This is the sort of bullshit you get from the left... I was incensed to see it under my name.[336]"

Although the story itself was a load of cobblers, the incident is very revealing. There had been a serious error on the part of Bercow's press operation, headed up at that time by the journalist Tim Hames, who was being paid an estimated £100,000 to do his job. Clearly Bercow's advisers were well used to distancing the "new" Bercow from his activities and views of the 1980s and 1990s, but this time they had acted too hastily in making the point that Bercow had long since changed.

But there is a deeper point, too. Much of Bercow's life, both political and personal, has been driven by his struggle to settle down; and, later, by the consequences of finally getting married to Sally. The *guide to women* tells us so much precisely because it was put in Bercow's name in the first place. It was, after all, not as Bercow claimed a leftist plot but a puerile practical joke perpetrated by Bercow's friends in the FCS. They had taken an excerpt from a tasteless book in the General Store in Covent Garden, plagiarised it, and put in his name. They then published it in *Armageddon* – an FCS magazine which made *New Agenda* look about as genteel as *The Lady* before Rachel Johnson became its editor.

The whole point of the *guide* was to poke fun at Bercow's utter hopelessness with women. The reason why Bercow was targeted was not because he was kicking girls out of bed every night of the week; rather, he'd be one of the people least well-placed to write the *guide* that was in his name. The joke was essentially no different to Stephen Pound's jibe more than twenty years later in the House of

Commons, saying that rather than know all of the facts Bercow did, he'd prefer to have a sex life.

The *guide* is symptomatic of the fact that for a long time, Bercow's love life was a pretty abject failure. Back in school he hadn't managed to have the long-term girlfriend he wanted – but then as someone resembling one of the characters from *The Inbetweeners*, it was no surprise that Bercow was hardly cutting a ready path through the girls at Manorhill. Millions of schoolboys up and down the country have shared a similar plight. Despite being surrounded by Essex girls – at least by education if not by breeding – at university, Bercow failed to do much better there either. He did have one or two encounters with women, but there was nothing that lasted.

Nonetheless, despite what some of his friends and colleagues over the years have thought, Bercow's difficulties with women were not a cover for hidden homosexuality – as Bercow put it when he turned up to a party with his mother, "I am a rampant heterosexual[337]". Instead, as one friend told me, "He did have relationships with women [but] he was probably just incompetent." Although Bercow could charm any number of blue rinsers, his obsession with politics made it difficult for him to relax around girls of his own age. As an FCS hack told me, when it came to women, "Bercow was a joke. Once he came back to the group and said about a girl, "Oh, whoosh!" and chucked his hands in the air to indicate the strength of his ardour. He was completely clueless. He was pleasant to girls but incapable of turning it into a romantic approach."

In the late 80s, Bercow gave a further demonstration of his ineptitude with members of the opposite sex when he plucked up the courage to ask someone to marry him. His decision to pop the question came as quite a shock to the lucky girl, because she and Bercow had never even kissed – and she had a boyfriend at the time. Undeterred, Bercow bravely asked, "If I were to become the Parliamentary candidate for [a particular constituency], would you do me the honour of becoming my wife?" Unfortunately for Bercow, his potential wife considered that he couldn't have been serious – and declined the offer. However, in a twist of fate that's indicative of the incestuous nature of young Conservative politics – the boyfriend that stood in the way of

Bercow's romantic ambitions later ended up in a relationship with Sally, the woman who *did* accept Bercow's marriage proposal.

It was Sally, though, who did change everything. Suddenly, in 1989, when Bercow was at the grand old age of 26, the politics-obsessed perennial singleton from north London found himself in the arms of a stunningly beautiful, Marlborough-educated young Tory. It was at a Conservative student conference – where else? – that Bercow finally met the girl of his dreams. Sally Kate Illman, then a 19-year old student at Oxford, was at the conference in Nottingham, too. Readers of her twitter feed might be forgiven for thinking that she was there to shout abuse at the Tories she now derides near-daily. In fact, her mission was quite the opposite, as back in the late 1980s, as Mrs Thatcher neared the end of her time in power, Sally was a fervent Conservative – showing as much passion for the party then as she shows disgust for it now.

Sally was a prominent member of the Oxford University Conservative Association, so it was only natural that she would head along to Tory events. And just as Bercow had his own brush with a very sinister character in the form of the serial killer William Beggs, so Sally too had the misfortune to encounter a man who would come to national notoriety. Never a shrinking violet, at an OUCA social she jumped up on stage and began cavorting with a male stripper, "Terry the Minder", who shoved a phallic object into a blindfolded Sally's hands. Shrieking, she pulled back the mask to find it was only a banana. But later revelations would not be so amusing: "Terry" was in fact John Worboys, known as the "black cab rapist" for a string of sex attacks on women across London.

When Sally arrived in Nottingham, she was pounced on by the young, Tory-boy who was soon to make it as an MP. But it wasn't Bercow – it was his best friend Julian Lewis. "It was I who spotted Sally first during that students' conference," says Lewis. "I told John that she was the most beautiful girl at the meeting and when I saw the two of them chatting away later that evening I did the gentlemanly thing and left them to it.[338]"

And when Sally came to choosing whether the spotty young man who was a good few inches shorter than her could be a potential boyfriend, Bercow was in luck. On first impressions, things hadn't gone so well: "I thought: no, I'm not going to bed with you," says Sally. "I thought: this is ridiculous, I'm nearly 6ft, he's 5ft 7in, you know, this is *ridiculous*, a ridiculous-looking couple. I cared about things like that then.[339]" But as someone who was good-looking enough to be used to having all sorts of men try it on with her, Sally had decided to make her choice in a rather unconventional way. Fortunately for Bercow, Sally's off-beat approach meant she wasn't just interested in looks; her potential suitors needed to pass a rather unusual test. So it was that Sally asked John to make a dull topic interesting for her: the challenge was to sound off on her choice of subject for ten minutes. How lucky that was for Bercow – what better assessment could there be for him than speaking off the top of his head? Unsurprisingly, he readily agreed and eagerly asked her to give him the issue. Sally's choice, as she gazed around the room for inspiration, was "the spiral staircase". It was a challenge that Bercow took up with aplomb and he immediately held forth on this most mundane of subjects for fifteen minutes. In Sally's eyes, he came across as knowledgeable, witty and entertaining – putting Bercow well above her other suitors in her estimation. Even now when she recalls that verbal essay on the spiral staircase, there is a light in her eyes.

Bercow certainly couldn't believe his luck. Back in 1989, Sally was everything that an aspiring Tory politician could want in a political wife. She was obviously very clever, bright and had a good sense of humour; and more importantly she was a committed Conservative. Luckily for Bercow, Sally was pretty stunning, too. In 1989 Sally was really very beautiful and in unseen footage of her from the period she seems a different person. Although you can see the resemblance, in the late 80s she was extremely attractive – slightly curvier and with straight, dark brown hair to just below the neck, and thicker eyebrows. The overall effect was eye-catching and Julian Lewis was not exaggerating when he said she was the most beautiful girl in the room. For a Tory boy, Sally was like hitting the jackpot.

It was all the more remarkable because Bercow was not very much better looking than he had been at school, when the girls had poured scorn on his looks. He still had the remnants of his acne, his hair could still have done with a bit more shampoo and he was, of course, a good few inches shorter than his future wife. She could probably have gone for any man in the room (and of course, over the years she did go for a fair few men), but it was Bercow whom she picked. There was a physical attraction, of course, but she admits now that it was that conversation, that monologue on spiral staircases, that made Bercow the one that she wanted.

At first, it seemed perfect – Bercow was 26 and could well have ended up settling down; but the relationship did not last. Although he and Sally stayed together for around six months, Bercow eventually decided that she was too argumentative and called an end to things. It must have been a very hard decision, particularly because Bercow had never managed to hold down such a serious relationship in the past.

Sally was a very different person then, physically, mentally and politically. Her support for the Conservative Party seemed unwavering, bordering on the fanatical. At the 1989 Conservative Party Conference she and Bercow appeared on a BBC programme together, along with the future MP Dominic Grieve, to give their views ahead of Margaret Thatcher's speech. So, although she claimed on BBC 1's *This Week* programme in 2010, when she was billed as a "Labour activist", that it was her first live TV appearance[340], she had in fact been on television before, some twenty-one years earlier – but as a Tory activist instead. The trio were described as "deeply committed to the party", and Sally made no bones about her allegiance:

"I think the government has got to get the economy right before the next election, I think the government's going to do that," she told the cameras. "I think in Mrs Thatcher's speech she's bound to mention the greening of the Tory Party so to speak; we're moving with the times, we're going to get more environmentally conscious and basically I think we're going to win this General Election.[341]"

What makes Sally's views all the more astonishing is that she was speaking just one year before Thatcher was forced out of office. The Iron Lady had already implemented the vast majority of her policies. She'd privatised industry, allowed many traditional sectors to fail and had beaten the miners into submission. It was, perhaps, the high point for the sort of Conservatism that Sally so despises now. It was not the case that when the Tory Party moved to the right, she turned against it; rather the Thatcherites had thrown everything they had at the country, and Sally was still there, standing up for the cause. The hatred she now feels towards the Conservatives must surely, then, encompass her twenty-year-old self, speaking to the country about why Mrs Thatcher should be re-elected.

However, if her views are hard to tally with the Sally of 2011, the intonation certainly isn't. Sally was clearly nervous, and looked very young with red blusher on her cheeks. Next to Bercow and Grieve, who were much more experienced political operators, she seemed quite the amateur. She spoke hesitatingly, with lots of ums and ers, and she briefly broke the cardinal rule of television interviews by looking directly down the barrel of the camera.

Interestingly, the similarity to when Sally first started making media appearances after her husband became Speaker is uncanny. In 2010, the Sally who became known to the public was one who was frank, candid and spoke in a quite "un-political" way. She came across as refreshingly honest, but her manner could just as easily be put down to inexperience. In the twenty-one years between that original interview and the appearance on *This Week*, Sally had not appeared as a pundit on national broadcast media. So when she was thrown into the deep end on BBC1 after Bercow won the Speakership, she unsurprisingly sounded no more assured than she had done the last time she had been on TV so many years before. Unlike most MPs or political pundits, she had had no gradual apprenticeship and no real training in how to be interviewed without giving too much away. The Sally Bercow who is so indiscreet can be seen as a direct continuation of the Sally Illman who spoke so passionately for Mrs Thatcher in 1989. In recent times, as she has appeared more and more on television and radio, some of that naivety has fallen by the wayside. She now sounds less like the young Tory girl from Oxford and more like an experienced political operator, although the rough edges remain.

Amongst the political arguments, though, it is really quite touching to see the couple together in 1989. Even while they were being interviewed about politics, there was a clear frisson between them. In his double breasted suit, with a striped shirt with a white collar, and a spot above his eye, Bercow may not have been everyone's ideal man, but it was clear that there was something special between the couple. Sally stood noticeably closer to Bercow than she did to Grieve and their arms touched at times, while Sally would steal a glance at Bercow while he was talking. Looking back at them, it is easy to see why she would have been, in many respects, a perfect foil for Bercow. As he said in that interview, "People like myself, Dominic, Sally, [will be] explaining to the public why they should vote Conservative rather than any other party.342" For Bercow, Sally was not only a personal confidante, but a political one too.

The argument that he discovered women and New Labour at the same time is clearly incorrect – after all, when he discovered Sally, she was almost as strident a Tory as he was.

Bercow and Sally stayed friends after their break-up – and kept, briefly, getting back together – but for Bercow, the lack of a girlfriend was to become quite a curse. A recurring problem was that local associations tended to look favourably upon those who were married or who at least had a nice, respectable girlfriend to come along with them. In a world full of fundraising coffee mornings, a good woman was seen by many Tories as essential. That presented quite a dilemma for Bercow, who was so often without a long-term partner and for whom it was often the subject of much angst. For normal events, he could take his mother with him, but selection meetings were different, as the panel would scrutinise him personally. His love life mattered.

Not wanting to lose out, Bercow came up with a solution. An old friend recalls that at some selection meetings Bercow would be accompanied by a female friend. "He didn't have a girlfriend and had to borrow a woman and take her to the meeting." A former work colleague at RSC recalls, "John took a girl from [his] office to selection meetings...we all thought it a bit odd." These arrangements engendered so much confusion that this workmate even believed that Bercow was gay – although that is certainly not the case – but it does show that Bercow was prepared to go to some lengths to be selected. A female companion of Bercow's reported to his friends that, after one particularly good performance, he turned around to her, joyously exlaiming, "Oh... I'd love to see you on my manifesto!"

It seemed that he would really leave nothing to chance. A Conservative MP remembers, "A strange thing when you rang him at home...suddenly, once he started looking for seats, there was a female voice on the answer phone, saying 'Sorry, *we're* not at home.'" This behaviour was again misinterpreted so that the MP told me, "It was [wrongly] widely assumed he was gay". The blame might well be put on the closed-mindedness of the people selecting MPs – after all, what is really so wrong about a man in his early thirties being between girlfriends? – but the way Bercow approached the problem is indicative both of his sheer ambition and his attention to detail.

As Bercow was searching for a seat in earnest in the early-90s – and as Sally and her Conservatism began to waiver – his friends were excited to hear that he was getting close to a female friend at last, and a Labour one at that. But it wasn't Sally, the New Labourite, who was thought to be the lucky lady; instead it was a former member of a notoriously left-wing organisation against which Bercow had promised to "wage political warfare" in the 1980s. It appeared to his friends that he had now decided to make love, not war to the organisation. However, rather disappointingly for Bercow, despite widespread rumours in Westminster to the contrary, none of this was true as his alleged partner never had any sexual relationship with him[343].

Nonetheless, the surprise and excitement expressed at the thought of Bercow having a relationship is telling. Even as he was making a success of his PR career, he still gave off the impression that he found it difficult to relax around some potential girlfriends, and in some respects he was just as awkward around women as he had been back in his FCS days.

Moreover, that Bercow's friends were prepared to buy into the idea of a fling with a woman on the opposite side of the political divide also indicates that – even very early on in his career - he seemed willing to set aside the political when it came to the personal. While Bercow was as strident as ever in his right-wingery, on a romantic level he came across as much more flexible. He would not give an inch to the Labour side of the argument, but he seemed to his friends to be much less close-minded when it came to love. Perhaps, then, his eventual marriage to a Labour supporter was not so unexpected.

Nonetheless, it seemed that the search for lasting love would go on. Bercow did have one significant relationship in the period immediately before he entered Parliament, with Louise Cumber, but this too did not last. So with few serious long-term relationships – and despite the fact that Bercow was "chasing[344]" Sally over much of this period (her words, not his) – the problems with women largely persisted after Bercow became an MP. Instead of going home to a girlfriend, he often found comfort in the chamber with Eric Forth. A friend recalls that Bercow would often confide in Julian Lewis at his despair at ever finding a wife. "He would call Julian every Sunday to gossip – not political talk. John called Julian in a great state of angst because he wanted a girlfriend." As an MP says, "He was very dedicated in a way that others weren't. John just had Parliament, he didn't have outside interests."

The lack of a relationship was not for want on trying, either. In 2000, Bercow spotted Sarah Westcott, a young journalist from the Press Association, in the gallery above the Commons. She was one of the only things that could take his attention away from the business of the House, and he kept smiling up at her until he finally plucked up the courage to get the Serjeant-at-Arms to give her a note asking her out for a drink. On House of Commons notepaper, he scrawled: "Sarah, may I tempt you to a glass or two of Deacon's Estate sometime this week or next?"

Westcott agreed to meet up with him, although she was never really interested in him romantically. She says that it was quite an unusual experience:

"He was a very odd little man, socially quite gauche, restless and he found it hard to relax. He was hard to get to know and asked lots of questions... He was a bit funny with women...one night I kissed him on the cheek and he was terrified. But he was perfectly charming, a gentleman and not sleazy.[345]" Nonetheless, there was always a slight air of unreality about going out with Bercow. He would often take Westcott to Shepherd's, a Westminster restaurant where they were bound to bump into a group of MPs or one of Bercow's friends. "I felt he was on the hunt for a woman for the next step of his career, it would make him look better if he had a girlfriend or wife, [like he was] ticking a box. It just felt slightly cynical,[346]" she says.

HOUSE OF COMMONS
LONDON SW1A 0AA

3·7·2001

Dear Sarah,

Please excuse
the red ink! It is
both unconventional
and ideologically
unsound!

I shall be delighted
to meet on Monday —
Wednesday is the start of
the committee stage of the
Nice Treaty Bill! — and will
be happy to render vows
at 9.00m in the Central
Lobby. Is that OK?

'Please excuse the red ink! ...'

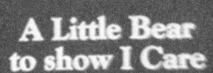

A Little Bear
to show I Care

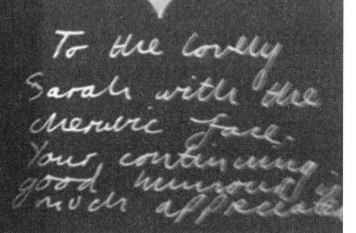

'To the lovely Sarah ...'

What comes through very clearly is that Bercow completely floundered when it came to women. He was nearly forty and yet seemed more like a clumsy schoolboy than a middle-aged MP. Once, he turned round to Westcott in the middle of a conversation and, out of the blue, said, "You look like Yvette Cooper![347]" – a rather cryptic compliment if ever there were one. Then there were his other letters to Westcott. Here was a woman he was trying to woo, yet his notes were always rather off-key and full of exclamation marks. "Dear Sarah", another on Commons notepaper went, "Please excuse the red ink! It is both unconventional and ideologically unsound! I shall be delighted to meet on Monday – Wednesday is the start of the Committee Stage of the Nice Treaty Bill!" On Valentine's day Bercow sent her a card entitled, "A Little Bear to show I Care," with an inscription to "the lovely Sarah with the cherubic face."

All of these missives are real hiding-behind-the-sofa, not-quite-being-able-to-watch stuff. They are not sleazy or nasty – just really very cringe-worthy. But more than anything else, they show a man who desperately wanted to share his life with someone. Of course it would have been politically convenient to have a nice girlfriend to accompany him to events, but Bercow very much wanted a companion. The letters show him to be both socially unaware and also, probably, a very nice boyfriend in waiting, if only he could find the right woman. Instead, for many of his early years in the Commons, Bercow had to be content with a life full of Parliamentary oratory but often devoid of romantic love, whilst putting up with constant untrue rumours about his sexuality. No wonder that when he bravely backed the equalisation of the gay age of consent, Bercow felt the need to remind the Commons that, "It so happens that I am heterosexual.[348]"

The intriguing question, then, is how the man who at the age of 38 was chasing after a lobby journalist, with little success, came to be engaged just a year later. And in answering that question, one also has to ask how one of the most fervent right-wingers of a generation ended up married to a Labour activist, former alcoholic and renowned good-time girl. It is this conundrum that has most captured the interest of the public as they attempt to dissect the relationship between John and Sally Bercow.

★★★

Sally and John had continued dating on and off over the years, but in the in-between times she was really very wild, moving from one man to another, seemingly with the same ease as she slid across the political spectrum from staunch Tory to ultra-Labourite. When Sally decided to finally make a go of her own political career by running for Westminster City Council, with a view to later becoming an MP, she gave an astonishingly candid, confessional interview, revealing that she had been an alcoholic in her 20s and had indulged in a series of one-night stands:

> I was a big binge drinker in my twenties. I started drinking at Oxford, being a party girl, and it got out of control.
>
> "I got a grip for a while, but in the mid-Nineties I was working in advertising and I would drink wine at lunch then go out and drink a bottle in the evening, most evenings really. I had no stop button… It was sometimes more like two bottles, except I promised John I wouldn't say that. Have I mucked it up already?
>
> I was an argumentative, stroppy drunk, picking arguments with my bosses over stupid things. Plus I'd lose my judgment and put myself in danger. I'd fall asleep on the Tube and end up in Epping or Heathrow. And I'd get into unlicensed minicabs in the early hours. All the things we'd tell our daughters not to do.

As for the one night stands, Sally said:

> They weren't romantic. They were more like flings. I wasn't looking for love. But it's true that I would end up sometimes at a bar and someone would send a drink over, and I'd think, 'Why not?' and we'd go home together. I liked the excitement of not knowing how a night was going to end. It was all very – work hard, play hard.[349]

Since that interview, life has not been the same for the Bercows. The revelations pushed Sally into the national spotlight and she has never looked back, although she will forever be known for those confessions. The strategy was simple enough: get the skeletons out of the closet so people can't use them against you. In that sense, it worked, and Sally is in a good position now to run as a Labour MP, free from having those events hanging over her. But revealing details about your private life allows the press to dig deeper into it. After the interview, it became known that in political circles she had been affectionately called "Sally the Alley" and for Bercow, too, the episode was immensely embarrassing, however much he believed in his wife's right to speak out as she wished.

Sally's excessive drinking started at Oxford. There, in the words of her spokesman, she "fell out with Oxford life and fell out with the tutors.[350]" In her first year, studying theology, she kept up easily enough, gaining a 2.i in her first year exams known as 'mods'. However, after she switched to history in her second year, her record went rapidly downhill. She found academic life hard-going, in part thanks to her heavy partying. After just over two years at Keble College, she left Oxford without finishing her degree.

Although she had left Oxford and the OUCA nights out behind, her Tory affiliation continued and in 1993 she even spoke on the platform at Tory Party Conference, where she wowed the faithful with her looks and her words. Sally's choice of topic was press freedom – and sex. "MPs are free to have affairs if they wish," she said. "After all...boys will be boys. But if those affairs conflict with their public image, carefully cultivated, of marital harmony, they cannot complain when the press catch them in their boxer shorts[351]."

By this time she had forged her relatively successful – but at times controversial – career in public relations and advertising. However, she continued to give in to a number of vices. As well as being a regular smoker, more worryingly Sally's drinking continued at a pace until 2000, when she decided "it wasn't fun any more[352]". Realising she needed to do something about her alcohol intake, she attended meetings of Alcoholics Anonymous. Typically robust, however, she decided she could handle it better on her own – and she hasn't drunk since. It is perhaps not surprising that a final reconciliation between Sally and John could only come about once her drinking had been dealt with.

But then, in 2001, came the decisive moment in John and Sally's relationship – which had, by then, become something of a long-running saga. Bercow ended up, finally, finding himself a serious girlfriend. It seemed that, like his father Charlie, John would end up marrying late. Sally's mother asked her how she would feel if he were to marry to someone else. She says that, after a bit of soul-searching, "I realised I would be devastated[353]," and she turned up on his doorstep imploring him to get back together with her. The pair moved in together soon afterwards and just six months later, during a dinner at the Cinnamon Club restaurant in Westminster, Bercow asked her to marry him. Finally, after 13 years, she said yes.

In a sign of his supreme devotion, Bercow also agreed to sell his much-loved cottage in Buckingham. The low ceilings proved no problem for him, but his 5'11 fiancee kept banging her head and Bercow did the gentlemanly thing. During the expenses scandal, that gesture would come back to haunt him.

Given Sally's political opinions, the fact that she was marrying the man who had been known as the Tory's Rottweiler-in-chief was the subject of much chatter around Westminster. Tongues wagged as to the kind of pillow talk that would flow with a woman who said, "John probably hates this, but I think Tony and Cherie Blair are superb. Labour has not let the country down and I think what they are doing on public services is right...I think the euro and Europe is right for Britain.[354]" Sally seemed to give some sort of reassurance by saying that in the previous election she, "Campaigned both for Blair and Bercow. I was thrilled that both of them won, but now I am lapsed from New Labour and I naturally support John on the important issues[355]." Although her support for Bercow himself has never waivered, to say that she was a "lapsed" supporter of New Labour would perhaps give a slightly incorrect impression to the casual observer. She had merely failed to renew her subscription and instead of "lapsing" back towards the Tory Party, if anything Sally's transformation went further as she moved ever leftwards in the years following her engagement.

Rightly or wrongly, the engagement crystallised a feeling amongst some in the Conservative Party that Bercow would quickly follow his wife leftwards across the political spectrum towards Labour. He strongly denied the charge though, as, "Utter balderdash, paranoid nonsense. I have always been a Tory and I will die a Tory. The idea that because I'm engaged to be married to someone who supports the Labour Party I'm somehow about to be influenced against the Conservative faith is ludicrous. It's based on the idea of the wicked witch in the background, which really is nonsense on stilts. Of course we talk, we influence each other – we're a partnership – but there's no link between us being together and my political views.[356]" But even amidst such strident words, there were signs that Bercow was moving away from his most entrenched positions as he admitted, "There are differences between the Conservatives and Labour but it isn't the yawning gap that it was.[357]"

Away from politics, there were going to be serious changes in his life – and not least that Bercow would no longer be seen turning up at parties with his mother as his plus one. In preparation for the end of his days as a single man – although it's not clear that he ever really enjoyed them all that much in any case – his best man Julian Lewis organised a stag do, at Pomegranates restaurant in Pimlico. It was a small affair, with seven or eight of Bercow's closest friends there, including Mark MacGregor, Gary Mond and the MP Alan Duncan. It was very much a civilised evening – a tasteful dinner rather than a raucous party with drunken escapades – although it had seemed that it might be very different when Lewis teased the newly-liberal Bercow about what he had up his sleeve: "How about a gay stripper?[358]", he asked.

Then, the night before the wedding itself, John's mother Brenda paid for a dinner in Knightsbridge for close family and friends, including Lewis and John's sister Alison. Sally was there too, but on her best behaviour. Despite the pressure of having the wedding the next day, she stayed off the cigarettes – having given up smoking shortly before – and clung steadfastly to her new-found sobriety by sticking to water all evening.

The big day was Saturday, December 7th, which was in itself a significant choice as Jewish weddings are not usually held on Saturdays. Bercow had ensured that he would marry the woman he loved most in the place that he loved most – the House of Commons – and had booked out the crypt for the ceremony. This, too, made a break from his Jewish heritage, as the service was being held in a Christian place of worship. Moreover, unlike his father, Bercow did not have his future bride convert to Judaism. As one of the guests explained to me, "It certainly wasn't a Jewish wedding."

The crypt was packed out and in the words of one guest, "Sally looked rather pretty." Despite her political views, a large number of Tory activists were there for the wedding, including some of the men who had been on the FCS National Committee with Bercow and who had subsequently voted to censure him when the organisation was shut down. Another guest was Michael Portillo – who was still something of a guiding figure for Bercow in Conservative politics. But one notable absentee was Norman Tebbit and his wife, who had withdrawn their acceptance after Bercow made his new, liberal views on gay adoption known. Tebbit told Sally's mother, "You will not be surprised to know that I believe it would now be quite wrong for my wife and I to be guests.359" Bercow was desperately unhappy about Tebbit's snub. "John was very upset," a friend told me. "The announcements were in the press and Tebbit sent him quite a curt note."

A press call followed, before the party made its way into the Churchill Dining Room for the reception. Soon it became clear that the seating plan was in a total mess: the numbers were in completely the wrong order and the guests were wandering round, bewildered. It was not what the bride would have wanted for her wedding day and Sally ran up to the Commons staff, red in the face, and shouted at them to, "Change it immediately!" Once that particular hiccup was sorted, next up were the speeches. Bercow's mother was, in the words of one of the guests, "Quite ballsy. I can see where he gets it from"; Julian Lewis retold his story about spotting Sally first at the student conference in 1989; then, when Bercow spoke, he regaled the guests with his impression of the Tory MP Sir Peter Tapsell – which he was to repeat some years later during hustings for the Speakership in the House of

Commons. It did not leave all the guests impressed: "I just remember how boring the speeches were," one says.

As the wedding came to a close, the couple were eager to view the pictures from the photo call and to see what the press had to say about their big day, so they despatched Julian Lewis and his date off to Victoria Station to buy the early editions of the next day's papers. Unfortunately, though, it proved to be a wasted trip as there was not a single photo of the wedding in any of them.

It was to be one of the few occasions when the new couple failed to make the headlines. Bercow realised that eyebrows would be raised at the political leanings of his bride, but few would have predicted their collective rise to prominence that has come since. Their wedding may have marked the first day of the rest of their lives, but it was also the beginning of something much more fundamental in Bercow's career. As he continued his political journey and Sally began to gain public attention, their relationship would only continue to raise difficult questions about Bercow's political leanings, his judgment and his relationship with his own party.

18

The Rise and Fall

"A pretty lousy frontbencher"

In 2001, as the Conservatives regrouped after yet another beating by Tony Blair, John Bercow was a man on the rise. He was sitting pretty in a safe seat and was about to be appointed to the Shadow Cabinet for the first time – and he was still a couple of years off turning forty.

But within a few years, Bercow was on the road to nowhere – stuck on the backbenches, with no prospect of a political recovery. As his personal fortunes suddenly improved with Sally coming back into his life, so his political trajectory nosedived.

It was Bercow's second Parliament as an MP and for the second time there was a leadership contest. Bercow managed to prove himself to be the political antithesis of the great World Cup soothsayer Paul the Octopus by – yet again – managing to back the loser. Bercow's choice in 2001 lay in stark contrast to his favoured candidates in 1997, when he backed the right-wingers Peter Lilley and John Redwood. This time around he was a devoted Portillista – and as Portillo journeyed from right to left, Bercow went with him. But Conservative MPs would put the spanner in the works, as they rejected Portillo in the final ballot selecting two MPs to be put forward to the party membership, opting for Ken Clarke and Iain Duncan-Smith instead. At a stroke, Bercow's best chance of fitting back in to the Conservative Party – one led by a man with a modernising agenda so similar to his own – disappeared.

Faced with the final two, Bercow did, at last, manage to go with the candidate who would emerge victorious. IDS was beginning to make the right noises about reform and importantly he was also, unlike Clarke, a Eurosceptic – and on Europe Bercow was scarcely any more relaxed than when he was a young man in the FCS. When Clarke came to address a meeting in Bercow's constituency during the election, Bercow awkwardly told the crowd that he was backing Duncan-Smith, although he did admit that his mother was supporting Ken[360]. In fact, Clarke pounced on Bercow's background as an example of Duncan-Smith's right-wing leanings, deriding his decision to put up a former "activist in the Monday Club[361]" on television to support him. Bercow retorted snottily, "I am sure Ken knows that I reject the reactionary politics of the Monday Club because he appointed me as one of his special advisers at the Treasury[362]."

When Duncan-Smith won the vote amongst the party membership, Bercow was finally able to realise the fruits of backing a winner. He was appointed as Shadow Chief Secretary to the Treasury, shadowing the role that Aitken had held when he was Bercow's boss. It was a big promotion, moving Bercow into the Shadow Cabinet for the first time and, with it, into the political limelight. Gone was the thrusting backbencher – here was a serious politician.

However, even though Bercow had been very keen on the job, accepting it was to prove a mistake. Significantly, the role had already been promised to Howard Flight and even though Duncan-Smith initially opted for Bercow, Flight had been told that the job would soon be his. It seemed from the very start that it would be just a matter of time before Bercow was squeezed out. Putting Bercow in an economics role was also a slightly strange choice – as his time at Hambros showed, he and finance were not an instinctive fit. "He did do himself damage," says a former colleague on the front bench. "He shouldn't have gone for Shadow Chief Secretary, it wasn't his metier at all. It wasn't that he let himself down but he didn't shine. I think that may have confirmed a view that he wasn't really a heavy[weight]."

Nonetheless, Bercow did approach the new position with his usual zeal, although it did not take long for him to spread his wings and start making some serious noises about reforming the party. In perhaps his first major step of the new Parliament, Bercow acted with a stark ruthlessness by turning his eloquent guns on his former friends in the Monday Club. He said that it would be "morally right and politically cathartic[363]" to kick Monday Club members out of the party – a policy which, if it had been implemented in the 1980s, would have meant getting rid of Bercow himself, not to mention a number of his friends. That did not seem to matter and Duncan-Smith soon jumped on the idea, effectively forcing a number of senior Monday Clubbers to resign their Conservative Party membership. Not surprisingly, they were furious at what they saw as Bercow's betrayal. "He's a hypocrite and a traitor," says Gregory Lauder-Frost. "People come and go in organisations, but it's quite another thing when…they condemn the organisation that they were a willing member of and to which they paid a subscription.364" Sam Swerling, the Club's former Chairman, was so incensed that he almost ended up coming to blows with Bercow when the two met, although Swerling later apologised for the altercation.

Bercow continued to push his social crusade, next declaring that the Tories could produce the first gay Prime Minister, but only if the party "embraced change". "In the last Parliament we were widely and justifiably denounced as shrill, homophobic and eerily detached from the reality of the lives of many of our fellow citizens," he said. "In this Parliament nothing we say should serve to reinforce that negative image.365" It was quite radical stuff – and it is hard to knock either the sentiment or the political position. It was the start of a process of Tory purification, continued the following year by Theresa May's "nasty party" speech; and the mantle was later taken on by David Cameron and his supporters. Bercow was right and he was ahead of the curve.

But amongst the radicalism, the John Bercow of old still existed. He was still loud and he still liked to get right up into the faces of opposition MPs. "I was very badly behaved," he says, recounting one particular occasion with his usual powers of mimicry: "I was beside myself with irritation at Tony Blair and I kept yelling and heckling and Speaker Martin eventually said, 'Order, Mr Bercow be quiet,' and Tony Blair said, 'Oh yeah, I'm bound to say, Mr Speaker, the honourable gentleman might find that quite difficult'.366" And when Bercow went skiing in Val d'isère that Christmas – the first time he had spent the festive season abroad – he vowed to use only French Francs rather than the nascent Euro.

Bercow also spent much of his time tabling Parliamentary questions – literally thousands of them. Such was his profligacy that he personally posed 10% of all the questions asked by MPs in total – and in one week alone in December 2001 he put forward 191 requests for information. Examples included finding out how many of his constituents had written to the International Development Secretary asking about overseas aid (answer: three); and asking if the Health Secretary had plans to visit patients in his constituency (answer: no plans)[367]. On one occasion, Bercow put a question to the Europe Minister, Peter Hain that was 10,195 words long. Hain replied in just 61[368].

Much of Bercow's effort was aimed at more weighty matters, including highlighting areas of government waste, but it was somewhat ironic that Bercow himself ended up costing taxpayers a fortune. Estimates put the total cost of all those questions at well over £500,000[369], but Bercow was unrepentant, saying that the civil servants were already employed and it was their job to answer – but there would have needed to be a serious recruitment drive if all MPs had decided to be as assiduous as Bercow.

Bercow was tasked with working under Michael Howard, who was the new Shadow Chancellor, and on the face of it the two men had much in common. Both were the descendants of Jewish immigrants from Romania and both were not high Tories; neither man was seen as "clubbable" in the traditional sense and they were not particular lovers of hanging around in the smoking rooms of the Commons. However, despite such common ground, the two men later had a very public falling out.

In that context, surprisingly it was Howard who often spoke up for Bercow, believing him to be able and worth keeping in the Shadow Cabinet. These interventions were much needed, as IDS was fast becoming frustrated with Bercow and the promise to Flight still needed to be honoured. There was a growing feeling amongst some senior Tories that Bercow was – in the words of one of them – "always stretching boundaries". His constant mea culpas – which usually included stinging criticism of his own party's positions from a few years beforehand – were not going down well and moves to sack him gathered at a pace. Howard – as one of the most senior members of the party and in his role as Shadow Chancellor, Bercow's boss – stepped in to save him more than once. However, it was a tide that could not be held back forever.

Bercow clearly found the constraints of collective responsibility challenging and time after time he made waves with his frankness. In January 2002, a letter from Bercow to his constituency party was leaked on the day of a keynote speech by IDS. "We are seen as racist, sexist, homophobic and anti-youth... In short, if we are to have a chance of winning, we have to change our ways,[370]" declared Bercow. The text came out just before IDS was to set out his own vision of what the party's core values should be, completely blowing the leader's speech off course. Then in May 2002, as Bercow was fast becoming the Conservatives' most prominent champion of gay rights, he abstained in a three line whip on gay adoption; and after the Central Office adviser Dominic Cummings said that the Tories should keep a low profile during a referendum on the euro, as "For many people, just about the only thing less popular than the euro is the Tory Party[371]". Bercow called Cummings – a fellow moderniser – "a brilliant man, [372]" although he did say that the Conservatives should campaign during the referendum.

Something had to give. "He was stepping out of line, saying things that were not the party line and that were mildly embarrassing," recalls a Shadow Cabinet colleague. "Not a problem unique to John Bercow, but he did it very deliberately and provocatively... It's his extreme self-centredness in a world that's full of self-centred people. He absolutely stands out, nobody comes close, it's about what's in it for John Bercow. It wasn't an inability to stay in line, it was a deliberate decision. Some people can't help themselves; with him it was a deliberate tactic."

However, Bercow's actions can also be explained by the continuing struggle between modernisers and the more traditional right-wing of the party. Like Cummings, Portillo had spoken out to advise Duncan-Smith to keep a low profile during a Euro referendum and many of Bercow's comments would have pleased the growing numbers of social liberals in the Conservatives. Many senior Tories were beginning to realise that the party had to change if it wanted to return to power – and they helped to set up think tanks like Policy Exchange and C-Change to make the shift. The liberal wing that has now found its comfort in David Cameron was on the march and has continued to push on ever since. That Bercow did not progress up the political pole with them is a clear indication that there was something different about him – both politically and personally.

When Duncan-Smith reshuffled his Shadow Cabinet in July 2002 he did – at last – decide to sack Bercow, although he offered him the less senior role of Shadow Minister under David Willetts at Work and Pensions. The rising star's trajectory had flattened out. Even so, Bercow did not let this setback get in the way of his concerted modernisation campaign. First he came out in support of gay marriage and against section 28[373], then at party conference in Autumn 2002, he said the Tories had, "Come across as an overwhelmingly rural, provincial and, dare I say it, prissy party.[374]" He also called for the Conservatives to disassociate themselves from the comedian Jim Davidson after he made a joke about asylum seekers at a gala dinner. Bercow had been at the event with Sally and she was very offended by Davidson's comments.

Things could not go on like this – Bercow seemed completely uncomfortable sticking to the party's agreed line when he took a much more liberal view than the leadership – and events came to a head as the Adoption and Children Bill went through Parliament. Duncan-Smith imposed a three-line whip to vote against gay adoption: even though such an issue would usually have been a matter of conscience, Tory MPs were being directed on which way their consciences had to go. It was a position that was completely untenable for Bercow.

The vote was scheduled for November 4th and Bercow wrestled with his dilemma for some time. It was one thing to speak out of turn against the party line, but quite another to resign from the front bench. He sought the advice of old friends, speaking several times to Brian Coleman, a friend from Finchley and later a GLA member, who was gay. As one of those who advised Bercow told me, "It's an equalities issue…he felt so passionate about it. It was clearly unfair and the Tory Party was wrong." Sally, too, agreed that Bercow was right in standing up for gay adoption and it was while Bercow was driving with her through the London traffic that he finally made up his mind. The next day, on the morning before the vote, Bercow told the Chief Whip,

David Maclean, that he could not stay away and would have to resign. Despite pleas from Maclean and then Duncan-Smith, Bercow said his mind was made up, although he did agree to make it clear that his resignation was on the single issue of conscience, not over Duncan-Smith's leadership as a whole. On the evening of November 3rd, Bercow wrote to IDS and resigned, saying: "I shall speak in the debate...and shall vote in favour of change."

Some of those close to Duncan-Smith felt that Bercow's decision was partly driven by a damaged ego – he had, after all, been demoted a few months previously. Bercow had also agreed to abstain rather than resign when the bill had first come before the House of Commons earlier in the year, when he was still Shadow Chief Secretary to the Treasury. However, that is to underestimate the strength of Bercow's feeling. As he put it after his resignation, "This issue is not about the rights of gay people, or of heterosexual people, or of married people, or of unmarried people – frankly, it is not about the rights of adults at all. It is about the rights, welfare and futures of some of the most vulnerable children in our society today.[375]"

IDS's decision was a significant blunder that weakened his party, causing a damaging resignation and helping to paint the Tories as socially illiberal, like the "nasty party" of old. Allowing a free vote would have been much simpler and more strategic. As Michael Portillo asked in the Commons, backing up his loyal supporter and embodying the view of the "mods", "Consider for a moment what your position would be if you found yourself in the minority in this party and whether you would feel happy that in order to vote with your conscience, you'd have to give up your front-bench position?[376]"

The fall-out was significant on all sides. Bercow's resignation was an undoubted blow to IDS – and it was only made worse when he turned down an offer to be the party's "campaign coordinator". Although Bercow won plaudits amongst the liberal wing of the party, he had completely alienated some of those who had been there throughout his political journey – and it was Bercow's resignation that led to Norman Tebbit boycotting his wedding.

The freedom of the backbenches seemed to suit him much better than the constraints of collective responsibility. He made good use of that liberty, speaking out whenever he saw fit to criticise the leadership on a number of occasions. When Duncan-Smith proposed lower taxes, Bercow argued strongly in favour of social justice and public services. Then he became one of the first to turn the screw on IDS's leadership, when he publicly declared that "our chance of winning the next general election is about as great as that of finding an Eskimo in the desert[377]".

By early 2003, rumours began to surface that Bercow was going to cross the floor and join Labour, although he always strenuously denied them. His marriage to Sally added fuel to the fire, but for now he was still very much an avowed Tory, just one who wanted the party to be more progressive. However, the process of estrangement from other Tory MPs was now well and truly under way. As John Redwood told me, it started with his resignation. "Colleagues started to get alienated. They didn't understand or sympathise with the reasons. He started to incur problems and it set a pattern." While Bercow was perfectly in tune with many of the other modernisers in the party over gay adoption, on other issues he began to irritate more widely as his views began to change. As one MP found, "He can't moderate his view. If he's not at the North Pole, he has to be at the South Pole. It's part of his peculiar character. By 2002-2003 he was clearly no longer at the North Pole. Europe was his only concession." Bercow was still very active in the Commons – in fact he gave more speeches than any other MP – but he devoted his time to causes wholly removed from those for which he campaigned in his early years in Parliament. It set him apart even from the modernisers.

But events would step in to give Bercow a helping hand, as a leadership challenge to IDS materialised in October 2003. It was the moderniser Francis Maude, who had advised Bercow over the gay adoption vote, who wrote to the Chairman of the 1922 Committee asking for a confidence motion. IDS was soon despatched and Michael Howard became the new leader in his place. Even though Bercow had been going nowhere fast under IDS, the situation was still far from ideal. For one thing, his great hope, Michael Portillo, had agreed not to run against Howard and had stood down from frontline politics. Once again, Bercow would not be able to rise within the party on Portillo's coat-tails.

More awkward was an interview that Bercow had given after resigning from the front bench. "One Young Conservative asked me recently," he began, "'what shall we do with Michael Howard, present him with a carriage clock or a set of golf clubs?' That's too harsh, he's an excellent Shadow Chancellor. However, sometimes there is considerable doubt as to whether he has signed up to the agenda of the modernisation of the Conservative Party.[378]" Even though there had not been a leadership election – so Bercow hadn't had the chance to back the wrong candidate – he had still trodden on the new leader's toes.

However, Howard did have faith in Bercow, believing him to be talented, and appointed him to the Shadow Cabinet as Shadow International Development Secretary. Despite Howard's deep reservations about Bercow's tendency to stray away from the official party line, he thought he was too good to be left on the backbenches. Bercow's career was resurrected; and soon after, a good year finished on an even greater high, when Sally gave birth to their first child, Oliver. "He's very handsome, a fact that is obviously down to Sally and certainly not me,[379]" said Bercow modestly. His son's birth was to be another key point in his continuing journey and the mellowing of his political opinions. Not only would it grant him a fresh perspective on life, but it would end up bringing him closer to New Labour.

But for now, everything was going swimmingly. Bercow threw himself into his new role and went on visits to Zimbabwe, Sudan and Burma, where he was obviously moved by much of the suffering that he saw. Ben Rogers, a campaigner for human rights in Burma, recalls that he was, "Impressed by his energy, enthusiasm [and] desire to get to grips with the subject and be helpful...John was one of the nicest and easiest politicians I've ever worked with.[380]"

Bercow wasn't afraid to take risks, either, and decided that he would enter Burma by an effectively illegal route so he could evaluate the situation there for himself. "I had warned him repeatedly about the nature of the trip," says Rogers, "and that the authorities wouldn't be pleased if they knew what we were doing... He said that this is not the sort of regime whose immigration laws we should respect.[381]".

Bercow certainly seemed to have been bitten by the human rights bug. Each trip abroad seemed to open his eyes a little wider to the injustices around the world and he would return with a desire to push forward the cause. At last, he seemed to have found his niche. However, the political honeymoon would only last so long and, inexorably, Bercow was soon stepping out of line again. A senior Conservative muses, "I suppose he thought one way of getting more attention is to be distinctive, so he may have thought…by taking his own line he was increasing his profile." Another theory was that Bercow was getting itchy feet as he felt that he should have been in a more senior job. A colleague remarks, "He was always obsessed with the view that his merits were insufficiently appreciated and the position he held was less significant than the position he should be in."

First, Bercow decided to publicly call for the Tories to match Labour's spending commitments on overseas aid and then – quite incredibly – he wrote a letter to Tony Blair praising his leadership. "Congratulations on your superb speech in the Iraq debate on Tuesday," he wrote. "On this subject, as on many other foreign affairs issues, you have provided outstanding statesmanship." This missive was all the more remarkable as Howard had been widely thought to have had a very bad day indeed in the Commons that Tuesday – thanks to Blair. "Most of the letter was fine," says a senior Conservative. "It was something to do with international development. [But the] paragraph which said how much I admire your leadership – he was in the Shadow Cabinet and it was completely unacceptable."

Howard was furious and he acted quickly. In a reshuffle just six weeks later, Bercow was unceremoniously dumped from the Shadow Cabinet. Although Howard did offer Bercow another less senior front role, he refused to accept it and the meeting turned into acrimony as Bercow told Howard that there was something in Ann Widdecombe's comment that there was "something of the night" about him. Howard was "sinister", said Bercow, and a "control freak" who was unable to "empathise with people[382]"; and Bercow added that when Howard arrived late at a meeting the pair both attended, "You looked at me in a strange and dark way.[383]" Howard retorted by telling Bercow he was not collegiate.

To all intents and purposes, Bercow's career as a front bench

Conservative was over – at least as long as Howard was in charge. Those near the top of the party thought he had stepped out of line once too often and believed him to be unreliable. Worse still, thanks to Bercow's sucking up to Blair, his increasing liberalness and his marriage to Sally, some seriously considered that he might even cross the floor. Bercow himself sums up part of the problem when he says, "I was a pretty lousy frontbencher. I was lacking in self-discipline. I was not willing to commit to a collective line. I was a poor team player.[384]"

This period marks a watershed which saw the demise of the old John Bercow. From around this time in 2004, Bercow began to go further than most of the Portillista modernisers: he was that much more vocal in his criticism of the party, that much more ready to step out of line. He sniped from the backbenches, criticising Howard for concentrating on immigration, lower taxes and Europe; and reiterated his support for Tony Blair over Iraq, saying Howard's attacks on Blair made him look "opportunistic[385]". Bercow went further still, and he announced that he agreed with the "broad approach" taken by Tony Blair and his Minister Alan Milburn on public services[386]. For someone who had for so long opposed almost anything that the Labour Party had said or done, it was remarkable.

Bercow seemed liberated by the freedom of the backbenches. He seemingly spoke and did largely as he wanted – voting against the party whip to oppose ID cards but then slating Peter Hain for calling Michael Howard an "attack mongrel". Amidst continuing rumours that he would defect to Labour – and in one interview Bercow refused to deny that he would cross the floor[387] – he did receive some vindication when he was voted Opposition MP of the Year in 2005.

When Tony Blair called a General Election for May 5th, Bercow's award featured prominently on his campaign literature, as if it were a sort of justification for the four years since the last election in which he'd annoyed many in the Conservative Party and raised eyebrows in Buckingham with his shifting views. His leaflets also featured Sally and Oliver very prominently, with some clever direction making Bercow seem a good few inches taller than Sally, who was sitting on a swing with her son. It was, as ever, an uneventful contest in the constituency, with Bercow increasing his share of the vote to over 57%. As for Blair himself, he returned with a reduced but still substantial majority, despite the protests at his decision to take the country to war – a choice that Bercow had steadfastly defended, even at the cost of his own Shadow Cabinet job.

But as the results were announced that night, some of the excitement of past elections was missing. Bercow's fledgling career had all but come to a halt and there seemed little future for him on the Conservative front bench. In just a few short years he had managed to self-destruct, going from a rising Tory star and – perhaps – a potential future leader to a relatively unpopular backbencher. Most Tories felt he was going nowhere – and some MPs felt that if he did end up somewhere, it would most likely be on the Labour benches. Bercow may well have thought it all worth it, as he had at times acted on principle, but to some in the Conservative Party, Bercow had come across as self-obsessed and disloyal. That feeling would continue to fester. But this, after all, was John Bercow: and soon he would be plotting a remarkable political recovery.

19

Making Enemies

"Cameron was absolutely furious"

"Well said," murmured Bercow approvingly, from his seat on the backbenches. This was the reborn Bercow – or in his own words, "Bercow mark three[388]". There he was, still in love with the House of Commons, still sitting through debate after debate and making one speech after another. But it wasn't one of his fellow Conservatives whom he was congratulating; it was a Labour MP. That's one of the MPs that he – who had not so long before been voted Opposition politician of the year – was meant to be opposing. Instead, Bercow was often heard muttering words of appreciation and agreeing vigorously when a Labour politician was on his feet. "He never sat easily on his side of the House," says the Labour MP Parmjit Dhanda. "He would nod in agreement to the Prime Minister or a Ministers' statements… some people on our side said he should be on our side[389]."

As for his own party – well Bercow would react to them, too. "Rubbish," he would bellow as an MP with whom he shared the party whip spoke. "Split infinitive!" he would shout at another. It was rude and it was inflammatory – and a lot of his colleagues were furious. Some couldn't stand the sight of him: the Members' Dining Room in the House of Commons is where MPs go to have lunch and in a spirit of cooperation they come in from one of the two entrance doors and sit at the nearest free seat. One MP told me that he so dislikes Bercow that every time he eats his lunch in the Dining Room, he walks past the first door to check Bercow isn't there and uses the other entrance if he is; such is his desire to avoid sitting next to him.

It would take a few years for Bercow to reach this low point, but the seeds were sown by yet another utterly disastrous set of decisions in a leadership campaign – although Bercow's conduct this time round was far more cataclysmic than ever before. Michael Howard resigned after the 2005 election, but not before Bercow had slated the party's manifesto as "embarrassingly thin" and called its policy on immigration "repellent[390]". As the runners and riders for the top job manoeuvred into place, Bercow declared his support for Ken Clarke, saying he was "the most impressive beast in the Tory jungle[391]". It was another volte face, having been involved in a spat with Clarke during the last contest, although the two had long got on well.

With the benefit of hindsight, Bercow's decision was a strange one. He chose Clarke, a renowned Europhile – and Europe was just about the only area in which Bercow had kept up his old beliefs. However, as a friend explains, "David Davis was favourite and right-wing. Given Bercow's journey, if he supported Davis he would lose credibility. Cameron was an outsider and also a toff. So Ken was the obvious choice – he had a chance of winning and [was] the most left-wing and if Clarke won it would lead to a plum job." Others think that Bercow's decision was driven in part by the fact that – in the words of a Tory MP – "to see someone who entered Parliament after you become Prime Minister is no doubt very hard."

However, it was typical of Bercow that he could not do anything by half. He might have arrived at the South Pole, but he then kept trying to dig down even deeper. When Cameron criticised Clarke's position on Europe, Bercow responded by saying that it was "ludicrous hyperbole". But then, he went further and in doing so finally destroyed his career in Conservative politics. Bercow launched a stinging attack on Cameron, saying that, "In the modern world the combination of Eton, hunting, shooting and lunch at White's is not helpful when you are trying to appeal to millions of ordinary people.[392]"

In politics, insults are usually veiled or made through innuendo. But Bercow used no such subtlety as he went for Cameron's jugular in a very personal attack. "Cameron was absolutely furious," says a member of his team. "Firstly, White's, his father was Chairman and it was getting personal. Secondly it was very effective. Cameron is very self-conscious about it [class]. Labour has played that card crudely and ineffectively and has overestimated people's chippiness. But at that point he was acutely aware of it." One MP calls it an, "Extraordinary attack. He was striking a match that was going to burn." Laying into Cameron was wholly unnecessary, a ridiculous gamble by Bercow – and even Clarke, the man Bercow was supporting, doesn't approve of the attack. "I don't know what he said that for, but I didn't agree with that," says Clarke. "It doesn't matter a tuppeny damn one way or another whether Cameron went to Eton or not, it's always been firmly my view.[393]"

In part, one might put down Bercow's savaging of Cameron to his own thoughts on class. After all, he had not benefited from the advantages with which Cameron had been blessed. Instead of going to Eton, Bercow was stuck in a comprehensive where he stood out like a sore thumb. Whilst Cameron's father was chairman of White's, Bercow's drove cabs, and for perhaps the least clubbable of Tory MPs, the White's connection was totally invidious. No wonder that Bercow argued, "If you've never known a day's disadvantage, material discomfort in your life and you don't regularly mix with people who come from the school of hard knocks, you can say, 'I care about these people' – and I'm sure David does – but it's much more difficult than if you have, frankly, a much more ordinary existence."

But more than anything, Cameron's advancement marked a sea change in the Conservative Party – moving it away from the self-made Tories that had formed a line from Heath through to Howard. Bercow had been schooled in the FCS – he had developed alongside 1980s Tories, full of ambition and a desire to make the best of themselves, whatever their background. They had been brought into politics by Thatcher, not by tradition. However much Cameron reached out to the disadvantaged, his election – and the rise of George Osborne with him – took the control of the party away from aspirational Tories like Bercow who came from relatively unprivileged backgrounds.

Whatever his reasoning, Bercow had made a huge tactical mistake, but the full scale of his miscalculation did not emerge at first. In fact, at the time, everything looked rather peachy – Cameron was very much a long shot, while Bercow had made himself Clarke's most prominent cheerleader and would doubtless have been rewarded with a top role if he'd won the contest. Meanwhile, those close to the Davis campaign believe that Bercow would also have been put back on the front bench if he had been victorious. Cameron seemed inconsequential.

However, a brilliant Conference speech by the outsider turned the race on its head, with Cameron's personal rating doubling in a matter of days. He was on a roll and when the first round of voting was held he came within six votes of Davis, who had been the early frontrunner. The curse of Bercow struck again and Clarke was eliminated. The momentum was with Cameron and in the second round just two days later he easily topped the poll. By now, it was clear that Cameron would win when local Tory Party members had the final say in the national ballot. Bercow had transferred his allegiance to Cameron, but it was not enough to heal the wounds gouged by his inopportune words. Bercow realised how badly he had alienated the man who was by then likely to be the next Tory leader, but friends recall that it was only some weeks after his "Eton, hunting" statement that he asked them for advice. He had been relatively unconcerned until Cameron became a realistic candidate.

Bercow's front bench career was over. "Cameron is well-balanced and it is very unusual for him to hate someone so much," says an aide. "John Bercow is an exception. I remember at the time he was very angry and subsequently when John Bercow's name comes up he spits blood, and says things like, "What a little shit.""

Having been consigned to the backbenches, Bercow continued to cultivate his interest in international development and threw himself into campaigning on a whole host of issues across the globe. Burma was at the top of the list, but Bercow also began making a lot of noise about Sudan, sub-Saharan Africa and Guantanemo Bay. He had more time for constituency work, too, and was constantly to be found popping up at one local event after another. It was a dedication that might have been seen as unnecessary by other MPs in as safe a seat as Buckingham, but Bercow stuck at it and would receive his reward in the choppier times to come. Meanwhile there was a further welcome distraction at home, with Sally giving birth to their second son, Freddie.

But away from the international sphere he also began to turn, much more obviously, against his own side – even comparing his old comrade

Eric Forth to Victor Meldrew for his opposition to lowering the voting age to 16[394]. For Bercow, "from about 2005 onwards…I think I could argue I became the model of exquisite Parliamentary behaviour.[395]" Certainly he was haranguing Labour politicians less often – but he was still calling out from the backbenches, although often just to criticise a Conservative. Nadine Dorries – perhaps the MP who dislikes Bercow most of all – recalls, "It was appalling and shocking how calculated it was…[Once] I was debating with a Minister. Bercow nodded furiously for the Minister and just sat there for me. It was very disconcerting.[396]" As one senior Conservative MP said at the time, "he is a cuckoo in the nest," and MPs made complaints to the Tory Whips' office about Bercow's behaviour.

Then, in the summer of 2007, just after Gordon Brown had become Prime Minister, a Tory did defect to Labour – but it was Quentin Davies, not Bercow. Inevitably, a flurry of speculation followed, but Bercow again denied that he was thinking of crossing the floor, although many Tories continued to believe that Bercow might follow suit. As Dorries says, "The day that Quentin crossed the floor, as we rose and walked out [of the Commons], everyone was talking about Quentin and the rumour that Bercow would cross too. Bercow's head was swivelling around, trying to capture everything everyone said. I thought, he's thinking 'is that what they'd say about me?'[397]"

Brown had been keeping watch for potential targets for defection for some time and thought that Bercow might take the plunge. In part, this was because he had expressed greater disillusionment with the Tories in private than even Davies. However, Ed Miliband met with Bercow several times but came away with the impression that he was not interested.[398] Although he never completely closed the door on the idea, Bercow's ambitions lay in a different direction: towards the Speaker's Chair. Despite all the rumours over the years, Bercow never did decide that he wanted to join the Labour Party.

But from what might have been considered a nadir in terms of his reputation amongst Conservatives, Bercow managed to alienate his side further. This time it was because he agreed to work as an adviser to Brown, leading a review of services for children and young people with special communications needs. Bercow had to work closely with

Brown's key ally and the Schools Secretary Ed Balls – a friend of Sally's and the candidate she trumpeted in the 2010 Labour leadership contest. A large number of senior Conservatives were absolutely incandescent at Bercow's decision, and it only reinforced the belief of those who thought that Bercow would have been more at home in the Labour Party. As one MP told me, "People were very angry about the Bercow Review. It was regarded as disloyal." However, Bercow had first consulted with his Chief Whip and Michael Gove, the Shadow Schools Secretary. Moreover, the review gave him the chance to influence policy at last; and Bercow also had an important emotional driver behind his choice: his son Oliver had been diagnosed with verbal dyspraxia some eighteen months before.

Bercow's appointment – along with another Conservative, Patrick Mercer – as a member of Brown's "Government of all the talents" created something of a mini-crisis for David Cameron. At this time, Brown was still riding high in the polls and questions were beginning to be asked about the new Tory leader's future. Bercow announced that he would not be going to party conference that year – and in an inflammatory move, decided to spend one of the days visiting a school on a joint visit with Ed Balls instead[399], although he later had to cancel. The defection rumours continued, however much Bercow made it clear that he was not interested in joining the Labour Party.

Nonetheless, in those few days around party conference, something far more fundamental happened. Brown had been in his honeymoon period as the public lapped up a man who was "not flash, just Gordon" and he had been building up the idea of a snap General Election – and all the signs were that he would win it. However, George Osborne pulled off a political masterstroke by announcing a new policy of reducing inheritance tax. The polls that had been consistently showing a lead for Brown began to waver slightly and Brown's resolve wobbled even more sharply. He didn't call the election; and never recovered his credibility as one event after another – including the economy crashing down around him – took its toll. His failure meant that, in reality, summer 2007 was a Tory MP's last chance for finally taking the plunge and joining Labour. No sensible politician would consider joining a party as it stuttered towards the end of its time in office, not least because it would be harder for Labour to find Bercow a safe seat. "John is not from a wealthy background," says the former MP Derek Conway, "and by that stage he had a wife and young family. To throw that all up if you're not a Notting Hill trust fund baby is quite a risk, as an MP's pay is better than being down the pits. There were personal calculations to take into account.[400]"

As Labour floundered, Bercow continued his review of communication services for children. An interim report was published in March 2008, with the final version of the Bercow Report coming out in July of that year. How apt it was that in perhaps his final significant act as a backbencher, Bercow dedicated himself to communication. It was his peculiar ability for speech that had allowed him to rise above his competitors, to stand out as someone different – even if his unusual style had also made him the target for abuse. It was speaking that brought Bercow from the streets of Dollis Hill to Westminster. Now, having spent many years teaching speaking skills to others in classes with Julian Lewis, he would sign off his active party political career by helping to shape the future of children who were not blessed with anything like his natural ability.

Bercow argued that children with speech difficulties faced "multiple risks", including falling into crime, and found that 7% of children started school with speech or communication difficulties. He recommended the implementation of his "Action Plan" designed to remedy the situation, which included the appointment of a "Communication Champion." The government pledged £52 million for the project and it was, for Bercow, a job well done. He argued that, "For far too long, speech, language and communication have been elbowed aside by policy makers in favour of other aspects of the child development agenda.[401]" Perhaps Bercow knew the benefits of erudition better than any other MP; and the review allowed him, after eleven years in Parliament, to see a policy position implemented at last. It was, he said, "The most stimulating endeavour of my parliamentary life.[402]"

Whilst the subject matter of the review was very close to Bercow's heart, it still came at a political price. It was perhaps the tipping moment when Tory MPs finally wrote him off as not being one of them. Nonetheless, it seemed that the political journey still had further to go. The conclusive moment arrived when Bercow began to turn on the one issue on which he had held firm: Europe. In 2008 Bercow wrote to a constituent telling him that he did not believe that there should be a referendum on the Lisbon Treaty as it did not "involve any significant transfer of powers from the United Kingdom to the EU". Tory Party policy was in favour of a referendum and any Euro-sceptic worth his salt thought that Lisbon should be opposed at all costs. That Bercow did not believe in a referendum was a sign of how far he had come – and for many it was the last straw. "He's abandoned everything" says a former friend.

By March 2009, the intense dislike of Bercow within the Tory Party had crystallised. Nor did he seem to care either, as he stoked the fire of resentment. When he was asked about Theresa May, a senior shadow minister, Bercow replied: "Who? I wasn't aware she was still around. Amazing.[403]" What, in truth, was amazing was that Bercow could be so brazen in his attitude towards his own party. Not all Conservative MPs joined in the antipathy, but it was undoubtedly widespread, with four, often overlapping categories of MPs who disliked Bercow.

First, there were the instinctively repelled. Bercow had always come across as an odd fish to many Tory MPs; they simply felt that he was not one of them; not the clubbable type. "There was a sort of bigotry about someone small and physically not attractive," says one MP. "His Judaism was not a problem, but the furtive look, the sloping gait makes him a target. He's not quite normal." Bercow was different and many MPs were repelled or simply made slightly uneasy by his bizarrely good memory and odd manner of speaking. Inevitably, though, some in this category were driven by snobbishness.

Then there were those who pointed to Bercow's personal behaviour rather than his political leanings as the root cause. As one current Minister told me, he was "perfectly pleasant" even in the period 2005-2009 when it came to discussing Tory policy, but what angered this MP was Bercow's, "Nauseating behaviour. It was cumulative, the oily insincerity." Another MP says, "You never quite feel you're reading the person…never feel you're meeting eye to eye. You always get a peculiar front… He is oddly insensitive to other people." One MP insists that the collective dislike crystallised "just after 2001", indicating that many of the problems that some MPs had with Bercow came before his political shift. This is not to suggest that Bercow is unlikeable as a person and very many people speak positively of him. Rather, he is an acquired taste.

Next there were those who felt they had had their fingers burnt – people like Michael Howard, who through their experiences of working with Bercow have come to mistrust him. These MPs disliked Bercow for his self-promotion and for his problems working in a team. An associate of Bercow says it's about his "total duplicity, his lack of principle, unpleasantness, self-absorption. Any incident is fine if people think you're doing it for a genuine principle. [But] people questioned the motives of every action, he was not a team player".

Finally, for policy purists, it was simply too much for Bercow to have made the shift from right to left. For them, it was the sheer disloyalty. As Ken Clarke says, "I think they couldn't forgive Bercow because he had been one of the head-banging extreme when he started and was now consorting with the likes of me, and there were all the stupid rumours that he was going to cross the floor, so that made them very resentful.[404]" Inevitably, though, Bercow's personal behaviour overlaps with policy – as after all, when Bercow was waving across the House of Commons at Harriet Harman and nodding his head at Labour Ministers' speeches, some might blame him personally and some might point the figure at his political journey. As a former political friend told me, "John is detestable on two levels. First, he's oily, creepy and an insincere character. Secondly, others took offence at his political positions." The tribal feeling amongst some MPs was undeniable, but for others like John Redwood, "People have a right to change their minds and it's right they do develop their thinking. I'm happier if they are on my side, but I don't assume they will be.[405]" Whilst Redwood remained on good terms with Bercow, others who might have also accepted his changing views in other circumstances were appalled by the way in which he went about the conversion – publicly criticising his leaders and not being afraid to support Labour politicians. As Dorries says, "We're there as opposition MPs to hold the government to account, to give colleagues support when they're speaking on behalf of the cause people elected him to represent. We support each other and there was none of that from him.[406]"

The question, then, is *why* Bercow changed his views so starkly. The oft-repeated refrain is that John Bercow "discovered sex and New Labour at the same time", although Bercow's past history clearly disproves this theory. In truth, Bercow's views have been fluid throughout his life. Back in the 1980s he made the initial shift from authoritarian Monday Clubber to libertarian in a relatively short space of time. Having changed once, it's perhaps unsurprising that he changed again.

Bercow has always been a pragmatist, too, as is evidenced by the wholly practical approach he took to dealing with Tebbit and the FCS and the way in which he became a mainstream Thatcherite. Bercow is therefore as much descriptive of the change within the Tory Party as being the driver of his own journey, and while he says that his conversion is genuine, he also admits it was influenced by circumstance. "I thought to myself, wait a minute, [there have been] elections in which we've done rather badly and instead of just sort of ranting perhaps one ought to ask oneself, 'Is one's party doing it the right way? Am I doing it the right way?' So I thought about it very carefully.[407]" The subject of Bercow's dissertation was Edmund Burke, the great conservative who argued that one ought to "change in order to preserve", and in a sense Bercow has done just that. Some of the key players behind progressive Conservatism are now significant figures in Cameron's Tory Party; and some of Bercow's contemporaries from the FCS are now happily ensconced in the higher Conservative ranks, having also understood the need to change. For at least the first part of his journey, Bercow followed the example of politicians like Michael Portillo and his shift can be seen as part of a general trend in Conservatism. For much of the time, his political antennae were in good working order.

But Bercow was different; and he went far further than almost any other reformer. It is partly because he seems to be unable to do anything by half: his essence is captured by the MP who told me that he is always at one of either the South Pole or North Pole. When Bercow takes on a challenge, he is like a dog with a bone. Sally seems to share much of this intensity – and she has undergone an even more extreme conversion than her husband. In her case she switched from being a speaker at the Tory Party Conference to being a Labour Party member in just four years – a startlingly rapid reversal. Like his wife, Bercow loves politics and when he takes a position, he then runs with it ad extremis. In every leadership campaign, Bercow has been the most vociferous, bang-drumming supporter of whomever he has backed, even though it was usually the kiss of death. It's the same with particular issues – if Bercow backs something, he then likes to be at the forefront of the campaign. But for many Conservatives this has been his undoing – they see him as an opportunist, who jumps on a bandwagon if he thinks it will take him to the right place.

Clearly Sally and his children have also had a vital role to play in his changing ideas. In 2008 his third child and first daughter Jemima was born, completing the family idyll for which Bercow longed for many years, and his home life has calmed him and worn away at the hard edges. "A lot of the explanation lies in his family circumstances,[408]" says Redwood – and it's a theory that Bercow himself subscribes to. "I married and so on," he says, "and I began to think, 'how do we combine effective scrutiny with being rounded people who live normal lives?[409]'" Having lost some of his hard-headedness, Bercow's political views changed accordingly and there is a sincerity in many of Bercow's positions – on gay rights and international development in particular. Sally clearly has a significant influence over Bercow, as any wife would over her husband, and key points in his career have been affected by her advice. It was Sally who was with him when he finally resolved to resign from the Shadow front bench and it is she who is his chief confidante. But it is facile to say that Sally alone has caused the change, not least because Bercow had already made some significant shifts in his positions long before they married. The whole Conservative Party, the "nasty party", had realised it needed to change and so it did – politicians who want to win elections are opportunists and Bercow was no different in that sense.

But in analysing the tracks of his political journey, which form a gradual process over 20 years, the train suddenly judders to a halt. There is a disconnect between Bercow's gradual liberalisation and his sudden friendliness towards Labour MPs opposite. Undoubtedly Bercow was moving ever towards the left of the Conservative Party, under Sally's eye, but his behaviour – if not his policies – then went further. For some MPs, Bercow's extremes – and the very acts that made him so unpopular within the Tory Party – were all wrapped up in a brilliant plan. Having set his sights on high political office for so long, Bercow turned his back on progressing within the Conservative Party and began to eye a different prize.

20

Mr Speaker

"Our view was anybody but Bercow"

"Could you help me find a job?" asked John Bercow, around the time of the Tory leadership election in 2005. It was during a lunch at Sheekey's restaurant that he turned to his old friend, Kevin Bell of Fleishman Hillard, the political consultancy firm, in the hope of getting some work. But he was out of luck. "It's just not practical,[410]" Bell replied.

This "astonishing[411]" behaviour, as Bell calls it, sheds some light on Bercow's inner turmoil as the 2005 Parliament got under way. Having sat in the Shadow Cabinet and found the experience to be rather an uncomfortable one; and having killed off any further prospects of a front bench career, Bercow was somewhat stranded. The burning ambition that had fuelled a trajectory from the FCS to Lambeth and on to Parliament was suddenly directionless. His fellow MP Derek Conway recalls, "At the time he was a bit lost, I'm not sure he knew what he wanted to do. There were lots of changes in his life, on the domestic front, in his political stance…a lot of turmoil going on in John's life for quite some time.[412]"

The decision to ask Bell for work was symptomatic of his changing priorities. Bercow had new-found responsibilities, with a wife and child who were relying on his earning capacity. His simple life of 1997, when he was an ambitious, single backbencher, was a world away. Perhaps this explains Bercow's rather odd choice in asking for some consultancy work. After all, the Parliamentary rules are strict. The Code of Conduct states:

"When a Member is taking part in any parliamentary proceeding or making any approach to a Minister or servant of the Crown, advocacy is prohibited which seeks to confer benefit exclusively upon a body (or individual) outside Parliament, from which the Member has received, is receiving, or expects to receive a financial benefit, or upon any registrable client of such a body (or individual).[413]"

It is hard to see how Bercow could have worked as a political lobbyist without approaching ministers on a client's behalf. It is, in many ways, the whole point of the job.

Bercow might well have taken the job and stuck strictly to the code, but he would not have been much use to his clients. Alternatively, if the approach to Bell had progressed further, he might have realised the conflict and backed out before starting any work.

In asking for work he was also going back on the explicit assurance he made in the run up to the 1997 election that, "I intend to take a parliamentary salary and no consultancies or directorships whatsoever.[414]" His opponent at that election, Labour's Robert Lehmann, remembers, "One thing that sticks with me...the question was asked to all candidates, 'will you take other paid employment to deflect you from your job?' Bercow at that time gave a categoric assurance. He broke that promise tons of times.[415]" Although Bercow did not end up working in public affairs, he had previously taken up a role as an adviser to the charity Christian Solidarity Worldwide, for which he received a fee of between £10,001 and £15000[416]; and he later became an adviser to Priory Holdings Company No.1, a company linked with the Priory Group, best known for its rehabilitation clinics. For this, Bercow earned a fee of between £35,001 and £40,000[417]. Even though the Priory Group was a UK company and pays UK taxes, the holding company itself was registered in the Cayman Islands.

Money was seemingly more important for Bercow, but there was also a sense that he no longer knew where he was going politically, and the idea of becoming Speaker had been burbling away in the back of his mind for a couple of years. In 2003, it was Bercow's old boss, Jonathan Aitken, who had first suggested to him that he follow the path of Aitken's godfather, Selwyn Lloyd, who was Speaker in the 1970s. In many ways Bercow was a natural fit for the job: he had a brilliant memory, was a true House of Commons man and would enjoy the high profile. But being Speaker would mean the end of Bercow's frontbench ambitions, which were still very much a goer in 2003. Bercow noted the suggestion, but did not seriously consider pursuing it. However, by 2005, and after the "Eton, hunting, shooting, White's" debacle, the available paths were more limited. Suddenly, the Speakership loomed large on the horizon.

Bercow was torn and he knew that he often felt that the benches were greener on the other side: when he was a backbencher he wanted to return to the front line, but when he joined the Shadow Cabinet, he longed for the freedom of the backbenches. "I thought, this situation is a recipe for discontent and unhappiness and that's wrong because Parliament is a great privilege. So I thought: 'Come on, pull yourself together. You're over 40. Make a judgement about what you think you should do and stick to it'.[418]"

In June, Bercow made a decisive step by joining the Chairman's Panel, a rather sedentary place where MPs go out to graze at the end of a distinguished career, but which also provides a useful stopping point for those who want to become Speaker, as panel members chair committees and debates. Bercow's friends were concerned, and Conway confronted him about what he saw as a bad choice. "It's an indication that your active political life is over," he says, "and John had always been partisan[419]." However, Bercow was not to be dissuaded: "I made the judgement that I [would] prefer to work away on the Chairman's Panel and if the chance came to stand as Speaker, I would take it.[420]"

At the time, Bercow was seen as a complete outsider for the job. A whole host of other names, including Sir George Young, Sir Alan Haselhurst and Conway himself were all thought to be in with a chance, but Bercow was not on the radar. Nonetheless, he set out on an underground campaign, making sure he complimented MPs on all sides of the House when they made a good speech and making an effort to get to know as many MPs as possible, including using his fabulous memory to remember their birthdays.

The key point of contention, however, was Bercow's friendliness with the Labour Party. As Ann Widdecombe says, "He decided he wanted the Speakership and went for it, he ingratiated himself with Labour.[421]" For some, this has cast doubt as to whether Bercow's conversion was genuine – they point to his support for Labour's Equality Bill; his friendliness with Harman, Balls and other key Labour figures; and his not-so covert support in the chamber when some Labour MPs spoke as evidence that Bercow's journey was merely a mask for his desire to become Speaker.

However, Bercow had definitely changed his mind on a whole raft of issues – and particularly on social rights, he was far to the left of the Conservative mainstream. As the former Cabinet Minister Peter Hain says, "It wasn't just a tactical thing. It was a genuine conversion on issues like apartheid, race, gender, sexuality and all those things on which he'd actually become more radical as he got older.[422]" It was also unsurprising that with as opinionated and as forthright a wife as Sally, pillow talk would inevitably help to influence Bercow's views. As Conway says, "John's clear close relationship with Sally suggests he's not a closet right-wing Thatcherite posing as a socialist.[423]" Bercow's position had undoubtedly changed – but, for his detractors, this merely provided evidence for their belief that he rarely had well-entrenched ideological positions on any issue it all.

Bercow was indeed a pragmatic politician – and he knew that he needed Labour MPs' votes to become Speaker. His stance in his defection talks with Ed Miliband[424] showed that the Speakership had become his priority and he changed his behaviour accordingly, encouraging Labour to see him as being on their wavelength. It was Bercow at his realistic best, using his new-found political ideas to his advantage, and realising that his future in the higher echelons of the Conservative Party was extremely limited. He did encourage Labour support; he emphasised his areas of agreement with the Labour Party; and he played up his credentials to them; but that does not mean the whole conversion was a mere fabrication designed to win their votes in the Speakership election. Bercow's views had changed – but perhaps they were always less entrenched than his public persona had made out. However, there's no doubt that Bercow made a great play towards the Labour Party, showing them his new-found liberal plumage, knowing that they held the key to his election.

What does, however, separate out Bercow from all others is that he set about winning the Speakership in a manner that was unparalleled in its drive and its organisation. He was determined that the job would not just be decided over drinks in the smoking room – he was not, after all, the most popular MP there; instead he would run a structured campaign and leave no stone unturned in achieving what he wanted.

Having relentlessly set about this task, by 2009 Bercow was in a position of both strength and weakness. He was very popular on the Labour benches and unpopular amongst many Tories; but the real spanner in the works was that Gordon Brown's poll ratings had imploded. As long as Labour had a majority in the House of Commons, Bercow knew that his popularity amongst the government's MPs would give him a very good chance of victory. But by 2009 it had become clear that the incumbent Speaker Michael Martin wanted to hang on till after the 2010 General Election; and Labour was on course for a defeat in that poll. A newly-constituted House of Commons with a Tory majority would be able to pick its own man – and that would almost certainly mean someone – anyone, in fact – other than Bercow. The great gamble would have failed: Bercow seemed set to miss out, leaving little option but to sit in the political wilderness for the rest of his career unless he changed his mind about crossing the floor.

But then, on May 8th 2009, the political world changed.

"The truth about the Cabinet's expenses," roared the front page of the *Daily Telegraph*. It was the culmination of an investigation by the paper based on leaked details of the expenses claims of every MP, but it was also just the beginning. Over the coming weeks, the *Telegraph* would release more damaging details, day by day, of the abuses perpetrated by MPs. The drip drip drip of scandal would send shockwaves through the British political establishment, finishing off the career of one longstanding MP after another and undermining the public's confidence in the politicians who represented them.

The man who acted as the lightning rod for the unrest was Michael Martin. He had managed to completely misjudge the public mood from the start and had spent tens of thousands of pounds of taxpayers' money mounting a legal challenge to the publication of details of MPs' expenses in the first place. Even after losing that battle, the plan had been to publish only a redacted version of MPs' claims, which would have hidden a number of the worst abuses, as key addresses and other information would have been blacked out. The *Telegraph*'s copy, which contained all the gory details, bypassed that decision.

Then Martin signed his political suicide note by calling in the police to investigate the leak of the information to the *Telegraph*. By Sunday 17th May, the Lib Dem leader Nick Clegg was openly calling for the Speaker to resign, whilst the Tory backbencher Douglas Carswell gathered signatures for a motion of no confidence. To make matters worse, the *Telegraph* reporter Jon Swaine discovered that some of the Speaker's officials in the fees office had given permission for an MP to claim interest on the full size of his mortgage even though part of it had been paid off[425]. Martin gave another statement to the Commons, saying sorry "to the extent that I have contributed to the situation,[426]" but in a sign of his disappearing authority, backbenchers repeatedly asked for a motion of no confidence in the Speaker to be debated. That was the final straw and within 24 hours Martin became the first Speaker to be forced from office in 314 years. He told the Commons that he would resign on June 21st, with the new Speaker to be elected the day after. Martin had sounded the starting gun for what would prove to be the most keenly fought contest for the Speakership in history

It was John Bercow who would flourish from the ruins of a Parliament brought to its knees by scandal. So what of Bercow's expenses? In his initial pitch to be Speaker after Martin resigned, Bercow wrote to his campaign manager Martin Salter, "I am asking people to vote not for a Conservative but for a Speaker who has what it takes to restore trust in Parliament and politicians."

But some question whether Bercow can be the one to restore trust in Parliament. After all, he was one of the offenders, having flipped the designation of his second home, thereby avoiding paying tax. From 1997 to 2003, Bercow had quite correctly stated that his second home was in his constituency; and then in May 2003 he sold his constituency home. You might say that as with many things related to John Bercow, it was all Sally's fault. It was she who was too tall for his cottage in Buckingham and Bercow had chivalrously agreed to sell the much-loved property for £162,000. Then, in September of the same year,

Bercow sold his flat in Victoria for £335,000 and bought another nearby for £540,000. Having sold two properties in such a short space of time, one might have expected Bercow to pay capital gains tax on one of them if he had made a profit on them both, as CGT is payable on any home that is not a primary residence.

But not Bercow – he had flipped the designation of his main home so that he did not have to pay any capital gains tax at all. He claimed that he had done nothing wrong and was just following his accountant's advice – and he had acted perfectly legally – but after the *Telegraph* contacted him he volunteered to pay back more than £6,500 in tax[427]. Avoiding CGT, even legally, was a serious charge – and a similar case involving the Cabinet Minister Hazel Blears had done great damage to her credibility.

But Bercow, as if coated head to toe in Teflon, managed to get away with it. It was, in part, down to luck and in part to brilliant timing. When the *Telegraph* team went through his expenses, they saw that Bercow had flipped his main home designation, but they were unsure whether the most damaging allegation – that he had avoided paying tax – was true. He had told them "as I far as I can remember[428]" that he had not paid the tax as his accountant had told him there was "no chargeable gain" and had promised to seek written confirmation from his accountant the following day. Unable to ascertain whether Bercow had made a profit on the homes, the *Telegraph* had to hold fire and ran a page five story headlined, "Would-be Speaker is another "flipper"[429]". It was damaging to Bercow, but in the sea of expenses stories, it did not stand out.

CGT avoidance was a whole other matter and the next day the *Telegraph* reporter Gordon Rayner chased him up, asking for the promised written confirmation on the CGT point. For nine and a half hours, Bercow didn't provide any details. The clock was ticking as the *Telegraph's* printing deadline loomed; there was still nothing from Bercow and the paper was all ready to go to press. But then, at 7.21pm, Bercow finally emailed his reply.

It was quite astounding: he admitted that he had avoided CGT, perfectly legally, but the timing of this admission potentially saved his campaign for Speaker. The decision was taken to put Bercow into the following morning's edition, which meant shoehorning the story in wherever there was space. As it was so late in the day, the production team could only find room for four paragraphs on page 7. If Bercow had replied earlier, his tax affairs would have been a prominent, headline story; instead they were well and truly buried. Rayner was annoyed at seemingly being outwitted by the MP and ruefully told a colleague: "I suppose the only consolation is that everyone'll have forgotten who he is by this time next month.[430]"

Even then, the CGT was not the end of it. The *Telegraph* also discovered that Bercow had tried to charge the taxpayer nearly £1,000 for accountancy advice[431], as well as more than £1,000 in plumbing fees for repairing a blocked lavatory. The receipt shows that the plumber, "Stripped down pump...to find sanitary towel blocked in pump. No responsibility to ourselves. This problem is not down to the installation whatsoever.[432]" The claim was allowed by the Parliamentary fees office, even though under the Additional Costs Allowance payments are to be made "wholly, exclusively and necessarily" to enable MPs to carry out their parliamentary duties[433]. It is not clear how repairing a blocked loo, caused by the fault of Bercow or one of his visitors, helped him to carry out his duties – or at least his Parliamentary ones.

Then, after Bercow was elected as Speaker, it was revealed that, in November 2008, he had claimed £978.51 over and above the cost of his mortgage for his second home – after Bercow switched his mortgage to one on a lower interest rate[434]. It was an accident, but it was no doubt an embarrassment to have to repay the money.

Bercow had also employed Sally continuously from July 2002 until he became Speaker[435] – and although the practice of employing family members has been criticised, this was perfectly within the rules. However, it does seem a little odd that Sally, a New-Labourite, was willing to work for a Conservative MP, even if it was her husband, and the work was non-political. Bercow's research assistant – even on constituency matters – would have had to help him to carry out his work as an MP and the fact that she worked for Bercow indicates either how far his political journey had come, or alternatively an admirable level of self-restraint on Sally's part in being prepared to work for a member of the party she so despises.

Inevitably, employing any spouse can raise eyebrows, however innocent the arrangement and however hard-working the spouse. After Bercow became Speaker, it was announced that it would still be permissible for wives to continue to be on the payroll. But, rather surprisingly, Bercow took great umbrage at the decision: "A complete ban on family members working for MPs, while involving some rough justice for hard-working spouses, would be preferable,[436]" he said. For someone who had spent thousands of pounds of taxpayers' money employing his wife over a period of some 7 years, it was a quite remarkable volte face. Sally had been working for Bercow for their whole married life and yet now Bercow was making clear his opposition to such arrangements.

Then there were Bercow's views on MPs' pay itself. In 2006 he had argued that MPs should be paid on a par with GPs and local authority chief executives[437]. Although a perfectly reasonable view, the effect of Bercow's plan would have been to bump up MPs' salaries by around £45,000, putting them on six figures each for the first time in history. No wonder that Bercow had felt he should look elsewhere for work when MPs' pay was so far below what he thought it should be. But in the light of the expenses scandal, any notion that MPs should be given more money was – for better or for worse – wholly out of kilter with the thrust of public opinion.

Bercow himself admits that his expenses claims were not perfect. "I 'fessed up to the situation," he says. "I am not saying I am some sort of saint but I am certainly saying that it is possible for all of us to put the past behind us by accepting responsibility and committing to thorough and immediate change.[438]" Bercow told Martin Salter in his initial pitch to be Speaker: "The spate of revelations about expenses has infuriated the people." But it was Bercow himself who was part of that problem; he did nothing illegal and he was far from the worst offender, but in the heightened climate of the scandal he was found to be one of those who erred. Even so, despite such transgressions, Bercow has in some respects been proved right. Although his expenses were controversial and have given rise to claims of hypocrisy, they were not so bad as to be a permanent black mark against his name. As Speaker, he has, as promised, been able to put expenses behind him; and although many criticise Bercow's suitability for the role, very few in Parliament do so because of his expenses claims.

***

After Martin resigned, the Bercow camp sprung into action almost immediately. By May 2009, it was an open secret that he wanted to be Speaker and a number of prominent Labour MPs had decided they'd do their best to put him in the chair. Bercow's two greatest allies in the contest were his closest emotional friend Julian Lewis and his closest Labour ally Martin Salter, the MP for Reading West. Although many felt that Lewis would be a natural campaign manager for Bercow as the pair's friendship was sincere and longstanding, Salter was put in charge. What he brought to the role was a decidedly old Labour approach and if there was ever anyone who could deliver the great mass of the Labour Party for Bercow, it was Salter. Theirs was not a natural pairing – in their youths one had been an anarchist and the other a Monday Club member, but it worked. As Salter explained:

"If someone had said to me 30 years ago I'd be running a campaign for someone that held the views that John Bercow held, if only briefly in his teenage years, then I'd have laughed them out the room, but John was quite clearly the most radical, most reforming candidate...I really saw John as a candidate worth working for, worth getting behind – and that's how our rather unique and strange partnership evolved.[439]"

There was also a seemingly spontaneous eruption of support for Bercow's candidacy, with Labour figures like Paul Flynn declaring early on that Bercow would be their preferred choice. "I vaguely knew in the background that he might be interested in the job," recalls the Labour MP Anne Begg, who also declared her support for Bercow in the hours after Martin resigned. "There were rumblings on the Tory benches that John wanted to be Speaker. He never said that to me, but obviously there was a knowledge out there in the ether.[440]" As Bercow stalked the corridors around the Commons, one Labour MP after another came up to him to tell him that they'd back him if he went for the job. The sheer weight of support was overwhelming, and Begg remembers Bercow looking "dazed" and muttering, "that's another

MP who's stopping to support me."[441]

However, although support was growing in Parliament, Bercow was not considered to be a likely winner at that stage – and was not even included on some of the bookmakers' lists. That evening he bumped into *Newsnight*'s Political Editor, Michael Crick, who had earlier tipped Bercow as the frontrunner during a live BBC News special. Crick advised him to get a friend to put a big bet on him to ensure his name was included in the odds list. "His eyes lit up at this and he thanked me," Crick told me.

There had never been any doubt in Bercow's mind that he wanted the job – the big question was whether he would win – and the avalanche of support allowed him to announce his candidacy just over twenty four hours after Martin had resigned. By that time, he had already received the backing of 100 MPs, putting him in a commanding position as the early favourite. A typical view from the Labour side comes from Peter Hain, who says, "He was the only candidate who really understood and was prepared to do something about the need for Parliament to change and come closer to the people[442]."

In his open letter to Salter, Bercow promised to be an advocate for Parliament, saying, "We must make no mistake: Parliament is broken. Disengagement from politics and indifference to what we do have given way to outright public ridicule and contempt." His key promises included two subjects close to his heart: reducing the power of the whips, whose stranglehold he had long disliked; and bolstering the influence of backbenchers. Nor could Bercow avoid having what many might perceive as a jibe at some of those on the Tory benches, saying, "For far too long the House of Commons has been run as little more than a private club by and for gentleman amateurs". Not only would that sort of language further endear him to the Labour MPs whose support he was quickly winning, but it also seemed to be a perfect revenge on the Conservatives who had always treated him as an outcast because he was not "clubbable". Here, Bercow had the chance to tell them that their club was what had put Parliament in the mess in the first place.

But much as Bercow was talking a good talk, party politics was never far from the thinking of some MPs in the election of a supposedly impartial figure. "The Tories have tried to stuff us by taking down one of ours," said a Labour whip, "So we're going to stuff them by voting for someone they hate. But they can't complain; John Bercow is a Conservative MP, if only nominally.[443]" Meanwhile, the Conservatives were desperately searching around for a candidate to stop Bercow. Sir George Young had always been a popular choice, but he was an Old Etonian and some doubted whether one school should produce the Speaker as well as the leader of the Tory Party and the Mayor of London. Crucially, Young was unlikely to persuade enough Labour MPs to back him to be able to overturn Bercow's advantage amongst the biggest party in the Commons.

Ann Widdecombe had already announced that she would stand down from Parliament at the next election, but she agreed to run as a stop gap candidate. "I was opposed to John for a number of reasons," she says. "Our view was anybody but Bercow...the campaign was run by the Labour Party on a 'stuff the Tories" ticket.[444]' But despite topping the popularity stakes in a poll of the public at large[445], Widdecombe was winning little support in the House of Commons. Not only was she a partisan figure, but many were unconvinced by her plan to be in the post for less than a year.

Sir Alan Haselhurst, one of the deputy Speakers, was also a Tory who might have been in with a shot. He had acquitted himself ably as a deputy Speaker, but was another MP to be affected by the expenses scandal, having claimed £12,000 from the taxpayer for his gardening bills. The other Conservatives were Sir Michael Lord – also a deputy Speaker – Sir Patrick Cormack and Richard Shepherd, but none of them was able to win a significant amount of support. Sir Alan Beith, the only Lib Dem, was also considered an outsider.

There was not much choice if Labour wanted to back one of their own, either, as only two members of the party decided to stand. Frank Field, who might have been a popular choice amongst the Tory benches, withdrew because he lacked enough support from his own side: in many ways, he was a mirror of Bercow and his position in the Tory Party. Parmjit Dhanda, who at 37 made Bercow look like quite the elder statesman, was never a likely winner. That left only Margaret

Beckett, who had recently been Foreign Secretary – and had genuine support in the Labour Party. She, too, had been damaged by claims about her expenses and many MPs objected to her perceived lack of impartiality thanks to her long stint as a Cabinet Minister. "She was seen as a status quo candidate who would do the Speaker's job as it had been done," says a Labour frontbencher, "and people thought especially after the expenses stuff that a new chapter was needed."

Most importantly for Bercow, the vast majority of Labour MPs seemed to be wholly untroubled by his controversial right-wing past. They – like Salter – accepted his conversion as a genuine one and seemed to have no qualms backing a man who had once been in the Monday Club. Peter Hain's lifelong interest in South Africa put him at complete odds with Bercow's old mentor John Carlisle, who had called Nelson Mandela a "terrorist", but his view was that, "As a sinner, he'd repented on the apartheid issue,[446]" and, for most Labour MPs, Bercow's views from twenty-five years beforehand were not relevant in deciding whether he would make a good Speaker. The Speakership election therefore provided a cathartic moment where the old John Bercow, the one who had minuted the meetings of the Immigration and Repatriation Committee and who had stood for a place on the Monday Club Executive over issues including immigration, was finally kicked into touch. His reputation had finally moved on.

With such strong support for Bercow from Labour, a number of Conservatives began to look to Beckett as a potential solution – as they would certainly have preferred her to win instead of Bercow. If she won enough support in the first round of voting to squeeze out George Young, she could then come through the middle and take on Bercow in a straight fight. Beckett had the crucial backing of John Spellar, a member of the Labour whips' office, who was trying to corral votes in her favour. As one MP told me, "A whips operation was going on for Beckett [but] others obviously wanted John to succeed, there were groups in the whips office supporting one person or another." In a straight fight between Beckett and Bercow, she might have had enough support from Labour, combined with anti-Bercow votes from the Tory benches, to take her to victory.

The Bercow and Young campaigns took on very different styles, with Salter turning the Bercow bandwagon into a well-oiled machine. "Martin was obsessively campaigning," says Dhanda. "I don't think the Tory grandees know how to campaign for votes, but it was different for John. Martin Salter was the best campaigner, they were like little and large, an odd couple, he never left his side.[447]" It does seem that at least some senior Conservatives underestimated just how likely Bercow was to triumph. "I thought it would be a fight between Haselhurst and George Young," says one. For Widdecombe, the Bercow campaign was "initially very aggressive. At some point they realised that the major concern was not to alienate. There was a visible point where the tone of the campaign calmed down.[448]"

Bercow was throwing himself into the task with his usual vigour, meeting one MP after another for coffee in fifteen minute slots. Nonetheless, despite the relentless approach to winning votes taken by Salter and the Bercow team, it's interesting that Bercow made less of an effort to win over some of his fellow Tories. In fact, many Conservative MPs were not spoken to at all by Bercow, despite the coming vote. As Peter Kilfoyle says, there was, "No attempt to get the Tories to vote for him".[449] Although Bercow did speak to some Tories, even relatively sympathetic MPs like John Redwood, who initially told Bercow he had not made up his mind, did not receive a follow-up.

The decision to concentrate on Labour can be put down, in part, to the fact that the Bercow team knew they were fighting an uphill struggle on the Tory benches. Often when Bercow made the call to ask for their support, the conversation did not go well. One Conservative asked Bercow if he would wear the Speaker's traditional wig and garments, to which Bercow replied, "It isn't me." That did not go down well: "That's the point. It isn't about you, John," the MP replied.

However, there was also a sound tactical reason: Salter and Bercow knew that if Labour delivered, they would win. It made little sense to waste time on the Tories, many of whom hated Bercow with a passion, and run the risk of alienating the Labour supporters who liked Bercow specifically because he was a Tory whom the Tories did not want.

With around two weeks to go before the Speakership election, Bercow had become the odds-on favourite to win – or in the words of

Dhanda, one of his rivals for the job, "John was a shoo-in.[450]" But in the intervening time before the crucial vote on June 22nd it seemed that the contest might be tightening. As the Tories became reconciled to the fact that Young might not be able to win, an increasing number were falling into line behind Beckett. "The weekend before it was hard to make a calculation," says one Tory MP. "We didn't know what Labour MPs were up to, there was speculation that Beckett could pull through."

When nominations closed on the morning of the contest, Bercow put forward a technicolour list of MPs who backed him, with representatives from Labour, the Lib Dems, the SDLP and Plaid Cymru. There was also a Tory on the list – but only one – Charles Walker. Although Bercow could count on the support of both Julian Lewis and his old FCS friend Nick Gibb, both were on the shadow front bench and did not nominate him. If he had failed to secure three nominations from the opposition parties, he would have been ineligible to stand; but any number from his own party sufficed.

At 2.30pm the phony war of the past month finally gave way to the heat of battle. Each candidate addressed the House of Commons, with Bercow recounting the story of one Tory MP whom he had rung up to ask for his support – his powers of mimicry were so strong that MPs were immediately aware that he was aping the Tory grandee Sir Peter Tapsell. "Certainly not, Bercow. You are not just too young, you are far too young, given that, in my judgment, the Speaker ought to be virtually senile.[451]" But behind the laughter, there was a serious amount of work going on, with Salter – assisted by the MPs Andrew Dismore and Jim Sheridan – totting up the numbers. Bercow was also trying to make a serious point, telling his colleagues, "Even youngish men can acquire wisdom as time goes by. In any case, that is all irrelevant to the role of the Speaker whose own political preferences must be permanently cast aside. Throughout my 12 years in this House I have always been passionate about Parliament.[452]"

As Salter added up the figures it was looking good, but nothing could be certain until the first round of ballots had been counted. When MPs eventually voted and the results came in just after 5 o'clock, it confirmed many Tories' worst nightmares – as Bercow supporter

Anne Begg says, "At that stage we thought we were ok.[453]" Bercow topped the poll with 179 votes, easily beating Young into second place with 112. Most importantly, despite vigorous whipping, Beckett had done worse than expected, as the Salter campaign worked its magic on the Labour side. She scored a measly 74, meaning the Tories had little choice but to back Young as the "Anyone but Bercow" candidate, even though it seemed as if Bercow was unstoppable.

Shepherd, Cormack, Lord and Dhanda were all eliminated in the first round, with most of the votes from the first three, Conservative, candidates seemingly switching to Young, and most of Dhanda's – including his own – going to Bercow. When the second round of voting was completed, Bercow was again in the lead – 221 to 174 over Young, with Widdecombe eliminated and Beith, Haselhurst and Beckett all withdrawing. As Bercow was expected to pick up most of Beckett's votes, it seemed inevitable that he would win in the final run off against Young. The Tory benches were in increasing despair and it was at this point that a gloomy David Cameron spoke of his dismay at the events unfolding before him.

Nonetheless, although very many Tories were utterly aghast at their impending doom, at least a few were still backing Bercow. While only four Conservatives – Lewis, Gibb, Walker and Bercow himself – were known to vote Bercow, it's believed that a small number of others did also cast their ballots in his favour. Derek Conway, who had by this time had the party whip taken away from him by David Cameron, was also full-square behind Bercow and was urging his friends in the Tory Party to follow suit. Conway estimates that around 20 Tories in total came down in favour of Bercow, including one member of the Shadow Cabinet. As there was a secret ballot it is impossible to know the exact number, but it was certainly higher than four and almost definitely in double figures. But, despite this support, there can be no doubting the real and visceral dislike of Bercow amongst a vast number of Conservative MPs.

★★★

For Bercow, however, Conservative votes were not his major concern and he knew that the moment of triumph was soon to be upon him. At around half past eight, the final tally was announced to a packed House of Commons. It was to be the result not just of a frantic month of campaigning but also of a number of years of planning. In some ways, too, it was the end result of Bercow's attitude to his life and to politics; of the political journey and of the inability to stay on the Tory front bench, which had collectively pushed him towards the Speakership. Somehow, against all the odds, the eccentric little man had beaten all-comers. To loud cheers, Bercow was announced as the winner, by 322 votes to 271. He had not won over all of the 350-odd Labour MPs, but enough of them had been persuaded – whether by his personal virtues or a desire to stuff the Tories, or both – to carry him to victory.

Bercow sat there on the Tory benches, flanked by Lewis and Walker, literally gulping at the result, seemingly both in relief and in trepidation at the enormity of the victory. From the Labour side there were loud cheers and near-unanimous applause, whereas the reaction from the Conservatives was much more muted. Many Tories sat there in stony-faced silence, refusing to applaud the man they did not want. Bercow was dragged to the Chair by Walker and, at last, the small man was able to sit in that very big seat for the first time.

Bercow thanked MPs for granting him "the greatest honour that I have enjoyed in my professional life", and paid tribute to Sally and his children, before turning to thank, as MPs laughed along, "my beloved mother, who has been keenly interested in the proceedings". Then, to more wry amusement from the Conservatives down below him, Bercow told MPs, "My commitment to this House is to be completely impartial as between members of one political party and another. I will do my best faithfully and honestly…to serve this House in the period ahead.[454]"

For his part, Cameron graciously told Bercow, "It goes without saying that you have the support of those on these Benches," and he summed up the mood amongst his party as he joked, "I also noted, as all colleagues did, what you said about casting away your past political views, and I think that on the Conservative Benches we would say, "Let's hope that includes all of them."[455]"

That night, John and Sally made use of the Speaker's apartments for the first time as they held a celebratory dinner for those who had made the day such a triumph. The atmosphere was understandably euphoric, with plenty of wine and good humour, and Bercow gave a speech thanking each and every person there that night. It was a strange occasion and some guests couldn't escape the feeling that Speaker's House didn't quite feel like home just yet. It was, "All very awkward but very nice,[456]" recalls Begg. As Bercow toasted his remarkable victory, surrounded by some Conservative friends but also a number of left-wing faces across the table, it was as if he had taken on Everest and had at last reached the summit – despite having a number of former friends throwing away his oxygen tanks on the final tilt for the top. 4 years earlier he had been in the wilderness, written off in Parliament as he had been so often in life; yet now he was Speaker. But just as there was unbridled joy in the Speaker's rooms, elsewhere in Parliament anger and dismay abounded. There was a new king, but already his subjects were plotting to take his crown.

21

Learning to Speak

"You can't be a Tory Speaker and common"

"Your reflections and thoughts on precisely how many people voted for me from my party are of no consequence whatsoever," snapped the new Speaker, John Bercow, the morning after the night before. He was giving an interview to ITN's Political Editor Tom Bradby and he was beginning to get angry. As Bradby ran out of time, Bercow snarled at him again: "Briefly, if you want to ask about the second homes allowance, you're very welcome to do so, the answer's very simple – you want to go? Well yes or no? Do you want to ask the question?[457]" As Bradby reflects, "I still don't know quite why he decided to get so cross.[458]"

However, the temper and the anger were a well-known side to Bercow's personality amongst some politicians and friends. "He could be absolutely charming but he was a bit of a Jekyll and a Hyde, says one Conservative MP. "He changed and could become very nasty and rude to colleagues." A friend who was at Bercow's wedding told me he could get, "Disproportionately angry [and] use brutal debating techniques on people who were supposed to be friends. It leaves a very bitter taste. [People] don't expect a perfect specimen of manners and behaviour but he crosses the line."

Equally, though, there were tens of MPs who had just spent the last month working day and night to see Bercow become Speaker. For them and for very many others in Parliament he was, as his Speakership rival Parmjit Dhanda says, "Incredibly courteous and kind throughout.[459]" It seemed that John Bercow as Speaker would be no less divisive than John Bercow as a Conservative MP.

Bercow was certainly very keen to stamp his authority on the role right from the start. First up came his decision to ditch the traditional robes that had been worn even by Labour's Michael Martin. Bercow opted for a simple suit and gown, surprising a number of MPs who have compared his get-up to that of a master at a minor public school. Ken Clarke says he would have preferred the traditional attire, but understands the dilemma. "John in the robes and wig would look a bit comic as he's on the diminutive side. So perhaps from that point of view it's wise he hasn't tried to bring it all back because he'd look like the sorcerer's apprentice.[460]"

The move certainly didn't please the popular former Speaker Betty Boothroyd, who accused Bercow of "letting the side down." She told him: "Nurses like their uniform, boy scouts, girl guides – you've 700 years of history behind you,[461]" but Bercow replied that "he didn't feel comfortable[462]" in the traditional garb. For the Tory MPs who thought that Bercow – the loudmouthed north London boy – didn't fit in, his choice of attire only added to the feeling that he was a little upstart who shouldn't be there in the first place. "They can't believe someone like that would occupy the chair," says Derek Conway. "They understand that Michael Martin was a Labour man – why wouldn't he be common! So he's not above himself. But you can't be a Tory Speaker and common, so there is a large class element.[463]"

At Prime Minister's Questions the day after becoming Speaker, Bercow had his first chance to show what type of Commons he would try to shape. More than once he spoke out, urging MPs to be quiet, saying, "Calm yourself…it is not good for your health." He told them, "There is simply far too much noise. The public do not like it, and neither do I.[464]" It seemed that the man who had once been one of the loudest, most belligerent backbenchers was about to stamp out his former pastime.

Bercow also set down a marker by cutting short a question from a Labour backbencher, saying, that Prime Minister Gordon Brown had "got the gist of it." He was determined to move more quickly through the order paper and give more backbench MPs the chance to ask questions – not just in PMQs but in all debates in the Commons. In this regard Bercow was, and is, a success and business generally moves much more smoothly than before. It's a powerful argument in favour of his style of Speakership. As Julian Lewis likes to say when cheer-leading for Bercow, it's hard for MPs to complain about him when they get to speak more often than before.

The next task was to make the Speaker's rooms fit for a young family. Bercow and Sally had decided to make the apartment their full-time home – complete with its giant antique bed – and although Martin had spent hundreds of thousands of pounds on refurbishing the rooms under Big Ben, there was still work to be done. Despite coming into office on the back of the expenses scandal, the Bercows sanctioned a significant programme of works, totalling £45,000 – nearly double the original budget[465]. It was Sally who seemed to be in charge and she sent in a list of requests after Bercow was elected. Then, just four days later, she emailed in with yet more demands, including for a larger television, with Sky and a DVD player as well as for a number of "scatter cushions". "Having visited today and thought a bit more, I have a number of comments/changes," she wrote. Sally agreed to keep the bathroom carpet, but wanted to update the decoration in a study that was being turned into a playroom for the children. "The existing wallpaper is very office/board-roomy. So, if at all possible, can the walls be redecorated? A wipeable paint strikes me as the best option in here as there may well be lots of sticky fingers?.(!)[466]" A reply came from the official in charge, but he expressed some reservation at the increasing list of requests, saying, "I know you are very mindful of the costs[467]."

Initially, the budget for the work was £11,929 for the refurbishment and £11,500 for "routine maintenance" of rooms that had not been redecorated in the previous five years. Over the next three weeks, the budget for both sets of work increased dramatically, to £20,659 for the refurbishments and £24,923 for the maintenance. Although Bercow did publish the refurbishment figure out of "transparency", the maintenance figure was not revealed – although a spokesman told journalists that, "A lot of the other [renovation] work is beyond the control of the Speaker and is determined by English Heritage and other bodies.[468]"

In the context of past spending on public rooms, the Bercows were relatively reserved – they were certainly counting their pennies by ordering some of their furniture from IKEA; and there was a need to make the rooms safe for their children, including their dyspraxic son Oliver. However, the scale of the works inevitably left them open to criticism – and while the Bercows may have felt totally justified in undertaking the redecoration, the incident demonstrated their increased level of scrutiny; and that knives would be sharpened at even the slightest foot out of line. It was perhaps in recognition of the increased public interest in his life that Bercow decided to hire his own special adviser, the journalist Tim Hames. But at a cost of an estimated £107,000 a year, the appointment itself only brought more criticism in the press – and raised further questions as to how Bercow could reconcile such expenditure with his claim to be the "clean break" candidate.

Hames's appointment also marked a change in emphasis of the role of the Speaker. In years gone by the Speaker had tended to be more introspective and concerned almost solely with the running of the House of Commons. The irony for Bercow, who seems to be most alive when speaking himself, is that the Speaker rarely has much to say in Parliament – and it was a concern that had been raised by some of his friends in the Commons when he decided to go for the Speaker's chair. As Peter Hain told me, "He was incredibly vicious in the Commons, a good Parliamentarian, one of the most impressive speakers without notes. I said, 'You're used to doing that. Are you going to be able to do the job of Speaker when you can't really be very vocal in policy issues and on political questions?'" Although Bercow was more than willing to accept the constraints of the job, it is hardly surprising that he focussed more on the Speaker's role as the House of Commons' ambassador, touring the country to promote Parliament. While some colleagues might have sneered, it is hard to deny that Bercow has had much success in this way, talking about the House of Commons to schools and community centres up and down the country. Just as Bercow enjoyed touring round as the FCS leader, so as Speaker he has taken up that mantle once again. While the policies of his time in the FCS have long gone, the same zeal is there.

Even with this increased role, the confines of the Speaker's Chair were – in some ways – restrictive for Bercow, who had for so long been outspoken on so many issues. So it came as no great surprise when the old Bercow came through – albeit momentarily – in the autumn. During a session of the British Youth Parliament – which was being held, thanks to Bercow, in the House of Commons chamber for the first time, Mr Speaker criticised a British political party. Despite the supposedly independent nature of his role, Bercow felt confident enough to call the BNP a "poison which we could well do without." Although few would disagree with the opinion, it was nonetheless a breach of the Speaker's impartiality. For Bercow, he was, "Under absolutely no obligation whatsoever to be impartial as between the forces of democracy on the one hand and the forces of evil on the other,[469]" but it was still a decision that flew in the face of a long-held tradition.

Bercow, though, did genuinely seem to want to use the power of his position as Speaker to make a positive impact. He allowed charities to use his apartments to hold receptions; he privately supported the election of select committee chairmen, thereby helping to shore up their role as critics of government action; and he set up the Speaker's Advisory Council on Public Engagement, which looked at how to restore public trust in politics. His desire for reform was genuine and he wanted to take the message out to ordinary people.

The more difficult challenge, though, was winning over MPs, with many – particularly Conservative ones – waiting to pick on any sign of bias from their new Speaker. When Ed Balls – with whom he had worked on the Bercow Review – made a number of pronouncements about his education white paper to the press before telling the House of Commons, Bercow failed to tick him off. For some Conservatives this was a sign of Bercow's friendliness towards those who had put him in the Speaker's chair, but the incident also shows that Bercow faced an almost impossible task. As someone who had to intervene against MPs on all sides of the Commons, it would always be easy for his enemies to point to particular decisions and argue that they showed Bercow's bias.

Even so, Bercow did not make things easy for himself. By early 2010, when he was beginning to settle into the role and starting to assuage some of the concerns held by the less strident anti-Bercow

MPs, Mr Speaker suddenly seemed to up the ante. First came an unseemly clash with the ardent Bercow-hater Simon Burns, who had been his whip earlier in the Parliament. As Burns shouted from the benches during Prime Minister's Question Time, Bercow turned to him and said that his heckling was, "As boring as it is boorish,[470]" an incredible and inflammatory insult. The response from the Tory benches was very telling, with a number of MPs jokingly slapping their order paper on Burns's head and shouting "naughty boy!" in brazen defiance of the Speaker. Then, the Shadow Education Secretary Michael Gove – one of the key members of David Cameron's inner circle – made a point of going over to Burns to shake his hand. By the end of PMQs, Burns had received at least four texts of support from fellow MPs and he heard not a word of reprimand from the front bench.

Soon afterwards Bercow faced more claims of bias as the question of party funding cropped up in the Commons. When the Tory front-bencher Theresa Villiers questioned the Labour Party's links to the Unite union in the context of the British Airways strike, Bercow ruled the point as out of order, saying that the urgent question before the Commons was about the strike and not party funding. Soon afterwards, the old Labour MP Dennis Skinner was called to speak – and asked about the Conservative donor Lord Ashcroft's tax situation – without any objection from Bercow, despite much anger from the Tory backbenches. One of those backbenchers, Mark Pritchard, then told the Commons that Unite leaders should be cutting their own pay, at which point the Labour Minister appeared to pause and to glance at Bercow, who ruled the question out of order. Pritchard was furious: "Moments ago you rebuked me, I think unfairly…after my question there was a pause, whereupon I saw the Minister of State appear to prompt you. I'm sure that was not the case because of course you can rebuke me in your own right.[471]"

Bercow became equally angry, telling Pritchard, he would be "sensible and rational" to move on as Bercow had seen "no sign whatsoever" from the government bench[472]. It did little to help Bercow's standing amongst Conservatives, although the irony is that Bercow had been allowing many more urgent questions – which call a minister to account by forcing him to take a question on a particular topic in the Commons – and with Labour in power, the Conservatives were the beneficiaries. But perception was perhaps as important as reality, for the Speaker relies on having the respect of MPs. Rightly or wrongly, many Tories still believed that Bercow had it in for them.

However, perhaps the most important change in the life of the Bercows came when Sally joined the social networking site twitter in January 2010. A month earlier she had "come out" as a politician by giving her full and frank interview – in which she admitted to having been an alcoholic who had one-night stands. Joining twitter was partly a reaction to that interview – she told me she did not want to be pigeonholed by her confessions[473] – and also part of the same plan to increase her profile. Sally was sick of not having her own voice and like her husband she could hardly be described as a shrinking violet. She had always played second fiddle to him but now he was Speaker, it was her turn. Sally wanted to be a bona fide Labour politician and was – in the words of a friend – "wound up like a coil" about the idea; she was determined to get her skeletons out of the closet and then build a career for herself.

By joining twitter, Sally certainly got her personality across, giving her ever-increasing band of followers all sorts of insights into her life. Most things seemed to have an anti-elitist, anti-Conservative slant, with a typical missive being: "Told off for propping open door of Speaker's House with Tesco bags. Would Waitrose bags have been more seemly?[474]" She also started coming up with uses for old Hansards – the record of the business of the House of Commons over which her husband presided – with suggestions including, "Place a pile in front of loo = a handy stepstool for your toddler"; and, "Wrap in a sheet of fine-grain cork. Stick photo of fave Tory on front (optional). Hang on wall. Throw darts.[475]"

Unsurprisingly, Sally created quite the furore when she talked about her life and that of her husband, or "Mr B" as she liked to call him. Now the public had insights into their daily routine, their political "ding-dongs" and their mother's day arrangements. Traditional Tories were horrified, thinking that Sally's tweeting was completely inappropriate for "Mrs Speaker". For Sally, she had the right to speak out.

Inevitably, though, her "personal" views began to impinge on her husband's role. Shortly before Bercow was due to welcome the polygamist South African President Jacob Zuma to the Palace of Westminster on his official visit to the UK, Sally tweeted, "President & Mrs Zuma are here later... Pretty sure it's the same Mrs Zuma I met last night... If it's not the same Mrs Zuma, I'll feel as if I am being disloyal to the one I met last night.[476]" Her comments were indiscreet at best and were potentially politically embarrassing for her husband. "What a stupid thing to say," says one former friend, who was a guest at the Bercows' wedding. "It flies against every diplomatic principle, it's so puerile."

Nonetheless, Sally's decision to tweet was welcomed by many in the Conservative Party, who saw it as a stick with which they could beat her husband. In the early days, a number of Tories tried to convey positive messages to her in the hope that she would tweet on and continue to cause problems for Bercow. Sally has kept going and she has, as predicted, embarrassed her husband at times. He says that she is not his "chattel" and that she should be free to do as she wishes, but a number of his close friends have been very worried about Sally's effect on Bercow's political profile. Clearly, in private, there were serious discussions between the Bercows about the direction Sally was taking. Her burgeoning public profile was beginning to have an impact on his – with some rather uncomfortable results.

But in early 2010, Sally was not Bercow's primary worry, as he came under attack on two other fronts. Sally's twittering certainly didn't help when there were enemies out there, but there was a much more disturbing bigger picture: it seemed that having fought his way to the Speaker's Chair, Bercow could end up being kicked out before he'd even managed to warm the leather of the seat.

22

The Battle for Buckingham

"My Hero"

It was the morning of May 7th in Aylesbury, and the Parliamentary candidates for Buckingham were gathering to hear the result. A plane crash the day before had almost killed one of those on the ballot paper – and had nearly cost John Bercow his job – and the eyes of the media were firmly fixed on the dull civic centre, waiting to see if a political career would come crashing down in front of their eyes as dramatically as the plane the day before. But when the acting returning officer announced the results, the Speaker seeking re-election came out on top, with a majority of more than 12,500. The question is how, in the face of a concerted and high-profile attempt to unseat him, John Bercow was still flying high.

★★★

In the 2005 election, John Bercow had been elected in one of the safest seats in the country, with a majority of more than 18,000. Having been through such a monumental battle to become Speaker, Bercow might have thought that he would, at the very least, face an easy ride in Buckingham, where the three main parties announced that he would not be opposed. It was to be the most politically compelling election of a lifetime, but in Buckingham the voters were sheltered from this political fire-fight. Only there, of all the constituencies in Britain, was there no possibility of voting for someone who might end up in a future government.

The convention that Speakers are unopposed is one that has only been observed irregularly at best – particularly when there is a former

Conservative in the chair. Bercow would have been all too aware of
this, as his inspiration, Selwyn Lloyd, was twice opposed in his constituency. Moreover, the reason given for opposing Speaker Peel back
in the nineteenth century and then Lloyd himself was that their constituency boundaries had changed – meaning voters in the new areas
should have the chance to give their verdict on their new MP. Bercow's
Buckingham constituency had likewise been significantly altered since
the 2005 election by boundary changes.

If anything, Bercow might have had an easier time of it if Labour
and the Lib Dems had run against him in defiance of the somewhat
flimsy precedent. Even standing as the Speaker seeking re-election
rather than as a Conservative, Bercow would have had a much more
predictable battle to fight if the other two main parties stood in his
way: after all, the true blues of Buckingham simply wouldn't stomach
a Labour or Liberal Democrat MP.

Bercow was vulnerable, and a number of Tory MPs began working
on the idea of putting up a Conservative against him – either in an
official or unofficial capacity. Some members of the whips' office
proposed approaching Howard Flight, who had been beaten by
Bercow and his helicopter back in the selection meeting in 1995. Flight
had since become an MP before being deselected as a candidate by
Michael Howard in 2005 for suggesting that the Tories would go
further in their spending cuts than admitted in their manifesto. Flight
was credible and known and liked by the Buckingham Tories, but he
did not want to go along with the scheme as Bercow had been
personally loyal to him after his de-selection. The idea soon died a
death, not least because the party leadership were not keen on it either.

When the main parties vowed to stay away, a number of independents began to declare their interest. First amongst them was Patrick
Phillips, a former High Sheriff of Buckinghamshire, who wanted to
offer a "Conservative" alternative to Bercow. As Phillips explains:
"The prospect of Mr. Bercow being returned unopposed was deeply
unappealing to me...we all resented having our right to vote denied,
and...Mr. Bercow's political views have changed significantly from
those on which he was originally selected for the seat... Far from being
'Son of Tebbit' he, accompanied by his Labour activist wife, now

seems rather more like 'Son-in-Law of Gordon Brown'.[477]"

The election was becoming increasingly unpredictable and there was a chance that a particularly high-profile independent might be able to corral enough anti-Bercow votes to unseat him. The new Speaker was all too aware of the danger and he gathered an experienced campaign team, including his former agent Gordon Bell, with the aim of shoring up support amongst local Conservatives.

However, an even greater threat soon emerged as Nigel Farage, UKIP's charismatic leader, announced in September 2009 that he would resign the party's leadership to run against Bercow. The decision was not made out of personal animosity – Farage barely knew Bercow, although their paths had crossed some time beforehand at meetings of the Eurosceptic Bruges Group. It was rather that Farage spotted an opportunity. "My philosophy has always been give things a go," he told me. "I'm a gambler."

Farage knew that his decision would cause a media circus – but as a credible and high-profile politician he also had high hopes of actually winning. He was a perfect fit for Buckingham – an affable chap who set about getting to know the constituency by having a pint in each of its pubs. Importantly, David Cameron had not yet endorsed Bercow and Farage hoped that local Conservatives would support him instead. At least some Tories seemed open to the idea – and there was some serious organising going on amongst those who saw Farage as the perfect weapon with which to finish off Bercow. A number of Conservatives discussed a vote swapping plan, which would have allowed Tory voters in Buckingham to cast their ballots in favour of Farage in return for UKIP voters backing Conservatives in marginal constituencies across the country. As one Conservative activist told me, "It's a useful indicator of how much [Bercow] is hated." The idea was given serious consideration and a PR agency was commissioned to determine how the plan could best be put into action. However, it ultimately floundered, because, as Farage says, "A chap with a 1st in PPE from Oxford thinks it's frightfully clever, but in reality it's never going to work...every person in the polling station knows it's a first past the post system, so what happens next door is not their affair."

But even if all this had worked out for Farage, he would still have

faced an uphill struggle – not least because he had badly underestimated the popularity of his opponent in Buckingham. While Bercow may
have been one of the least popular Tory MPs amongst Conservatives
nationally, he was undoubtedly extremely well-regarded by many
people in his constituency. As Farage says, "I have never been
anywhere and met a more popular local MP. He worked very hard in a
way that most MPs wouldn't. You can paint it in a positive or a negative
light, but you can't deny it exists. I came face to face with it and was
very surprised…not just with the local Tory blue rinsers, [but] also all
the old dears shopping in centre of Buckingham.[478]" Such was the
support for Bercow that even amongst UKIP supporters, Farage was
finding it hard to get people to back him over their sitting MP. "There
was one response that sticks in my mind very strongly. A door we
knocked on, there was an old boy in his 80s, a Navy veteran. We
chatted away and he said, "Mr Farage, I absolutely endorse and
support everything you stand for, but of course I've got to vote for John
Bercow." "Why?" "Because John's done so much for the [Royal
British] Legion."[479]"

Speaking to Bercow's constituents, this author has heard one tale
after another of his brilliance as a local MP. A typical story comes from
Sue Farrington Smith, who runs the charity Brain Tumour Research.
"He's my hero!" she declares. After Farrington Smith visited Bercow
in a constituency surgery, he decided to help her raise funds for
research into treating brain tumours. Bercow organised an
adjournment debate in Parliament, held a reception in the House of
Commons and even set up the All-Party Parliamentary Group on brain
tumours, becoming its first chairman. "I am more than happy to stick
my neck out and say what a fantastic chap he is," she says. "When he
gets behind something he puts a lot of effort in, he always makes time
for us even though he is very busy.[480]" She says that – in part thanks to
Bercow's contribution – funding for brain tumours has increased by
millions of pounds a year. Another example comes from a constituent
who had financial difficulties. "I met him when I had a problem with
the VAT authorities," he told me. "They owed us £75,000 and they
wouldn't pay – it went on for 2 years. I got John's help, he wrote and
although he didn't absolutely resolve it, he was totally on my side.

[Eventually] I got the £75,000 back."

The final nail in Farage's coffin came when David Cameron decided to publicly endorse Bercow. For someone who found Bercow's election so unpalatable that he briefly congratulated an MP for quitting the House of Commons, Cameron hardly seemed a likely ally for the Speaker. But while Bercow may not have been Cameron's favourite person, he was annoying rather than dangerous. "The heart says kill John Bercow, the head says not," an aide close to the Conservative leader told me after Farage had said he would run. "Cameron wants John Bercow to win...the Tories fear UKIP. The nuisance factor of Bercow is outweighed."

So it was that in February 2010 Cameron issued a statement urging, "All Conservatives – and, indeed, supporters of all parties and of none – to vote for the Speaker, John Bercow." The intervention was decisive. Although the Buckingham Association had largely been supportive of Bercow, it was now impossible for any of them to publicly back Farage and hope to have a future in the Conservative Party. Likewise national Conservatives who might have spoken out – and many had, including Conservative Home's Tim Montgomerie, who said he would be "tempted[481]" to vote for Farage – were firmly warned off from doing so. Farage says, "In the end we came up against a campaign of 'Oh of course we want Cameron to win.' For your average working family or retired couple in Buckingham, they can't stand the Labour Party and wanted Cameron to be Prime Minister. They saw Bercow as being their man... Pre-Cameron, he was very nervous, post-Cameron he was very relaxed.[482]"

But Bercow's problems weren't over quite yet. In early 2010, the former Tory MEP John Stevens announced he was planning to run in Buckingham. Stevens's campaign was joined by a number of others from across the political spectrum, including some Liberal Democrats – although this was hardly a surprise, as Stevens had joined the Lib Dems after resigning from the Tory Party over its position on Europe. It was clear, though, that they were united by one thing only: a desire to get rid of John Bercow.

There were a number of initial problems with Stevens running. Primary amongst these was that he was an avowed Europhile – putting him at odds with both the good, Conservative-minded people of Buckingham, and UKIP itself. Moreover, Stevens had also left it late to enter the campaign: with only 5 months or so before polling day, Stevens had barely even got going.

Nonetheless, Stevens was convinced that he might win. He set up the "Buckingham Campaign for Democracy", sending out thousands of leaflets to voters across the constituency. He also deployed Flipper – a man dressed up in a dolphin costume – to follow Bercow around as a reminder that he had 'flipped' his second home on expenses. As a tactic it was juvenile and unsubtle, but people began to sit up and take notice. We must, however, spare a thought for whoever had the job of being inside that dolphin costume. With an election in late spring, it must have been sweltering in there – although the lucky volunteer did receive a fair amount of airtime. Flipper was last seen making an appearance on *Newsnight*'s "Motorway Man" segment after the Election: as Lembit Opik played a disconsolate refrain on the harmonica, the two compared their bad luck in being out of a job.

Soon Stevens began to outflank Farage – but Bercow was a much harder nut to crack. If anything, it seemed that by crowding the field Stevens had served only to improve Bercow's chances in the contest, as the anti-Bercow vote was split between two credible alternatives. However, the contest was definitely narrowing and key figures began to back Stevens's campaign. Amongst those was Bercow's predecessor in Buckingham, George Walden, and Martin Bell, who had seized Tatton from Neil Hamilton in a famous victory in 1997. Bell told the press, "We need to restore public trust in public life. I believe that the Speaker's constituency would be a very good place to start.[483]"

Amidst all this, one must feel a large amount of sympathy for Bercow. Stripped of his party organisation and funding, he must have felt somewhat stranded on his own. With Gordon Bell and a large number of local Conservatives helping his campaign, there was a degree of continuity, but there was also a significant danger. As Selwyn Lloyd had put it back in 1974, "The difficulty lay in explaining in sufficiently clear terms the unique position of the Speaker: why, on election as Speaker, he had to become non-party; why he had to be re-elected as an MP; whether, if he was, he would be re-elected Speaker;

whether voters…were voting for him as MP or Speaker or both. Quite a number thought I would continue as Speaker even if defeated in the fight to continue as MP[484]".

For Bercow, the challenges were the same. His riposte was to say that as Speaker he was uniquely well-placed to stand up for his constituents, arguing:

"I have continued to represent all my constituents, taking up thousands of new cases over the last year… The unparalleled access to Ministers that I enjoy has enabled me to provide an enhanced service to the people of the Buckingham constituency.[485]"

Although Bercow said that little had changed, a series of errors on his website gave the lie to his position. The text said, "He [Bercow] has been a member of the International Development Select Committee since November 2004. He is co-Chair of the All Party Parliamentary Group on Burma, vice-Chair of the All Party Groups on the Prevention of Genocide, Africa and Sudan. He is also Secretary of the All Party Group on Human Rights." After the election, his personal website continued to carry many of the same claims.

However, this paragraph is incorrect. Bercow had been a member of all these groups, but resigned on becoming Speaker. Although these unintentional errors arose from a bad copy and paste job, they also showed Bercow's dilemma. He needed his constituents to accept that he could still lobby on their behalf, because if they didn't, their next question would be: 'why should I vote for him?'

No wonder that Bercow raised the prospect of the Speaker being immune from challenge at General Elections, under a system which would make him the "Member for St. Stephen's", elected by the House of Commons and with no need to go to a constituency and ask for their votes[486]. It reflected the essential unfairness of the position – that the Speakership made him a target, but his hands were tied by that role, too. Although he had to ask the people of Buckingham to vote for him, Bercow realised that there was a certain absurdity about the whole process. The system was at fault and he had to make the best of a bad job.

One notable absentee from the campaign was Sally, who rarely went to Buckingham in the lead up to the election. As she put it with her usual openness, "I freely admit to having escaped, once again, the political wife "stuff" – basically because: a) my husband is no fool – his constituency is overwhelmingly Tory, so I, and it, are hardly a match made in heaven; b) I can but dream of being a Sarah Brown or a SamCam – namely more of an asset than a liability.[487]" Clearly her husband's opponents agreed, with a UKIP insider saying, "The more Sally Bercow speaks the more she inadvertently becomes one of UKIP's most potent political weapons in recent memory.[488]"

Sally had also been concentrating on running for Westminster City Council – as a Labour candidate of course – but inevitably found herself in hot water. Her twitter posts had continued and her frankness was again controversial. She wrote one update saying that while out canvassing she had been "heckled by a couple of smack heads in a stairwell[489]", before deleting the comment. Nonetheless, it was too late, and she was forced to admit it was "just another Sally cock up," tweeting, "Wish I hadn't used term smack head now – gives wrong impression. Pls don't think I'm being judgmental – def not as far as drugs concerned [sic].[490]"

That wasn't her only set-to over twitter during the campaign, either. Another run in was with the "Cameron cutie" Joanne Cash, the Tory candidate for the marginal seat of Westminster North. Sally claimed that Cash had said canvassing was "like a ghastly cocktail party", which Cash vigorously denied. She accused Sally of lying, writing, "How dare you, actually. Bloody cheek.[491]" Sally responded by promising to campaign for Cash's opponent, Karen Buck. It would hardly have been a surprise move – Buck and Sally were to be found in a pretty similar position on the political pendulum – but it showed that even in the run up to a tricky vote for her husband, Sally had no intention of keeping quiet.

Back in Buckingham, as election day neared, Bercow was soon to find out if the first major threat to his position as Speaker would succeed. On the morning of May 6th, as the voters started going to the polls, Nigel Farage began his final electioneering push. Never one to go quietly, he had hired a plane to carry a UKIP banner. But after take off, the banner became tangled in the tail and the plane dramatically nose-dived to the ground. A photographer who was meant to be capturing the banner in its airborne glory instead had to run towards the wreckage, where he feared both Farage and the pilot were dead. Miraculously, both survived, and Farage was pulled, bloodied and dazed from the plane, still in his UKIP rosette, pinstripe suit, blue shirt and tie. He suffered broken ribs, a chip to his spine and damage to his sternum, but the injuries were not life-threatening. They did, however, put him out of action for some time and he had to watch the rest of proceedings from his hospital bed. Bercow behaved magnanimously and rang Farage to wish him the best and check on his prognosis.

Bercow must have been grateful that Farage survived. Clearly on a personal level he would have wished his opponent no harm, but Farage's death would also have come at a very high price to Bercow himself. If Farage had been killed as the plane came down, the election in Buckingham would have had to have been postponed for a number of weeks. That would have been catastrophic, as the Commons elects its Speaker as the very first act after it returns for the new Parliament. Bercow would have still been hanging around in Buckingham, waiting for the election to happen. In 2005, the contest involving the MP Sir Patrick Cormack was postponed following the death of an opponent; but he was deemed to have still been in "continuous service" as an MP, allowing him to maintain his place in the queue to be Father of the House. However, Bercow's situation would have been very different, as when it came to electing the Speaker, he would simply not have been a permissible option. Bercow would not have been an MP, and so the Commons would have been forced to elect someone else. There may well have been a great deal of protesting from the Bercow camp, but with so many opponents in the Commons looking for a chance to get him out, it's unlikely that the Tories would have been in any mood to stretch the rules for him. So whilst Bercow had ridden out the opposition of countless political figures over a period of twenty-five years, all that was so very nearly undone by a light aircraft and a UKIP banner.

Interestingly, that loophole had in fact been spotted by some of the strongest Bercow-haters a short time before Farage's plane had come down. They briefly considered the idea of putting up a candidate in Buckingham who was likely to die soon after nominations had closed.

But there was not enough time to put the plan into effect – finding a willing person who fitted the criteria would obviously be very difficult – and there were also some obviously serious ethical problems with the plan.

★★★

When voting closed on Election night, the position across the country was uncertain. The exit polls predicted a hung Parliament, with Cleggmania having seemingly come to nothing. It was a long night, but in the small hours, as the Tories saw one high-profile candidate in London after another fall short – including, pleasingly for Sally, Joanne Cash in Westminster North – it was confirmed that the country was heading for a hung Parliament.

However, as election night turned into election morning, it was still unclear which party, or parties, would form the government and it was to be many days before the coalition finally gave the country a new Prime Minister. In Buckingham, too, there was no news. That was because, even at 5am, the count had not yet started. Buckingham had to share a counting hall with the neighbouring Aylesbury constituency, which had first dibs on the space and declared its own result overnight. Buckingham had to wait until the next morning to begin. There were around 20 constituencies due to declare on the Friday afternoon and Bercow's result was by far the most high-profile. With a continuing marathon of television coverage taking place, it would be a very public humiliation if he were to be unseated.

However, as the journalists, candidates and assorted political hacks gathered at the civic centre early on Friday morning, it was obvious that Bercow was home and dry. Stevens had the look of an angry man as the news came in that the real battle was between him and Farage for second place, and he told me, irritably, "We should have done much better". UKIP too, devoid of their talisman, seemed to be both bereft and dejected. Eventually Bercow and Sally arrived at the count, all smiles and seemingly relaxed. Sally kept saying that she was much more worried about the vote the following week in the House of Commons, where MPs could yet bring Bercow back down to earth.

When the results were announced, there was no surprise as to the winner. The Parliamentary green rosettes bristled with joy as John Bercow, the Speaker seeking re-election, was duly re-elected, with a reduced but still substantial majority of more than 12,500. There was nonetheless an air of discontent, not least amongst the huge pile of spoilt ballot papers, which numbered more than one thousand. Bercow himself recognised the, "Surprise, confusion or plain discontent" of many voters at the rather bizarre choice that had been put before them at the election.

Certainly Bercow must have been immensely grateful that both Stevens and Farage were on the ballot. Stevens had come second, with 10,331, beating the ailing Farage into third with 8,401. Their votes together would have run Bercow much closer – and if the other independents and spoilt ballots were added into the equation, Bercow might even have lost. If a truly unifying independent candidate had stood in Buckingham, Bercow would have been in more serious danger.

The figures suggest that Bercow is therefore not out of the woods yet – he could still be in trouble in Buckingham at the next General Election. While he is very popular with many constituents, the maths shows that he will have a very close battle on his hands if the anti-Bercow vote is united behind a well-funded, plausible and charismatic figure. Nobody, though, knows who such a person might be and both Farage and Stevens have indicated that they will not run again in Buckingham.

The AV referendum adds another dimension to the story. Sally is a highly vocal supporter of switching away from the first past the post system, but it could cause immense discomfort to her husband if she is granted her wish. In Buckingham, perhaps more than anywhere else, the impact of AV can be readily divined, thanks to the fact that the main parties did not stand there. The votes in 2010 were broadly divided along the lines of 'a vote for Bercow' and 'a vote against Bercow', but the anti vote was split by the large number of independent candidates. Although Bercow maintains significant support, he did not quite make the 50% threshold. AV would allow anti-Bercow voters to pass on their second and third preferences to other independent candidates, helping to crystallise the vote. It might not be enough to unseat him, but it would make the result much closer and therefore lead to a much more nervous campaign next time around.

Bercow's victory in 2010 was nonetheless a moment of triumph. As he gave his acceptance speech this author could not help but notice Sally's behaviour on the floor of the civic centre, just a metre or two away. When Bercow spoke, she clapped and nodded her head with a zealot-like vigour. But more than that: Sally was surrounded by Tories – the very people she barracks every week on twitter. Yet here she was putting on a display of backslapping camaraderie that was totally irreconcilable with the Tory-bashing rhetoric she churns out. Although she has often backed both Bercow and Labour, it still seemed a little bit like she was back at Conservative Party conference, singing the praises of Mrs Thatcher. Or else, she was putting on a very good show.

23

Survival

"He doesn't have two horns and a tail"

Even as the newly anointed Mr Speaker was being dragged to the chair, the plots against him were beginning to take shape. Bercow's allies worked hard to shore up his support and close down any possible challenges, but there was also a real and significant groundswell of opinion against him, led by a rump of MPs who would do just about anything to get rid of him.

In the days after Bercow's election up to 50 MPs fell into this most hardcore category – led publicly by Nadine Dorries and Simon Burns, who both refused to shake Bercow's hand when they took the oath as Parliament resumed in 2010. There were certainly other MPs who felt as strongly, even if they did not express their views in the open. The group was not large enough to organise a coup by itself, but it was a significant power base from which to start.

There were a number of possible options open to the plotters, but for the hardcore Bercow haters the equation was simple. Bercow was foist upon the Tory Party by Labour, they thought, and the majority of Tory MPs did not want Bercow. Simply, then, they just had to wait until the Tories won the 2010 General Election, and the new, Conservative majority would kick him out. The battle lines were drawn, with D-Day set for May 2010, when the House of Commons would re-convene after the election.

Sally's attitude at the count in Buckingham was quite telling and the Bercows were obviously worried. The ideal opportunity for the plotters – and the biggest threat for Bercow – presented itself in the shape of a House of Commons formality, whereby the Speaker has to be re-elected at the beginning of each Parliament. Normally, MPs just shout their agreement and no division is called, but if enough MPs were to go against the convention and signal their opposition to Bercow's re-election, a formal vote would be required – and then, all bets would be off. MPs who would have just nodded their re-approval of Bercow, albeit through gritted teeth, might well change their minds if they were given an active choice whether to back him or knife him. If Bercow were to lose that vote, he would be out – an unprecedented humiliation for a Speaker.

A significant degree of pressure was being brought to bear on the Conservative leadership in the months before May 2010. In March, around the time of Bercow's controversial attack on Simon Burns and the furore over the BA strike, Cameron had a meeting with Sir Michael Spicer, the Chairman of the Tories' backbench 1922 Committee, at which Sir Michael urged his leader not to force Conservative MPs to back the Speaker in a public ballot. Around the same time, one MP tells me, "Cameron was in the Members' Dining Room and got an earful from people at lunch saying that there had to be a free vote and they [didn't] want him." When questioned about Bercow's position, a spokesman for Cameron said he "supported the office of the Speaker"[492], rather than explicitly supporting Bercow himself – and the response mirrored Cameron's words in the dying days of Michael Martin's Speakership.

But the sands had shifted by the time Parliament finally reconvened after the General Election on May 18th 2010. It was a momentous day, on which David Cameron entered the Commons as Prime Minister for the first time, taking his seat alongside his new coalition partner, Nick Clegg. However, those who disliked Bercow were ready to make their protest; and Dorries and the Labour MP Kate Hoey had been openly proposing alternatives for the job, including the former Liberal Democrat leader Ming Campbell and the Tory Sir Alan Haselhurst, in the hope that these choices would tempt MPs to vote against Bercow.

But the positives for the plotters ended there. For one, their campaign was distinctly disorganised, a collection of like-minded MPs rather than a synchronised unit. Like most MPs, they had also had other significant battles to fight in their own constituencies over the previous few weeks. If the plotters had had more of an opportunity to work on their colleagues in the corridors round Westminster, they might have had a better chance of success. Instead, the group was disparate.

Another factor standing in their way was the Conservative leadership. Just as David Cameron had stepped in to shore up Bercow's position in Buckingham with an endorsement, once again the potential fate of the Speaker lay in the hands of the man he had so insulted a few years beforehand. There had never been an appetite amongst Cameron's inner circle to get rid of Bercow – for, as a source close to him told me, "The reputational risk of being seen as interfering outweighs the benefits." It was inconceivable that after thirteen years in opposition, the very first act of a new Conservative government would be to get rid of an incumbent Speaker. It was for that reason that the MP James Gray felt that there "was no chance whatsoever of a challenge[493]". John Redwood agreed. A few months before the election he told me: "There's still unhappiness, but...it's not appropriate and would look very unreasonable. It is a strange use of the Conservative majority to make the first row of the Parliament to depose a Speaker. A new government will need all the political capital it can get, I wouldn't recommend doing it.[494]"

On a purely personal level, the General Election result could scarcely have been any better for Bercow. If there had been a huge Conservative majority, Cameron might well have felt bullish enough to allow his MPs to tackle Bercow head on. Instead, needing to broker agreement for a coalition, the Tory leadership was inevitably focused on shoring up its political capital with the public for more important moments. There was no chance whatsoever that Cameron would agree to an attack on Bercow in the unchartered territory that faced him in the earliest days of the coalition. The large number of new members in the Commons – well over two hundred – also stacked the odds in Bercow's favour. Many of them had had no prior dealings with him and so had no appetite to depose him on their first day in Parliament.

However, by May 2010, the biggest obstacle to Dorries, Burns et al was that support for the anti-Bercow camp had gradually fallen away in the crucial eleven months following his election. The first, initial blow to the potency of their case came from the very fact that Bercow had won: many MPs did not like the result, but they felt they should respect the wishes of the House of Commons and give him the chance to make a go of the job. Having thrown out Michael Martin, it would be a bold step to force another Speaker from the role and it could establish a very dangerous precedent. Many MPs felt more strongly about the sanctity of a vote in the Commons than they did about Bercow himself. Ann Widdecombe explains that after he was elected, "The party was savage. It felt that for the second time, first with Michael Martin and now with John, its wishes had been ignored. It was a very partisan appointment but...we must uphold the office of the Speaker, we can't get into the habit of turfing them out.[495]" John Redwood, who also voted for George Young, says that, "When someone has just pulled off a triumph with a good majority, it behoves all of us to give him a fair wind.[496]"

Many Tory MPs also had to face up to the reality that Bercow was actually doing a fairly decent job. After all the hype of the Speakership campaign, during which Bercow was thoroughly demonised within the Tory Party, the reality was somewhat more mundane. As Widdecombe told me before the 2010 election, "the savage mood has calmed. He's getting on with it – he doesn't have two horns and a tail[497]". James Gray says, "At the time of the [Speakership] election, the view was, 'Can he achieve the kind of respect that he needs?' We're slightly changing our views and he is beginning to command a certain amount of respect.[498]" Ken Clarke goes further: "He runs the chamber very well, he's greatly improved the conduct of proceedings on the floor of the House; he gets more people in; he gets more discipline; he's keener on the order and he's got all the views Speakers should have about the rights of backbenchers, the rights of minority parties... So he's doing that very well.[499]"

That is not to say that all of his detractors were convinced – far from it – or that the Tories had forgotten the times when he crossed them from the chair. But as Bercow had been portrayed as the ultimate bogey man it was perhaps impossible for him to live up to that billing. For some, the anger subsided.

When it came to the moment itself, Bercow was able to rely on Sir Malcolm Rifkind, a senior Tory MP who was widely respected amongst the party, to re-propose him as Speaker. He told the House that Bercow was a "modern Speaker for a modern age," and that since voting for Young, he had been "impressed" by Bercow as he had "shown himself to be splendidly robust at intervening with both Prime Ministers and Leaders of the Opposition if they are going on too long and interrupting the smooth business of the House... I think the House can be reassured that if it chooses him today we will, indeed, have some experience and gravitas in the Speaker's chair.[500]" It was a ringing endorsement.

The key man in all this was Sir Peter Tapsell, the new Father of the House whom Bercow had parodied over the years, perfecting his impression not only at his wedding but also in his hustings speech for Speaker. With Sally watching from the public gallery, Sir Peter cut to the chase and proposed that Bercow be re-elected. The vast majority of MPs shouted "aye" and then a few, audible and heartfelt "noes" followed. It was a crucial moment, when Sir Peter might have called for a formal division, but instead he declared that Bercow had been re-elected. For the Tory leadership and for Bercow's supporters, the outcome was to be welcomed; but for the plotters, it was a failure – not unexpected, but a big blow nonetheless. Having won in Buckingham, Bercow had faced down a second challenge to his position in as many weeks. 11 months after he had become Speaker, it was only now that he seemed secure in the job at last.

When the new Prime Minister spoke for the first time in the Commons, he offered his congratulations to Bercow. But he couldn't resist a dig at Sally, telling Bercow, "I have to say there were times during the General Election when I was a little concerned about your safe return to Parliament, but I'm glad to see the mostly Conservative inclined voters of Buckingham stuck with you. And I hope there won't be too much family strife if I welcome the fact that similarly inclined voters in St. James's ward in the London Borough of Westminster did the same thing.[501]"

★★★

Since Bercow has been freed from the sword of Damocles that hung over him from the first day he took the Speaker's Chair, we have begun to see more of what he hopes to be as Mr Speaker. He has continued to move through the order paper at a lightning pace – which is much welcomed by MPs – and has fought to increase the rights of back-benchers. He has carried on acting as an ambassador for Parliament, taking his message round the country – as if the constraints of not being able to speak in the chamber require him to let loose his tongue elsewhere.

Bercow has also taken it upon himself to try to reform PMQs, which he says is "unappealing" to the public. He has tried to increase the time for questions from the backbenches and has stepped in to stop the more raucous exchanges between the party leaders, clamping down on heckling. He has frequently intervened to stop questions – or answers from the Prime Minister – that he feels have gone on too long. For some MPs, though, Bercow is taking away from the theatrical splendour of PMQs. They feel that he is too keen to have his say and is trying to destroy the essence of the clashes in the Commons. This underlying feeling came to the surface when Cameron controversially joked to a group of lobby journalists about Prince William's wedding. Saying that he was sure that the Queen would find a place for the Speaker "and Mrs Bercow", Cameron laughed that Bercow might be tempted to stand up and interject in Westminster Abbey when Kate Middleton said "I do." Turning the tables on Bercow by mimicking his tone, Cameron wondered whether he might bellow: "Order! I want to hear what the Prince is saying![502]"

Bercow has been looking at other ways to reform the Commons and has called for new measures to entice more MPs into the chamber. With attendance often being as low as twenty out of more than six hundred MPs, Bercow – the perennial attendee of Commons debates throughout his time in Parliament – is trying to pass on his enthusiasm to others. Likewise, he has been successful in persuading MPs to shorten their three-month summer break, and he has allowed more points of order – causing critics to say that he has only done so because they give him a chance to opine on whatever question is put before him. However, more accurately, points of order are the bread and butter of someone who loves Parliamentary procedure. The young John Bercow who sat on the wall outside his house, lapping up *The Times*, still exists. He has always been obsessed with politics and remains so. Bercow's love for the Commons remains undiminished – despite his political journey – and his desire to improve the Commons and to reform it is a genuine one.

It is too early to judge Mr Speaker Bercow in totality, but the signs so far are very promising. While many Tories may not like him personally, he has, by and large, done a good job. Although he could have been a more revolutionary reformer, he has nonetheless steered the tiller with a commendable firmness. It *is* easier for backbenchers to speak and he does have a sincere desire to improve the public standing of Parliament. He has been unafraid to innovate and to speak his mind and it is no bad thing that Parliament now has a Speaker who is more willing to be the public face of the Commons.

But even so, controversy continues to dog Bercow everywhere he goes. Even since his re-election in 2010, there has been a constant stream of stories in which he has come in for criticism. First came the row over the appointment of the Commons' Chaplain, when Bercow prevented Canon Andrew Tremlett being promoted to the position, favouring instead the Jamaican-born Rev Rose Hudson-Wilkin. Many MPs criticised Bercow's supposed political correctness, saying that whilst they recognised the capabilities of Rev Hudson-Wilkin, they felt that Bercow only picked her because she was not a white man. Mr Speaker then only served to exacerbate the row by personally issuing an order vetoing the release of documents relating to his role in the appointment under the Freedom of Information Act[503]. There were also continued rumblings about the approval of a crèche in Parliament – at a cost of nearly £600,000 and – perhaps more importantly to MPs – in the place of the popular Bellamy's Bar. With many of the crèche places remaining unfilled, significant public money has been spent not only on the refurbishment but also on maintaining the facility itself[504].

There is also no denying that, despite a slight thawing of relations with some Tory MPs, Bercow has remained a deeply unpopular figure amongst a large number of Conservatives. Once again it was a spat with Simon Burns that illustrates the point best – although this time it was Bercow who was on the receiving end of the insult. During questions in the Commons, Burns turned away from the despatch box to address a backbencher and Bercow intervened to ask him to face forwards, saying, "I am sure that opposition members will want to see his face[505]" – which some took to be a dig at Burns's appearance. Then, half an hour later, Bercow interjected again, asking Burns to face forwards once more, telling him in a typically dismissive tone, "It is a very simple point; I have made it to others and they have understood it.[506]" For Burns, who hated Bercow in any case, to be told off like a naughty schoolboy was too much. Under his breath, he muttered that Bercow was a "stupid, sanctimonious dwarf." Bercow's reply was relatively meek, saying that MPs had to show "respect for the chair[507]". Sally's response, as ever, was much more animated, as she tweeted, "Low grade abuse" and, "So much for the 'new politics' eh Mr Burns."

That such enmity goes far wider than Burns himself was shown all too clearly when David Cameron gave a speech to lobby journalists in late 2010. The Tory leader recounted an apocryphal tale in which Burns's driver inadvertently backed his Ministerial car into the Speaker's vehicle in a courtyard in Parliament. The story as Cameron told it was that a furious Bercow told his old enemy, "I'm not happy!" to which Burns retorted, "Well which one [of the seven dwarves] are you?" That Cameron made the joke to an audience of journalists, who have newspapers and TV reports to fill, shows not only that there is no love lost between the pair, but also that Cameron is not afraid to show it.

But perhaps most damaging was the ugly spat between Bercow and the Tory Chief Whip, Patrick McLoughlin, when Bercow appeared to prompt Labour to say "object" at the correct time during business in the House. McLoughlin was furious and shouted "Give them an indication won't you[508]", before trying to make his way from the Commons. Bercow was incandescent, furiously calling back McLoughlin and ticking him off like a unruly child. The Mr Hyde that briefly emerged in the interview with Tom Bradby was back. The Chief Whip was having none of it, though, telling the Speaker, "We all saw you", as Bercow continued to try to put him in his place.

It was a very damaging episode, not least because it's vital for a

Speaker to keep on good terms with the whips. After all, it was McLoughlin who pressured Tory MPs to agree to Bercow's re-election, thereby ensuring that he wasn't thrown out when Parliament reconvened after the General Election. Moreover, for Tory MPs who might have been warming to Bercow's Speakership, it was a stark reminder of why he had been so unpopular at the time of the Speakership election in 2009, and it reignited the feelings amongst some Tories that Bercow might be biased against the Conservatives. The dark mood towards Bercow amongst many Tories was summed up when the much-respected Father of the House publicly approached McLoughlin in the Commons the day after the row – and heartily slapped him on the back. The First Commoner has to be careful that he does not – in the words of the Tory MP Mark Pritchard, during another ugly Conservative confrontation with the Speaker – act "like fucking royalty" in the eyes of Tory MPs.

Nonetheless, Bercow is safe in the Speaker's Chair – at least for now. Although there are still many MPs who would dearly love to force him out of office, the threats have largely passed. But as with most things in politics, the future is full of uncertainty. With the Conservatives back in power, Bercow has to tread a delicate line: if he tries to make Parliament more accountable, he could be seen as unduly favouring Labour at the expense of the Tories. As one MP argues, if Bercow does seem to allow too great a degree of scrutiny, that would, "Aggravate and irritate and I can see how it could cause the relationship to break down".

Although Bercow has built some bridges with the Tories since becoming Speaker, the underlying mistrust is certainly still there and it has been exacerbated by his recent public confrontations with Tory MPs. As one told me, "I got hauled up by him; he was indulging the Labour Party, he ticked me off. But the awful thing was I didn't really accept it. I was in the wrong, but I thought, 'You're being such a pompous prat.' This is dangerous because being Speaker is a little bit like being a head teacher or officer in the Armed Forces: you have legal authority but most of the authority as Speaker is moral authority; and if at the end of the day the majority of MPs don't accept it, you've got a problem." Removing Bercow is not on the agenda, but the residual levels of enmity could become a force again if Bercow either starts causing real problems for the government or continues to pick fights with Tory MPs. The gun powder is gradually falling away, but a large enough spark could well still ignite it. David Cameron has stepped in twice to help shore up Bercow's position already, but there are no guarantees that he would do so again in the future.

Most of all, it will be Bercow himself who controls his destiny. As one MP told me, "His record suggests he will have a massive blow out, that's what you have to look out for." The spat with McLoughlin was not a total "blow out", but it showed that one is certainly possible – and that could then make being Speaker a very hard task indeed. But without such a cataclysmic event, it is likely that Bercow will see his proposed two full Parliaments as Speaker through to the end.

However, the biggest change to Bercow's life – and the biggest source of uncertainty in the future – is that Sally's profile has risen exponentially since the General Election. Although she was becoming more of a public figure in the first half of 2010, she felt constrained by the obvious threats in Buckingham and the Commons. Once Bercow secured his position, she began to put herself around as a broadcaster, first appearing on the BBC programme *This Week* and – from there – becoming a regular fixture on the political punditry circuit, reviewing newspapers on Sky and the BBC and becoming a willing talking head. It's no surprise that Sally has done so well – broadcasters are always on the lookout for talkative, interesting pundits, particularly when they are female and easy on the eye – and the good news for her is that she is also getting much better at it. When she first started appearing on television she was inexperienced and it showed – now she is much more composed. Even appearing on *Have I Got News For You* proved to be a success – despite the somewhat barbed "good luck" message to her from Nadine Dorries, who said, "having turned it down twice I have to say, she's much braver than me.[509]"

Although Sally has become more measured, she has continued to be outspoken and has embarrassed her husband in the process. In one interview she admitted that she refused to meet the Pope[510] – despite the fact that her husband was introducing him in a speech at Westminster Hall, with the eyes of the world upon him. Instead, Sally had noted the Pope's visit by tweeting, "The Pope has landed! Mark the occasion by sponsoring my parachute jump for Stonewall UK and gay rights.[511]" It couldn't help but undermine Bercow's role in the state visit.

Equally controversially, Sally decided to say that George Osborne was "mental[512]" after he announced his programme of government cuts, echoing the disparaging term used a few years earlier by her husband in the House of Commons when he described someone as a "nutter[513]". Simon Burns, as Bercow's whip, was despatched to have a quiet word with him to ask him not to use a term that some people found offensive, but Bercow was absolutely furious with Burns – and it only added to the growing hatred between the two men.

Perhaps more troubling still was Sally's decision to speak out after Phil Woolas was found guilty of electoral offences and banned from being an MP. Viewers on *The Politics Show* were treated to the quite remarkable sight of Sally publicly urging her husband not to call a by-election in Woolas's Oldham constituency to allow him time for an appeal – even though it wasn't Bercow's decision anyway. And if it had been, it would have put her husband in a no-win position: either he'd have followed her advice, making it look as if he was under her thumb; or he'd have gone against what she said, creating an embarrassing media story in the process.

Bercow has publicly supported his wife in her endeavours, calling those who criticise her "snobs and bigots[514]". Certainly, even as Speaker, Bercow still feels very keenly the critical eyes of those who look down on him for his upbringing: "The snobs are those who regard themselves as socially superior because of their background, the person they have married, or the money they've got. The worst snobs are of no distinction at all,[515]" he says. But he maintains that Sally has the right to speak out, arguing that, "People say it's different because I am Speaker and that I'm impartial, but Sally doesn't have to be. She never uses the title Mrs Speaker and she has no desire to. She's not bound.[516]" But some of what Sally has said must have made Bercow uncomfortable, particularly because he personally has been criticised for many of her outpourings. Inevitably, it must be hard for him as Sally turns into the current equivalent of Cherie Blair, the woman whom Bercow called "Lady Macbeth". "Obviously, it would be much easier for him if I were happy to sit at home and look after the children[517]", Sally admits.

But beyond the tittle tattle of Westminster, the media appearances indicate that Sally has also moved on politically. Having run unsuccessfully as a councillor, after the election she then took on her husband's mantle of backing the wrong leadership candidate by becoming perhaps the most enthusiastic cheerleader for Ed Balls's campaign. Largely thanks to her husband's position, she has been able to build a role for herself as a well-known Labour campaigner. She has made no secret of her desire to be a politician and it is more than possible – perhaps quite likely – that Sally could be parachuted into a safe Labour seat at a future General Election.

For Bercow himself, the future is less certain. Even if he survives to the end of the promised two full terms as Speaker, he will still be a relatively young man. Well before he is 60, he will have to honour his promise and stand down from the House of Commons. It is not clear what he wants to do next – with one Conservative MP even telling me that he wouldn't be surprised if Bercow wanted to become leader of the Labour Party. In truth, though, such ideas are fanciful. More plausibly, Bercow may well want to take on more lucrative directorships, become an elder statesman and go round the country speaking to people – doing what he has always loved. But none of this will quite make up for losing out on the cut and thrust of daily politics. Bercow faces the possibility of once again being without a direction in life. "When he's an ex-Speaker, what does he think he's going to do?" asks Ken Clarke. "He'll wind up in the House of Lords; it's alright but it's kind of life after death. You shouldn't go there when he's whatever [age] he will be. It's a pity really.[518]"

But if Sally does become an MP, then it could be she who shapes John Bercow's future. It would not be so unlikely for her to make it onto the front bench and, if Labour are back in government, she could even become a Minister, having the power that eluded her husband throughout his political career. It will be interesting, though, to see whether she is any more comfortable under the binds of collective responsibility than Bercow himself was. The Woolas dispute showed this dilemma quite clearly – as Sally publicly differed from the line being taken by Labour's leadership. She and her husband are similarly outspoken and she could well fall down thanks to her frankness, just as Bercow did in the 2001–05 Parliament.

But Sally's profile is rising very quickly – she is making sure of that – and if she becomes an MP there is no telling how far she could go. It is an irony that the small man who has made himself stand above most others could end up being eclipsed by none other than his very own wife. If she continues to garner the level of coverage in the media that she has achieved so far, she could, eventually, become the one who wears the political trousers in the relationship.

However, as it stands, Bercow's remarkable journey to the Speaker's chair has lost none of its shine – and as time goes on it seems that he will only become more and more ensconced as Speaker. Now that Bercow is far removed from his Monday Club views on immigration, Jack Bercowitch would be proud of his grandson and what he has achieved. But nothing is simple with John Bercow and so the old tensions under the surface – and in some cases out in the open – mean that at the slightest hint of weakness, there will doubtless be a renewed attack on his position. To keep one step ahead of his enemies, Bercow will have to draw on his decades of guerrilla political warfare. As Speaker, he has a chance to make a real contribution to his country and his Parliament, taking it away from the choppy waters of the expenses scandal towards a more serene place in which politicians can win back the public's respect. Perhaps he will never rise from the shadow of the constant sniping from some of his critics; but Bercow does have all the ingredients to be a great Speaker if he puts his mind to it. With Sally at his side, his task will be an unpredictable one. Only time will tell how much further the small man with the big ambition can go.

References

1 Interview with author
2 Ann Widdecombe, interview with author
3 Sue Farrington Smith, interview with author
4 National Archives, file HO 144/2953
5 'Writing in Debit and Credit—The Jewish Question in Romania'
6 Carol Iancu, 'Jews in Romania, 1866-1919: From Exclusion to Emancipation, East European Monographs'
7 Given as his occupation on Jack's wedding certificate
8 National Archives
9 1901 Census
10 This and other details of the marriage come from their wedding certificate
11 National Archives
12 Ibid
13 *Jewish Chronicle*, 12.10.1965
14 Interview with author
15 Interview with author
16 Centre for Parliamentary Studies lecture, 6.7.10
17 *Hendon & Finchley Times*, 29.7.09
18 Ibid
19 Winnersgallery.co.uk
20 Guys & Dolls Casting Agency
21 Interview with author
22 *Daily Mail*, 28.11.09
23 Interview with author
24 *Hendon & Finchley Times*, 29.7.09
25 Frith Manor reunion, 21.11.09
26 *Finchley Times*, 1.3.74

27 Julian Baker, interview with author
28 Interview with author
29 Interview with author
30 Ibid
31 *Daily Mail*, 3.8.10
32 Interview with author
33 Julian Baker, interview with author
34 *Daily Mail*, 6.12.09
35 *Evening Standard*, 4.12.09
36 Interview with author
37 Interview with author
38 Conservativehome.com, 4.5.09
39 Ibid
40 Adrian Velasco, Friendsreunited.com, 25.10.01
41 Interview with author
42 Interview with author
43 Ibid
44 Interview with author
45 Interview with author
46 Interview with author
47 Interview with author
48 Interview with author
49 Interview with author
50 Interview with author
51 Interview with author
52 Interview with author
53 Interview with author
54 Interview with author
55 Interview with author
56 *Hendon & Finchley Times*, 29.7.09
57 Interview with author
58 Interview with author
59 Interview with author
60 Interview with author
61 Independent, 2.8.04
62 Interview with author
63 Interview with author
64 Interview with author

65 Interview with author
66 Interview with author
67 April 1982 and October 1981 respectively
68 Ibid
69 *Daily Mail*, 4.3.04
70 *Guardian*, 28.7.2000
71 April 1982 and October 1981 respectively
72 AP, 14.10.81
73 *Daily Telegraph*, 26.6.09
74 *New Statesman*, 13.11.00
75 Speech, March 1981
76 Interview with author
77 Times, 20.9.00
78 *New Statesman*, 13.11.00
79 Ibid
80 *Daily Telegraph*, 8.11.02
81 Interview with author
82 Guardian, 5.4.86
83 Interview with author
84 Ibid
85 *Jewish Chronicle*, 4.2.10
86 *Telegraph*, 9.11.02
87 Prof Anthony Barker, interview with author
88 Interview with author
89 Interview with author
90 Interview with author
91 *Guardian*, 5.7.86
92 Interview with author
93 Interview with author
94 She called the ANC a "terrorist organisation" at the 1987 Vancouver Summit.
95 Interview with author
96 Interview with author
97 Interview with author
98 *Independent*, 6.9.01
99 *Independent*, 31.8.01
100 Interview with author
101 Uni of Essex press release, 23.06.09

102 Interview with author
103 Uni of Essex press release, 23.06.09
104 24.6.09
105 *Daily Mirror*, 3.4.85
106 *Daily Telegraph*, 6.4.85
107 *Times*, 4.4.85
108 News Letter, 6.12.08
109 *Guardian*, 5.4.86
110 Interview with author
111 BBC News website, 12.10.01
112 *Guardian*, 5.4.86
113 *Guardian*, 3.4.86
114 Interview with author
115 *New Agenda*, Summer 1986
116 Interview with author
117 *Guardian*, 19.4.86
118 *Guardian*, 20.8.86
119 Ibid
120 AP, 19.8.86
121 Ibid
122 *Financial Times*, 20.8.86
123 *Guardian*, 20.8.86
124 *Financial Times*, 20.8.86
125 *Guardian*, 20.8.86
126 Interview with author
127 *Times*, 22.8.86
128 *Guardian*, 28.8.86
129 *Times*, 19.9.86
130 *Guardian*, 8.9.86
131 *Guardian*, 20.8.86
132 *Times*, 11.9.86
133 *Times*, 11.10.86
134 *Times*, 13.11.86
135 *Times*, 14.11.86
136 Ibid
137 Ibid
138 Interview with author
139 *Guardian*, 3.1.85
140 Council minutes, 27.5.86
141 Select Committee on Standards and Privileges Fifth Report, 1999-2000, Appendix 2
142 Annex C
143 Table 1
144 Appendix 1
145 PA, 16.2.01
146 Interview with author
147 *Guardian*, 6.9.86
148 Interview with author
149 Interview with author
150 Ibid
151 Interview with author
152 Interview with author
153 Interview with author
154 Interview with author
155 Interview with author
156 *Independent*, 2.1.90
157 Interview with author
158 Interview with author
159 Interview with author
160 Interview with author
161 Interview with author
162 Interview with author
163 Interview with author
164 Interview with author
165 Interview with author
166 Interview with author
167 Interview with author
168 Interview with author
169 Interview with author
170 Interview with author
171 University of Buckingham interview with students, 2004
172 *Total Politics*, issue 19
173 Interview with author
174 Interview with author
175 Interview with author
176 Interview with author
177 Interview with author
178 Interview with author's researcher
179 Interview with author
180 Interview with author
181 Interview with author's researcher
182 Interview with author
183 Interview with author
184 Interview with author
185 Interview with author
186 Interview with author's researcher
187 Ibid
188 Interview with author
189 Interview with author
190 Philip Stephenson, interview with author
191 *PR Week*, 21.10.93
192 Ibid
193 Ibid
194 Interview with author's researcher
195 By the Labour Chancellor Denis Healey
196 *Guardian*, 18.1.91
197 Interview with author
198 *Independent*, 9.10.91
199 *Guardian*, 18.1.91
200 Interview with author
201 PA, 25.3.92
202 Interview with author
203 Interview with author's researcher
204 Interview with author
205 Interview with author
206 PA, 12.10.94
207 Interview with author
208 Interview with author
209 Peter Rae, interview with author
210 *Sunday Times*, 14.11.10
211 *Daily Mail*, 25.11.09
212 Ibid
213 Ibid
214 Interview with author
215 Aitken, Interview with author
216 Interview with author
217 Interview with author
218 Interview with author
219 Interview with author
220 Interview with author
221 Interview with author
222 Interview with author
223 29.1.95
224 Aitken, *Pride and Perjury*, Continuum: 2004, p157
225 Interviews with author
226 Interview with author
227 *Guardian*, 28.4.95
228 Interview with author
229 Aitken, op.cit, p56
230 Interview with author
231 Interview with author
232 Independent, 5.9.95
233 Interview with author
234 *Guardian*, 30.8.95
235 Interview with author
236 Interview with author
237 Interview with author
238 Interview with author
239 Interview with author
240 Interview with author
241 Interview with author
242 Interview with author
243 *Times*, 5.2.96
244 Cora Stephenson, interview with author
245 Evening Standard, 8.2.96
246 Interview with author
247 *Times*, 9.2.96
248 Ibid
249 Interview with author
250 Interview with author
251 Interview with author
252 10.6.97
253 Nadler, *William Hague In*

His Own Right, Politico's: 2000, p43,
254 Ibid
255 21.5.97. Bercow was previously officially mentioned when he swore the oath and when he voted in divisions. This was his first "contribution" to a debate.
256 *Independent*, 21.5.97
257 Hansard, 4.7.97, Col 561
258 Ibid
259 Ibid
260 Hansard, 4.7.97, Col 562
261 Ibid
262 Hansard, 4.7.97, Col 563
263 Centre for Parliamentary Studies lecture, 6.7.10
264 Interview with author
265 *Independent*, 20.11.98
266 7.7.97
267 Hansard 19.11.97, Col 323
268 Record, 13.11.97
269 Interview with author
270 Interview with author
271 Interview with author
272 *Independent*, 24.4.98
273 *Observer*, 17.5.98
274 Ibid
275 Interview with author
276 Interview with author
277 Interview with author
278 Centre for Parliamentary Studies lecture, 6.7.10
279 Ibid
280 *Independent*, 17.2.99
281 *Herald*, 29.1.98
282 Centre for Parliamentary Studies lecture, 6.7.10
283 *Mail on Sunday*, 14.6.98
284 *Daily Mirror*, 2.9.99
285 *Daily Mail*, 31.8.99
286 *Evening Standard*, 4.12.09
287 Ibid
288 Hansard, 28.6.99, Col 5
289 *Independent*, 3.2.00
290 Hansard, 10.2.00, Col 455
291 Hansard, Col 456
292 Hansard, Col 457
293 Hansard, Col 455
294 Hansard, Col 462
295 Hansard, Col 495
296 Ibid
297 Centre for Parliamentary Studies lecture, 6.7.10
298 *Scotsman*, 13.5.00
299 Hansard, 25.5.00, Col 1121

300 *Sunday Times*, 28.5.00
301 *Daily Mail*, 17.7.01
302 Herald, 29.5.00
303 Ibid
304 *People*, 18.6.00
305 Hansard, 19.6.00, Col 36
306 *Guardian*, 20.6.00
307 *People*, 18.6.00
308 *Guardian*, 28.7.00
309 Ibid
310 Independent, 8.8.00
311 10.8.00
312 *Independent*, 9.8.00
313 *Daily Mail*, 28.9.10
314 Ibid
315 Interview with author
316 Snowdon, *Back from the Brink*, HarperPress:2010, p69 317   Times, 3.10.00
318 *Times*, 5.10.00
319 *New Statesman*, 13.11.00
320 Interview with author
321 Ibid
322 *New Statesman*, 13.11.00
323 Interview with author
324 Interview with author
325 *Telegraph*, 30.3.01
326 Hansard, 2.5.01, Col 865
327 *Daily Mail*, 3.5.01
328 Hansard, 5.4.01 Col 521
329 *Telegraph*, 21.12.00
330 *Independent*, 15.2.01
331 Hansard, 11.5.01, Col 393
332 Interview with author
333 *Guardian*, 6.6.01
334 *Daily Mirror*, 5.12.09
335 *Express*, 5.12.09
336 6.9.86
337 *Daily Mail*, 8.11.02
338 *Telegraph*, 3.7.02
339 *Sunday Times*, 14.11.10
340 24.6.10
341 BBC, 13.10.89
342 ibid
343 Interview with author
344 *Sunday Times*, 14.11.10
345 Interview with author
346 Ibid
347 Ibid
348 Hansard, 10.2.00, Col 455
349 *Evening Standard*, 4.12.00
350 *Daily Mail*, 25.11.09
351 *Daily Mail*, 8.4.93
352 *Evening Standard*, 4.12.09
353 *Telegraph*, 3.7.02
354 *Guardian*, 3.7.02

355 'The John Bercow Story', BBC News website, 24.6.09
356 8.11.02
357 Ibid
358 *Mail on Sunday*, 25.8.02
359 *Independent*, 7.11.02
360 *Evening Standard*, 22.8.01
361 *Independent*, 22.8.01
362 *Independent*, 23.8.01
363 *Daily Mail*, 28.9.01
364 Interview with author
365 Speaking at a Torche event, 10.10.01
366 Centre for Parliamentary Studies lecture, 6.7.10
367 *Mirror*, 11.12.01
368 *Guardian*, 11.7.02
369 *Evening Standard*, 19.4.02
370 *Guardian*, 17.1.02
371 *Daily Mail*, 10.6.02
372 Ibid
373 *Scotsman*, 10.6.02; *Yorkshire Post*, 7.10.02
374 *Independent*, 10.10.02
375 Hansard, 4.11.02, Col 66
376 Hansard, 4.11.02, Col 46
377 GMTV, 5.1.03
378 *Daily Telegraph*, 8.11.02
379 *Daily Telegraph*, 9.12.03
380 Interview with author's researcher
381 Ibid
382 Crick, *In Search of Michael Howard*, Simon & Schuster: 2005, p457
383 *Daily Mail*, 12.9.04
384 *Total Politics*, issue 19
385 *Independent*, 1.11.04
386 Ibid
387 Ibid
388 Centre for Parliamentary Studies lecture, 6.7.10
389 Interview with author
390 *Independent*, 10.5.05
391 *Independent*, 21.5.05
392 GMTV, 25.9.05
393 Interview with author
394 Hansard, 21.11.05, Col 1233
395 Centre for Parliamentary Studies lecture, 6.7.10
396 Interview with author
397 Ibid
398 Richards, *Whatever it Takes*, Fourth Estate: 2010, p262
399 *Independent*, 1.10.07

400 Interview with author
401 DCFS Press release, 17.12.08
402 Bercow Review, foreword
403 *Western Mail*, 16.3.09
404 Interview with author
405 Interview with author
406 Interview with author
407 Centre for Parliamentary Studies lecture, 6.7.10
408 Interview with author
409 Centre for Parliamentary Studies lecture, 6.7.10
410 Interview with author
411 Interview with author
412 Interview with author
413 Point 96, guideline 1
414 *Independent*, 27.10.96
415 Interview with author
416 Register of Members' Interests, April 2005.
417 Register of Members' Interests, 11.11.09 Bercow resigned in June 2009.
418 *Total Politics*, issue 19
419 Interview with author
420 *Total Politics*, issue 19
421 Interview with author
422 Interview with author
423 Interview with author
424 Richards, op.cit, p262
425 17.5.09
426 Hansard, 18.5.09, Col 1205
427 Winnett & Rayner, *No Expenses Spared*, Bantam Press: 2009, p289
428 Ibid, p288
429 22.5.09
430 Winnett & Rayner, op. cit, p289
431 *Daily Telegraph*, 21.06.09
432 Ibid
433 Ibid
434 *Independent*, 16.10.09
435 House of Commons Media and Info Service to author, 17.11.10
436 *Daily Mail*, 30.3.10
437 Submission to Senior Salaries Review Body, reported in *Daily Mail*, 21.6.09
438 *Total Politics*, issue 19
439 Profile, BBC Radio 4, 27.6.09
440 Interview with author
441 Interview with author
442 Interview with author
443 *Guardian*, 21.5.09
444 Interview with author
445 *Telegraph*, 1.6.09
446 Interview with author
447 Interview with author
448 Interview with author
449 Interview with author
450 Interview with author
451 Hansard, 22.6.09, Col 623
452 Hansard, 22.6.09, Col 624
453 Interview with author
454 Hansard, 22.6.09, Col 624
455 Hansard, 22.6.09, Col 626
456 Interview with author
457 ITN, 23.6.09
458 Interview with author
459 Interview with author
460 Interview with author
461 Straight Talk, BBC News Channel, 16.1.10
462 Ibid
463 Interview with author
464 Hansard, 24.6.09, Col 789
465 *Daily Telegraph*, 14.11.09
466 Ibid
467 Ibid
468 Ibid
469 30.10.09
470 Hansard, 10.3.10, Col 292
471 16.3.10, reported on BBC News website
472 Ibid
473 Conversation on 7.5.10
474 *Daily Telegraph*, 22.1.10
475 Ibid
476 4.3.10
477 Phillips' campaign website
478 Interview with author
479 Interview with author
480 Interview with author
481 Conservativehome.com, 3.9.09
482 Interview with author
483 BCD website
484 Lloyd, *Mr Speaker, Sir*, Jonathan Cape: 1977, p129-130
485 bercowforbuckingham.org
486 *Total Politics*, issue 19
487 *Guardian*, 6.5.10
488 *Express*, 8.12.09
489 Twitter, 27.4.10
490 Ibid
491 Twitter, 26.4.10
492 *Evening Standard*, 19.3.10
493 Interview with author
494 Interview with author
495 Interview with author
496 Interview with author
497 Interview with author
498 Interview with author
499 Interview with author
500 Hansard, 18.5.10, Col 4
501 Ibid
502 *Telegraph*, 25.11.10
503 *Daily Mail*, 24.10.10
504 *Daily Mail*, 25.9.10
505 Hansard, 29.6.10, Col 699
506 Col 714
507 Col 719
508 BBC News, 7.12.10
509 Twitter. 11.11.10
510 *Sunday Times*, 14.11.10
511 17.9.10
512 Twitter, 4.7.10
513 Hansard, 28.4.09, Col 843
514 *Independent*, 5.7.10
515 Ibid
516 Ibid
517 *Sunday Times*, 14.11.10
518 Interview with author

Index

Index

Index